DEAREST FRIEND

PIER PAOLO BELLINI | CHIARA PICCININI

DEAREST FRIEND

Enzo Piccinini in his own words
and in the stories of those who knew him

ENZO PICCININI—DEAREST FRIEND
Enzo Piccinini in his own words and in the stories of those who knew him

By Pier Paolo Bellini and Chiara Piccinini

Original Title: Amico Carissimo

Translated from Italian by: Fr. Matthew Henry

Edited by: Suzanne Tanzi

Copyright © 2024 Pier Paolo Bellini and Chiara Piccinini

Copyright © 2025 Human Adventure Books
17105 Longacres Ln
Odessa, FL 33556

www.humanadventurebooks.com

All rights reserved

ISBN: 978-0-9823561-5-9

To Giorgia
who smiles with Enzo

Contents

Introduction | ix
1. Enzo according to Enzo | 1
2. Putting Your Heart into Things | 4
3. With Feet Nailed to the Earth | 17
4. What the Heart Desires does Exist | 32
5. We Need to Not be Alone | 59
6. You Are Good as You Are | 88
7. That Naive Boldness that Characterizes Us | 116
8. If Changing Ourselves Means Making an Effort, We Give Up | 160
9. Lord, Make Happen to Him What Happened to Me | 183
10. The Poetic Must Become Epic | 207
11. Gusto for Life Is Proportional to Your Engagement with the Ideal | 228
12. The Day After | 252

Afterword | 263
Biography of Enzo Piccinini | 267

Introduction

I MET ENZO PICCININI IN 1984, WHEN I ENROLLED AT THE University of Bologna. I was 19 years old; he was 33. An older brother... but what a distance! He had a very strong impact on me, one that could hardly be believed. I came from his same Catholic education, from the same movement of Communion and Liberation, but I had the impression that we were talking about two different Churches, and (for each of us) we were certain of coming from the correct one. Being close to him gave me, and everyone, the sense of a constant and absolute hyperbole in everything that he did. There was a hyperactivity that always reached the limit and often surpassed it, going beyond the physical and psychological rhythms of a human being, whether it had to do with visiting a city, playing soccer, praying, engaging in culture, politics, driving, falling in love, working, using money, correcting errors, or accepting correction...

For me, this whole vortex represented a provocation that I sought to avoid for almost a year, dodging the blows as long as I could, until the day when, in one of the many trips we took together, when we were chatting, he told me that he had four children. Right there, an alarm bell went off. The time of the flower children was not so far off, as well as the time of the Red Brigades and the killing of Francesco Lorusso in Bologna,[1] and the fact that one could still live on the wave of ideology and anti-ideology did not seem so

---

1. A fighter in *Lotta Continua* (Constant Struggle), killed by a police officer in the disorder that broke out during a student demonstration in Bologna, March 11, 1977.

strange to me. That one could do it, though, while implicating in some measure the lives of one's own loved ones, was the detail that triggered a fundamental question in me that I could not postpone: "Either he is crazy, or there is something that I have not yet understood. Something [I had to admit] that fascinates me at the same time as it scandalizes me."

It was the decision to go to the depth of this second hypothesis, of understanding what there was behind that unwieldy, exuberant temperament, that marked a story of friendship, a sharing of life that was not interrupted for 15 years, and only changed in its form after May 26, 1999, when Enzo left us.

This book, in honor of the 25th anniversary of his passing and in the full progress of the process of canonization, aims to document what we heard and saw on a daily basis, being near him and in direct contact in those years.

This work was made possible thanks to the Enzo Piccinini Foundation,[2] which put the precious archive of the transcriptions of his public addresses at our disposal, and thanks to the many testimonies left by those who had the occasion to know him in person. All this was interwoven and stitched together on the basis of my own memories and those of Chiara, his oldest daughter. We desired, from the beginning, that the human and educational patrimony that Enzo poured out in the lives of those who spent time with him should not be lost.

This is an "insider" story, from those of us who, when young, beheld the explosion of an extraordinary and contagious humanity, registering what we saw and heard in the environment where this spectacle principally took place: the life of the university students of those years.

---

2. https://www.fondazionepiccinini.org/.

1.

Enzo according to Enzo

WHO WAS ENZO PICCININI? LOOKING AT HIM FROM THE OUTside, he was a "force of nature," a man who slept little, who traveled a lot, who worked hard, who had strong passions, who entered into the life of others, a leader, a courageous and provocative man... and we could list so many other exceptional human qualities. And yet, behind all this, for those who had the occasion of catching a glimpse within the phenomenon, there emerged a man totally passionate because he was totally embraced and, for this reason, infinitely generous. His temperament and his untamed character, moved by "the only thing that counts," that is, "the divine restlessness of unsatisfied souls,"[1] had found their most congenial environment in the encounter with a Christian experience that was integrally human, "carnal." From here, his personality developed into an explosive concoction that progressively shed its "spectacular" aspects in order to leave more and more space to what gave him life, the embrace of Christ. This embrace entered his life powerfully through the unique

---

1. Emmanuel Mounier, *Lettere sul dolore* [*Letters on Pain*], Rizzoli, Milan, 1995, p. 23 (translation: ours).

friendship with Father Luigi Giussani[2] in an encounter "that had transformed even some traits of his temperament, while it had exalted others."[3]

Enzo was a passionate, strong man, with a past that was both violent and sweet, a past that sometimes resurfaced, yet was more and more ordered and shaped toward the new love of his life. He was also a kind man, behind the brazenly gruff façade that he exhibited in a theatrical way, highlighting the contrast and paradox of his revolutionized existence. He had a funny way of describing himself: "I am an atheist who happened to become a Christian because, at a certain point in my life, I happened to encounter this 'thing.' I was totally on the other side. All the foundations were missing—like those who play soccer without knowing the fundamentals, have you ever seen them? They express themselves... only, they lack some of the fundamentals. I am like that, lacking some of the fundamentals. What can you do? But I love this life with a passion. Completely."[4] Enzo was "totally on the other side," he had passed through a radical ideology, an extreme left ideology that later had gone into hiding in preparation for the armed struggle, the anticlerical ideology that had left in his blood a natural reactivity in front of injustice, oppression, and intrusion, whether they be political, social, interpersonal, psychological, or clerical. He lacked "the fundamentals" of the faith. His was a totally practical Christianity; that is, totally "lived," and here was the fire, that surge of life that he loved. Completely.

On the other hand, from his native land one could only expect that mixture of opposites that always marked his life: "My

---

2. We have omitted publishing those meetings where Enzo found himself explaining directly the texts of Father Giussani (there were many Schools of Community dedicated to this). As will become clear, though, the thought of the founder of Communion and Liberation (now also Servant of God) will emerge in every word of Enzo who, in repeating and following them with total dedication, gave a totally personal and original stamp on those contents and on that friendship that had been at the origin of his extraordinary and endless arc of conversion.

3. Message of Father Giussani on the occasion of the first anniversary of the death of Enzo Piccinini, in "That Surge of Life," *Traces* (June 2000), http://archivio.traces-cl.com/archive/2000/giugno/surge.html.

4. Pesaro, April 6, 1998.

story begins from a place where atheism was born, the lowlands of Emilia that begin from Mantua. Atheism was born right there, and I grew up with the typical pragmatism of those from Emilia—from Modena upwards, to be clear—those people who always have to do, do do... They damn their souls in doing, and they don't dig deep enough, because for them metaphysics is just the opinion of some sick mind."[5]

Metaphysics was not a "cultural" preoccupation inscribed in the nature of Enzo, but in some way it became so. His entire existence acquired a different sense and enthusiasm in his "totally physical" impact with metaphysics. That impact revolutionized not only the present and its projects, but also his reading of the times that preceded it. In taking in hand the words spoken by Enzo in his last 15 years of existence, we notice the clarity he had in describing himself, his talents and his limits, his own passionate, confused, and sometimes contradictory road. This clarity came to him, as Father Giussani said a few days after his death, from that encounter with "metaphysics": "Enzo was a man who, from the intuition he had in a dialogue with me 30 years ago, said his 'Yes' to Christ with an astounding devotion, intelligent and total in outlook, and he dedicated his life completely to Christ and his Church."[6]

That which follows, therefore, is a kind of "autobiography" dictated by Enzo himself, the words that inflamed his existence, that made his perspective intelligent and integral, that illuminated his human structure, equal to the structure of each man and woman in this world, and that marked the life of so many young people, leading them to take seriously the metaphysical dimension through a very physical encounter.

---

5. Pesaro, April 30, 1999.

6. Luigi Giussani, "Father Because Intensely Son," *Traces* (June 1999), http://archivio.traces-cl.com/archive/giu99/piccinini.html.

2.

Putting Your Heart into Things

IN THE MANY PUBLIC MEETINGS THAT HE HELD THROUGHOUT Italy (an average of almost one a day, considering that he often held many of them in the same day), Enzo never spoke in the third person. He always spoke about himself, speaking always of Another, to whom he directed the attention and the affection of those who were listening. It is this Other who, retrospectively, clarified his own structure, his restless "heart," a heart particularly explosive but not structurally different from that of the young people who heard him.

"When I was a kid—and a bit of this childlikeness[1] remains in me—I was very enthusiastic about adventure. I loved above all those stories that took place on the sea, on great sailing ships. I breathed all that in. I set about reading those things and I saw them with my eyes—I was a kid who loved adventure novels—and I imagined the ship that sailed the sea, with three masts, people up above, the force that challenged nature. At a certain point, I was overtaken by anguish as I read the phrase, 'it stopped, coming to ground on dry land': a bank of sand. I was in anguish because that great thing that

---

1. Editorial note: While correcting grammatical or transcription errors, we intentionally left in the text the "colloquial" forms typical of spoken language. We thought that this gave value to the "direct" perception that these words left in the soul of those who listened to them live. We therefore suggest to the reader an attitude of identification with the living context of the situations in which these dialogues took place in those years.

challenged the forces of nature, that is, what man cannot do, suddenly, because of a bunch of sand, could no longer do anything! You see, our human potential, which the heart illustrates, is the same thing as the ship that challenges the sea: the sea is life when it runs aground on a little sand, in the sandbank of the conditional, 'I would like to, but am not able,' without hope, 'I would like to, but am not able,' 'if I were, I would...'"[2]

It's not just a bunch of feelings

Existence is this: a human potential "which the heart illustrates," made for great things and, at the same time, tragically uncertain about the good outcome of this endeavor. A revolutionary discovery for Enzo, derived from the Christian encounter, was exactly the discovery of the "heart," an awareness that, from then on, marked the originality of all his actions. But what is the heart? "The heart is not just a bunch of feelings, no! It is the biblical heart, it is that which makes a man a man, it is the ontological aspect of man, that is, that complex of evidences, of original needs, for which and with which we do everything. It is that complex of evidences and original needs, but which ones? We can synthesize them as four things: the beautiful, the true, the just, the desire to love and be loved. Everything is inscribed in these four things; every attempt that man makes is inscribed, from the day we open our eyes (when one's awareness opens up and one begins to ask, 'Why, why, why?'), to the day we give up the ghost. We will continue to ask, 'Why?' These four things point to the desire for happiness; it is that for which we get up in the morning, for which we fall in love, start a family, go to work, study, play sports, or do anything else. To be happy... we live our whole life for this."[3]

The heart feels, but it is not a feeling; it is the desire for happiness. Because it is not a feeling, it must constantly accept "correction" from its deepest, most objective needs: beauty, truth, justice,

---

2. February 23, 1995.
3. Summer vacation with Bologna university students, August 13, 1997.

love. And from all four of these together. From here comes the great work, the great law: to compare everything we come across with that natural endowment. This is called "experience." "There is something within us that almost unintentionally notices reality and compares it with itself. This 'something' is a criterion that gives us our identity. In short, it is a need for happiness; we have done and we do everything for this. To be aware of the criterion that we carry within ourselves, and to follow it to the very end in what we do, this is experience. There is no alienation, because that criterion is in you, it is born with you. There is a nature that characterizes us within, like the face we have outside. I have black eyes, you have light eyes, she has blonde hair, but there is a nature within that characterizes every human, whatever latitude or longitude and culture one may have. It is born with us. It is there from the beginning and will accompany us to the end. In short, it is structural."[4]

There is a face within that characterizes the "human type," and this face is not a vague and unstable sentiment. He repeated this to us many times: an emotion helps man only insofar as it is not detached from its "meaning." The heart is a need for meaning. "Why is life so tremendous? Because, getting up in the morning, in some way you decide whether what you do has meaning or not, whether the meaning of what you do is the daily routine or something else. From this beginning, the day is decided. It is like this in every instant."[5] "When is life most beautiful and full of enthusiasm? When is there an enthusiasm to be with your family? When is there an enthusiasm to eat together? When is there an enthusiasm to work or to go on a hike? When it has a meaning. This is the problem. Meaning is what gives consistency to reality, whatever it may be: wife or husband, father or mother, book or beer, eating or hanging out."[6]

Meaning is an urgency that, by nature, is totalizing and inexhaustible, so much so that "if even the last page, the last line, the last question, the 999th question were taken out, if this were missing,

---

4. Catania, October 13, 1997.
5. Bologna, April 21, 1991.
6. Summer vacation with the Marche university students, August 15, 1997.

the last of the questions in the world… man would be as restless as when he opened the first page."[7] The need for meaning is therefore the root of the eternal "holy restlessness" of the human condition in relationship with things, with reality that "is never affirmed ultimately unless it is affirmed in its meaning. We say it with the most beautiful word: if it is not affirmed in its destiny, that is, the place from which it comes and toward which it is going. When we say 'I,' if we do not say from where we come and toward where we are going, or we do not at least imply this dramatic mystery, what does it mean? A series of reactions and sensations, condemned to end in ashes, in nothing."[8]

When we came back from our vacations and began to study again, there was a gathering that could not be missed, the Beginning Day, to which we invited hundreds of friends. It was the occasion to fix together the starting point, a key point that was able to sustain our involvement in the months of work that awaited us. The central word, most of the time, was that which defined a mysterious and demanding horizon, present in every moment, fascinating as it was mysterious, sometimes vague, sometimes even fearful: the word "destiny." And we heard about it not as a concept to learn, but as an attractive possibility in front of our eyes: "Tonight I want to tell you only this: starting university, I would like to understand where you put your head and your heart. Look (excuse me): everything is useful. Your studies—above all because you are here at university—your house, your girlfriend, sports, your favorite teams, Inter, Juve, whatever you want, everything is useful, but what do we want to do with all this? This is the concept. This is the problem of life. There is only one solution, and it's the possibility that there is something greater than what I feel and see, because what I feel and see and measure create fragments, while I need something in which my gaze is included, of which even my gaze is a part. In short, to give you an idea, think about the horizon and, in the horizon, all the things you normally see. You see houses, you see a man on a bicycle, you see a

---

7. Bologna, November 21, 1985.

8. Summer vacation of the Marche university students, August 15, 1997.

tree, you see an animal, you see a car, you see the road. Everything has its place. Take away the horizon and what remains? A house, a tree, a road, a man: everything is isolated. I believe that life should have the same key! I need to understand that yesterday is connected to today and that today will be connected to tomorrow, and that my gesture of affection for the person I love is connected to the sky, to the earth, to the sea. In short, it is part of the past, of the future, and it remains! Destiny is a beautiful word that expresses that from which we come, that toward which we are all heading. It is something that can be hated, can be felt like a threat, because it is something that we cannot measure. But, to the point in which we manage in some way to live within this horizon, life becomes more beautiful. It is as if the usual things took on a new light. When things are 'destined,' they acquire a greater value than they normally would, than we are normally used to giving them. It is like when one gives a bouquet of flowers to his girlfriend. What does it mean? They are not flowers; they become love. So the things that are connected to destiny acquire a different light, they are the usual things, but they have another taste, another intensity! You guys, we are in the world for this, not to throw away our dignity on some feeling or on some greater or lesser goal that is only partial. We are in the world for this, because we are destined."[9]

This was the heart for Enzo. From here was born the phrase that distinguished him in every meeting, his ID card, a phrase that I heard repeated and that I begin to understand now after 40 years of distance: "It is the phrase that I will always use, that I will never stop using: life is a unity if you put your heart into what you do."[10] I never thought that Enzo intended by this phrase to flavor his actions with good sentiments (it was a hypothesis opposed to his temperament). I considered it rather an exhortation not to spare one's energies (as he abundantly showed us). It had to do instead with another thing: "We are ourselves only if we can put our heart into what we do. The heart is that 'detector,' that infallible thing

---

9. Florence, October 20, 1989.

10. Cesena, March 12, 1999.

that we have within us that, instinctively, makes us recognize when others are oppressing our freedom, makes us get up in the morning and desire to be happy. This is what we have to use in all our work."[11]

"And to put your heart into what you do exalts the I. This is as true for the housewife who has to stay home to clean her baby as it is for the President of the Republic."[12]

The more we engage our heart, the more we inevitably arrive at the experience of its insufficiency. And, precisely in the recognition of this, our heart's congenital structural insufficiency, it is possible to understand its essential and unique function: the openness to something that surpasses it. "And then my family had grown; meanwhile, laughing and joking, I had found myself with four children. It was a serious problem, and my parents continued to give me money. It was a bit of a humiliation. Then, in the end, I told them this, and then they would give me maybe some cheese, or some clothes, in order not to give me money. In this way, I understood that we can put our heart into what we do if we are in front of something greater than ourselves. We need something greater than ourselves. This could help me put my heart into play in any situation, something greater than me, greater than my capacity."[13]

"When you look at it correctly, all these things that you see have an origin that is not you. There is something that is not you, without which, without the awareness of which, each relationship is made false by an instrumentalization that is called 'what you feel, think, see.' And 'the other' is never allowed in. 'You' is just a word, a way of speaking; it is never the dizziness that is experienced in recognizing an origin different from you: 'You.'"[14]

"I went to Boston to say goodbye to my professor, my supervisor during the time I had been there, vice-president of surgery, a great personality, who—for a strange paradoxical circumstance, but one that can happen—got sick from a tumor that we had operated

---

11. Bari, February 13, 1997.
12. Catania, October 13, 1997.
13. Rimini, December 12, 1998.
14. Bologna, November 21, 1985.

on together, pancreatic cancer. I went to meet him on the last day, the Saturday before leaving, and I was chilled by the scene that I saw. He was at the end of his life, by now, reduced to skin and bones, and next to him the psychologist—because American hospitals of a certain level send in the psychologist for therapy—made him talk in order to distract him, to make him not think. 'Without Me you can do nothing,' came to mind. Man needs more. I looked at him: even just because of my affection and the sign that he had been for me, he could not be reduced to being emptied by a psychologist. Man is like a sign of something else, he cannot explain himself by himself, with scientific techniques. You feel that it is too restricting, you feel it. It is amazing because 'we feel that even if all the possible questions of science had an answer, our vital problems—that is me and you, my life, my pain, my joy—our vital problems are not even touched.'[15] We need something else for you to be yourself, for me to be myself; we need something else that is not what I am able to do, what you are able to do."[16]

In other words, the original needs and evidences "imply something: that you cannot fill yourself by yourself. It is like one who, being thirsty, tried to quench his thirst by himself. He will have to go where there is water, right?"[17] "An interest, a desire, shows that we need something other than ourselves to be ourselves. We don't have to be philosophers, or theologians, or converts to whatever religion or whatever God, to admit this. It is enough to be loyal to ourselves. Constantly you are projected into a relationship with something other than yourself. Constantly. This is not something that priests or nuns, the Vatican or the bishops invented to hold you down. It is structurally like this. In order to be in relationship with this thing that is other than yourself, which your life constantly needs, in order to be in relationship with this, you have to recognize that something in you has to break, because it cannot be that you

---

15. Ludwig Wittgenstein, *Tractatus Logico-Philosophicus* [*Logical-Philosophical Treatise*], Carocci, Rome, 2006 (translation: ours).

16. Bologna, November 23, 1989.

17. Summer vacation, August 13, 1997.

just agree. The relationship with this other—give it whatever name you want—has to break something in us."[18]

"Whoever has been seriously in love knows all the fear and trembling that he had in making the smallest gesture toward the beloved, feeling like it was always inadequate. Whoever has been seriously in love knows this, knows the doubt that he may be always inadequate, incapable of the greatness that the heart desires. The more we discover our needs, the more we recognize that we cannot resolve them by ourselves. The sense of impotence accompanies every serious experience of humanity. This sense of impotence generates positive solitude; that is, the kind of solitude that asks, the kind that has need of the other."[19]

We were not spared uncomfortable, challenging words. *Desire* is a source of unease because it makes our ultimate, irresolvable impotence come to light, it makes us live a solitude. But, as Enzo often repeated, "we have to chase the unease." And he carried out this strange operation. I was often amazed by his conscious decision to face very disagreeable situations, situations that were also avoidable (above all, in seeking out tasks and relationships that were uncomfortable or thankless). He went in search of what was uncomfortable for himself and he did it also with us, with a mix of gestures that were in turn sweet and rough. Desire implies sacrifice, and to refuse this state of things is similar to Aesop's famous fable of the fox and the grapes, about which he often reminded us.

We felt ourselves provoked (in Latin *pro-vocati*, "called forth") to say "I" without canceling anything, without dreaming, without forgetting the evidence that desire is always accompanied by our limits as well as by our betrayal. "That episode of Pius XII is beautiful when, walking along the corridor, where there were people in audience and they were all stretching out, as happens, to kiss his hands or to greet the Pope, or to tell him a word or to ask his blessing, at a certain point he stops in front of the only one who, hanging his head, was not saying anything. A bit shocked, he stops to look at

---

18. Pesaro, April 6, 1998.
19. Bologna, June 21, 1992.

him, the secretary comes up to the Pope and tells him, 'Holiness, he cannot see you, he is blind, that is why he doesn't move.' The Pope is struck, comes close to the man, puts his hand on his head and tells him, 'Courage, we are all blind.' And this is a profound truth."[20] We felt the trembling of this profound truth, yet, strangely, we were not crushed by it. "Life has its limit, and if this limit enters within the normal awareness of our relationships, it creates right away a capacity for relationship that is otherwise impossible. It is the sense of limit that puts you in front of another man, immediately together, even if he has different ideas than you do, even if he doesn't understand you, even if he doesn't even look at you. Because, like him, you are also needy; in order to be yourself, you also have a need."[21]

"If one thinks about himself and closes his eyes for a minute, there passes in front of him the film of his life, and he recognizes how it has been a collection of endless attempts to do what is good, what is beautiful, what is just, what is true, and how he has always descended to compromises, and how he has always reduced this—in one way or another—to some betrayal or incoherence. You should see with the kids, what an effort it takes to make them understand that they are a structure of desire for what is good, and of the impossibility to fulfill that desire by themselves, structurally. Therefore, they think they don't need anything. Seriously, they think they don't need anything, except some details. This is also true for us. It is the same. At the end of the day, it is self-sufficiency that determines our position. We put things together by ourselves, we adjust them, we decide for ourselves the points of view, and, all in all, even when it comes to our so-called repentance, it is still a feeling of ours, not the objectivity of a position that needs something else in order to be saved. And this position is not there!"[22]

---

20. Florence, May 6, 1989.
21. Cesena, March 12, 1999.
22. Bologna, Apri 21, 1991.

BETTER RELIGIOUS THAN CLEVER

Desire presupposes an openness to "otherness," which is a universe without limits. The other is not just "what is different from me," with whom I can compromise so we do not step on each other's toes. Enzo taught us that to affirm the other means, sooner or later, to go beyond every measure, to overcome every calculation, every consideration, to surrender ourselves to a dimension that is not our own, and which we need in order to be saved. The use of the heart according to its nature leads inevitably to the great threshold that we can overcome only by recognizing an ultimate dependence: this is the religious experience. The heart leads there, and we must accept this dynamic because it is the only one capable of putting it in its right place, in the only dimension adequate to it. Enzo said, "Look, we do not have to be afraid of being religious. It is better to be religious than to be clever. This is the awareness that makes us pray, like the old nun in my hospital ward who says, 'Doctor, go pray, some morning, and you will see that it gets better'... 'Please, why don't you go, sister?' But she was right: in this way, things are given back their true value, their true proportion. We need this, we feel it, it is the heart of man that desires it."[23]

Religiosity, far from the understanding we had inherited from our traditional educational environments, is not the moment we close our eyes, abandon reality, turn off reason, and begin to dream of the hereafter. It is the exact opposite. It is the point of arrival for those who follow concrete reality all the way, by using reason, to reach the limit to which it inevitably leads, and to which desire also leads. "What is religiosity? It is the need for meaning, just as concrete as this table, just as concrete as the things you eat, in the same identical way, because a person cannot live outside of this. Well, this religiosity has often become either an atmosphere or a kind of moralism, but it does not touch the heart and it does not determine daily life–yet it establishes the dignity of living. We can lose everything, my friends, we can lose everything, but we cannot lose this

---

23. Bologna, October 6, 1990.

position, because sooner or later life will force you to an unbearable cynicism, or a repetitiveness that will make the issue go grey."²⁴ "We too fall into the trap of thinking that the most concrete thing is the most abstract, that the 'religious dimension' is something that has nothing to do with life. But this condemns us, because it makes us accept a superficial life in place of a true life; it makes us exchange what exists with what we feel. Truly! It makes us reduce things that repeat themselves to an incredible boredom, because we already know them, we already know."²⁵

We end up inevitably intuiting that there exists something "beyond," only and simply if we go to the depth of the things that are "here." In order to help us understand this, Enzo colored his descriptions with many earthy anecdotes: "The religious sense is not a problem for religious people. It is not a problem for 'those who have lived a sad youth.'²⁶ It is not a problem for those with some philosophical urge. It is a human problem. It is as if, meeting each of you, of whom I know more than half, and meeting a housewife, I don't know, who is 55 years old, I said, 'Look, your problem is the religious sense.' That would be something strange, because normally one thinks that this is a certain type of mental attitude, while instead it is a human problem. The religious sense is what determines the fact that our everyday actions may be human."²⁷

And neither is it the business of people who are exceptionally reflective or introverted: "These questions are not an invention to make our life more problematic. As one of my friends said, 'How many problems you create! Life is much simpler! All these problems are only for certain types of people. For us, it is enough to have two things: a couple friends, a nice evening, and we are set.' Certainly, as long as it all goes well. As long as things go well, it is enough. But

---

24. Florence, November 12, 1992.

25. Bologna, November 21, 1985.

26. He is referring to a song that accompanied us very often in our singing nights with the guitar, a famous song called "*Tema*" ("Theme"), by I Giganti, which Enzo used to help us understand that the religious sense is not just something for visionaries or depressed people.

27. Riccione, December 16, 1998.

because all of life provokes us again and again, and it is impossible to endure these provocations for long without getting wounded (just think about old age), so these questions are not something extra."[28]

Besides irony, Enzo often added to his explanations an attention to current events, above all to the ideas that came out of the newspapers, on which we exercised ourselves regularly in a type of critical gymnastics (this was learned from Father Giussani). At that time, the one who paid the price was a philosopher who was well known then: "Listen to what Lucio Colletti[29] says [and here we could imagine the pompous tone and the reverent gestures of his hands, a theatrical flair that always accompanied Enzo's words], a famous thinker, in his article on October 16, 1998, speaking about reason's need for meaning, regarding the questions that the Pope maintains are structural. And to the questions, 'Why do I live? Where do I come from? Where am I going? What is there after death?' some have already given a response while others pretend to seek it out, but no one really knows how to respond. If you ask me, 'Where are you going?' I respond, 'Where I was before coming into the world.' 'And where were you?' 'In the cells of my forebears,' you say. 'And where will you end up?' 'I am going to end up in the cells of your descendants.' The genetic patrimony passes from one individual to the next, like getting in and out of a taxi. Mr. Lucio Colletti allows himself this statement. I would like to ask him a simple question: Excuse me, but when you are with your wife, do you say, 'My dear, we are getting into and out of a taxi?' To your son do you say, 'You are a genetic patrimony'? Because these assertions are possible and allowed to pass for real laws, like a thought that sums up all the logic of life, only if you distance yourself from experience, because your experience will never make you say that an embrace is a transmission of genes. That is absurd. And yet, distancing ourselves from experience, it is possible, it is thought, and it is allowed to pass as correct for everyone."[30]

---

28. Riccione, December 16, 1998.

29. (1924-2001) Intellectual, editorialist, and philosophy teacher.

30. Riccione, December 16, 1998.

"Freedom is not just being able to choose (because someone lets you choose). It is adhering to what is true. Therefore, my friends, freedom implies being able to distinguish between what is true and what is not true. You are not free if you could not do it, if there are others who instill this in you. In fact, what amazes me most in those who espouse the so-called cliché is that they do not distinguish between good and evil anymore. Freedom is the energy with which we adhere to what is true, that is, to what corresponds to our destiny. We feel it when it corresponds and when it does not, what corresponds to our own destiny, what corresponds to what is moved in us. Because we are like a postage stamp that does not stick. Have you ever seen a stamp that doesn't stick?... On the envelope... Five minutes go by... *tuc*, it falls. We are like this, we are not able to adhere. My friends, it is like this."[31]

And here begins the true battle, every day: whoever notices he or she has a heart recognizes, immediately after, that all around "all things conspire to keep silent about us."[32] That is, we recognize that it is not just a way of speaking, a chat at the bar, the fact that people and systems "instill" in us ways of thinking that are educated and inhuman. In those years, Father Giussani warned us constantly not to be naïve in front of "power," in front of what Christ called "the world." There is a battle to be fought, not because we want to attain power, but because (abused) power becomes structurally the principal enemy of the evidences of the heart. And the religious sense represents the ultimate bastion against that power.

We speak much less about this today, even within the Church. Maybe power today is better, and more respectful than it was then. Maybe, though, after a little more than five minutes, the stamp that doesn't stick has gone *tuc*. And the world rejoices.

---

31. Bologna, November 22, 1986.

32. Rainer Maria Rilke, "The Second Elegy," https://www.poetrychaikhana.com/Poets/R/RilkeRainerM/SecondElegy/index.html.

3.

With Feet Nailed to the Earth

ENZO ALWAYS LISTENED TO FATHER GIUSSANI'S SUGGESTIONS, even those that clearly cost him a lot of effort: it certainly did not take much effort for him to discuss this topic (power) that he felt so close to his core, all the way to those vocal chords that swelled together with the veins in his neck every time he spoke about these things. Ultimately, his revolutionary youth had been spent for this war against every type of abuse of power, until he had realized that with that revolution he was doing nothing else but promoting the coming of a new power, more violent than the first. In the years of his youth, that impulse (which he was to continue to keep) did not have the instruments to understand where the true wound is, the violent character of power.

CHERNOBYL: DETACHMENT FROM THE HEART

If the heart is the precious pearl within each of us, the compass toward the goal, if we must put our heart into what we do, what can be the most violent action against a man? To separate him from his heart. The most dramatic thing that began in those years to pervade Western culture was the fact that this violence was perpetrated "without violence," with the consent of the violated. It was a violence that does not leave exterior signs, but changes the structure of a person. This was the heart of the problem, the heart of the new violence.

In 1986, the catastrophe at Chernobyl, a Russian nuclear station, happened because of the explosion of a reactor, which spread a quantity of devastating radiation throughout Europe. Father Giussani took a cue from this disaster to help us understand what was happening in our minds, in the structure of our very organism, by the hand of power, and what were the dynamics with which this massacre was taking place. Enzo told us in his own way about these same dynamics: "It was the year of Chernobyl, you understand? That is, the year when the nuclear reactor blew up, and spread radiation around, radioactive particles that came all the way to us. Do you remember? The older ones here surely remember that light rain. You had to go out in the car or with an umbrella, not go out with your head uncovered, not eat salad... The thing, though, substantially concerned the Adriatic coast, so much so that now we notice it—we do not say it in public, but I am a cancer surgeon—we notice that there is an increase in particular tumors that can be attributed to that period, above all on the Adriatic coast, your coast, to be clear, in Rimini (I'm sorry guys: it came to us in Emilia a little less). How does radiation function? It acts on the person without one becoming aware; that is, there are things you do not recognize. The "Chernobylized" person, the one hit by the radiation, is a normal person. We walk normally, we have two eyes, there are no huge alterations. But we are destroyed within, because the radiation hits us, but from within. It changes the genetic code, it changes genes, it changes other things you don't see, things that determine the whole individual. So, you see, the dominant mentality—Giussani said—functions in this way: it is as if there was a radiation that you don't recognize, but you absorb it. You are presumptuous if you think that you are an exception, that you reason with your own head, you are able to discern: 'Come on, other people are like that, but I know, I understand!' What nonsense; you are taken by the same thing, and destroyed within. The destruction consists in the fact that they have managed to distance us from our heart, they have separated us from our heart. These needs for the true, the beautiful, for justice, to love and be loved—these no longer enter into our everyday life, they are separated from us. We can do so many things without being aware of these needs. And what happens then? Our heart is clogged by partial answers. They have distanced us... we increasingly settle for partial answers, and life descends to a lower and lower level. 'But that's life,' we say this, don't we? 'My child, that's just life.' What does that mean? Seriously, what does that mean? Nothing. It is life, it is life, it is life... lower and lower. It is life... you no longer play, you no longer look up."[1]

It was unbearable for Enzo to think it possible to live without his heart at work in its totality, without it being able to react and to say "true, false, right, wrong, good, evil." Therefore, he set about in every way to stimulate us, to prick us into re-activating that detector that reacts inevitably when something concerns it, that risks being atrophied when it is not educated to perceive that "everything" concerns it. This is the great, new strategy of the "world": "Yesterday, I was in Bari. We had done a number of things in the community. I was even very happy, and at a certain point we had breakfast there with the small group,[2] a delicious breakfast, fantastic. At a certain point, we heard on the radio—they were speaking about the former Yugoslavia—that the war was starting again, a general mobilization, terrifying news... and we were frozen. I think that if one is minimally aware of himself, in front of something like that one is not able to eat anymore, because the true problem is that they have managed to take from us that sensibility, so that, almost without wanting to, one says: 'But what does this have to do with me? It's their business, they are always fighting,' or rather: 'They are black or they are Muslim.' That is, something has been taken from our heart and from our mind, so that I can say this about what happens:

---

1. Summer vacation, August 13, 1997.

2. This term, within the experience of Communion and Liberation, always indicates a group of leaders, not formal and not representative (for which there exists instead a structure called the "diaconia"). The small group is an "operative friendship" in which the leader can freely ask to share the care and judgement of the life of a community, as well as a reciprocal human attention.

'It has nothing to do with me.' Or, like those hundreds of people who died on the boats: they were a people, these people here, destroyed, and they keep coming now, hundreds, thousands of dead, drowned! How can we live like this? What is the dignity of any action of mine if I do not have an answer to this, if I do not have a minimum of an answer to this? This is how the mask of solitude, of cynicism, is drawn on the face of each of us, and we live everything with this mask, even our family relationships. There is something that questions us, but our life loses its dignity if it is only moved for a moment by these things that we have said, and then passes on."[3]

This is the most unbearable illusion: to manage to live day by day. The most effective system used by power to detach us from the heart is very simple: to distract us from what really counts. "When I was in America, all the secretaries where I was, of the school where I was, had on their desk something they displayed that said, 'Thank goodness it's Friday,' and that's how they began the weekend. And they all let loose on the weekend. Saturday, yeah, beer, everyone drunk... those beautiful bars (where I went once and came away dazed), deafening with music. It drove me crazy, *bum bum*... People stay there for hours and get drunk. They were not like the clubs we have here, that have a bit of style. These were terrible places, with a band that is completely "gone," playing non stop on its own, with no one paying attention to it. There were two or three who drank beer by the liter and they went on like this. Then came Monday, everyone straight ahead to work, and then they waited again for Friday, to have fun. Survival. It is a society like this."[4] "The world has only one weapon against us, and it is called distraction. Distraction manages little by little to estrange us from our heart. In what way? Literally by blocking it. Suddenly, everything becomes superficial, it passes over us like water over a rock, without leaving a trace."[5]

"The danger, in front of a situation like this, is to go into hibernation. To go to university in hibernation. That is, to endure it.

---

3. Bologna, June 21, 1992.
4. Bologna, October 1988.
5. Marche, October 22, 1995.

We leave the lamp of reason on the side of the street, we leave it to the side because… what do you want… that's society, right? To go into hibernation. And drugs… why have they become the emblem of our society? Because they allow one to walk around without feeling anything. If this problem has exploded now, it is only for this reason. Drugs allow us to walk around without feeling anything. In hibernation."[6]

Bourgeois, That Is, Safe From Risk

I have never known a more anti-bourgeois man than Enzo, not just in terms of aspirations toward the betterment of one's economic condition, but especially because of the type of mentality that is meant by the word bourgeois. Certainly, the peasant origins of his family, as well as his extreme-left ideals, influenced him on this. But I think that the bad odor of the bourgeois mentality bothered his sensibilities because it was structurally irreconcilable with Christianity and, maybe even more than that, because of a genetic incompatibility with his temperament. Power, for Enzo, was always that little voice that said, "Do not push desire beyond a certain limit," "Stay in your place and get in line without bothering anyone…," "When you reach your goal, you'll see…." Enzo was ruthless with people who proclaimed great ideals and then followed that little voice. "This is the serious problem that we have: bourgeois society is only worried about security and the elimination of risk, safety against risk. The supreme bourgeois mentality has as its criterion security against risk or, alternatively, the complaint and accusation of others that characterizes most everyone at this moment."[7] The problem had to do with a reduction of the heart that Enzo tried with every means to correct in us young people, using even those martial tactics we remember so well:

> I had a burning passion for Vespa, the mythic Primavera 125, and, after hammering away for a long time, I convinced

---

6. Bologna, October 1988.
7. Bologna, February 14, 1993.

my parents to buy one for me. "She" arrived when I still had an arm in a cast. Not able to drive it, every now and then I went down to the garage, started it up, gave it two or three revs, and watched it as if she was the most beautiful woman in the world. One day, I was invited to a concert of Bolognese singer and songwriter Andrea Mingardi. I bought a chain that weighed almost more than the Vespa, and arrived at the concert very early, in order to find the best place to park it safely. Enzo Piccinini was also there that evening. We all entered the small arena of the festival together . After the concert was over, I hurried out to get to my dear Vespa as soon as possible. Plot twist! The Vespa was not there anymore. I kept wandering from one area to another. At a certain point, I approached my friends, and Enzo looked at me with a defiant expression, and said, "Where did your Vespa end up?" Enzo had "commissioned" some of our friends to hide the Vespa. It was his way of loving me, because he was asking me, in that way, what I held most dear. He did not oppose what I cared about, my interests, to the Mystery that was within the companionship that had taken hold of me, but precisely starting from my dearest interests, he challenged me. After many years, Enzo told that story, something apparently banal, to some friends, saying that that kid (me) whose Vespa he had hid, was unhappy, deep down... It was true. (Luca Rossi)

Naturally, when he spoke to us he said that this bourgeois mentality was a peculiarity of our generation (and he was right); when he spoke to the adults he said the same thing (and he was right). In both cases, though, he emphasized different aspects and adapted his terminology: "What is the true sickness of us adults? It is called arteriosclerosis. It is an invalidating sickness that we suddenly start to tolerate, without fighting it anymore. In fact, psychologically you see it in us adults: we have allowed ourselves to settle into a certain kind of sedentary life, we no longer confront life, we no longer fight, we endure life. This psycho-physical decadence is favored by thoughts such as: 'Now, after 40 years, it's not like we can act like little children anymore. And as for enthusiasm, come on! Leave it to the university students, at most. I have my worries. I have a family. It's totally different. It's not like you can come to me and say that I have to... Enough. I have already done my part. Now you do something yourself. I already put in my time.' Arteriosclerosis has to do with the fact that we no longer love, even as we still participate in life. Therefore, ultimately, it is a mechanism; our lives just go on their own way. The alternative to a sedentary life is not neuroticism, or frenzied activism. It is a way of conceiving ourselves as in a battle."[8]

What made these words sharp was not only the force and the appropriateness of their content, but also their "practical" interpretation, the very life of Enzo that entered forcefully into the life of whomever he met, disrupting routines in other people's homes, in Bologna or in Paris:

> I was about to leave with a group of friends, law students like me, to go study in the mountains. The luggage was on the bus and I was stepping up into the bus... From one of the windows of the building in front of us, I seaw people hugging and shouting. Out of breath, a girl I didn't know showed up and yelled my name (I was starting to get seriously worried) and said, "Enzo is on the phone! Come quick!" I ran to pick up the call. "According to what the Church asks us," he told me on the telephone, "we are organizing a march for Bosnia [the war in Yugoslavia had just broken out]. I thought about you who are good at printing things and coordinating with the other associations at the school. Let's get together today. Bye." The bus left without me and with my luggage on board. I accepted because I trusted the friendship with him. It was often like that with him; plans changed and routines also. (Sara Bassani)
>
> Quickly, he broke through every comfortable, bourgeois criterion of family life. With Enzo you could never get comfortable. Our house became his general headquarters. He ate at our house, met people at our house, brought people to our house that he had met, or friends of friends, and we

---

8. Marche, June 10, 1997.

did School of Community[9] at our house! And dinner after dinner ended up in discussions that lasted late into the night. They were always heated discussions because he and I never agreed. He poked his nose into everything, into our life, but also into what to give our kids to eat, where to spend our vacations, with whom, for how long. With my 18-month-old son, he had no problem giving him a whole apple. And I rushed over and shouted: "What are you doing? And you're a doctor? Don't you know that he could choke?" Or when he went to pet the swans in the park, and I was always there shouting: "Are you crazy! Don't you know they can run after you and bite you? What kind of example are you setting for our kids?" (Alexandra Guerra)

It was the very life of Enzo that was incompatible with any bourgeois appeal, and he always told us clearly, even concerning the way to treat relationships among us: "We have to break through, to go permanently beyond the limit of what is comfortable, of convenience, of likes and dislikes. These are only brief stages that call us to the need for something more definitive, something that can finally, truly respond to what you are."[10]

"Brief stages" means that the transience of things is their unavoidable condition. Not to recognize this means to remain in prison. In those years, Father Giussani loved to re-read a passage from the Ambrosian Liturgy, which he appreciated so much: "Lord, in giving us the goods that pass away, you push us to the possession of a happiness that remains and, while you allow consolations in this present life, you already promise future joys, so that there may be, already now, a foretaste of everlasting life."[11] Precisely by starting from our dearest interests (the Vespa), Enzo challenged us, so that those goods that were "given" to us, those goods that pass, would

---

9. "School of Community" is a moment of catechesis, in guided groups, generally occurring once a week, on a text indicated by the center of the Movement. It is a fundamental instrument of the education to the faith that has accompanied, since the beginning, the educational proposal of Communion and Liberation, promoting personal and communal reflection.

10. Bologna, January 9, 1994.

11. Preface of Monday of the Fifth Week of Lent.

not imprison us. On the contrary, they should push us to a foretaste of everlasting life.

On this matter, I have had the occasion to hear some of Enzo's stories that unfortunately I have not found again among the available transcriptions. It is worthwhile to bring them out here, trusting my memory. For example, on a visit to friends in Turin, he told us that, when he was young, he had seen in a courtyard a blackbird that tried to take off with all the strength that it had and then, after a few meters, it crashed suddenly to the ground. A bit stunned by the blow, it waited a few seconds and then tried again, with the same tragic outcome. Enzo, curious about the phenomenon, got up close and saw that the foot of the bird was tied with a fishing line to a tree. We can aspire with all our strength to have this foretaste of everlasting life, but we will always fail, as long as something on this earth ties us in such a way that we are not able to take off. The second story (even further back in my memory) was that of the infamous "little rubber man" (I really don't know where he found this image) who, being nailed down to the earth as well, gave the impression of being able to stretch up to heaven... but then he would always bounce miserably back to the ground.

There was then another aspect that we had to resist: the attitude (very widespread, in those days, toward the truth of things) that exalts "doubt" as the only path to knowledge. We were being taught to face reality as a "problem," that is, as a transitory and difficult moment in which we must conquer the truth, a truth that was attainable and certain. Doubt, instead, cuts us down, takes the ground out from under our feet, and keeps us from abandoning ourselves to what convinces the heart. It was not only a battle of terms that often generated harsh debates at the time; it was the denunciation of an attitude that resulted in the radical solitude of the person. After the gray period of the great ideologies, there was now an opposite, discolored period of solitude respectful toward the opinions of others: "I am originally from the flat lands between Mantua and Reggio Emilia, a foggy zone six months of the year, something terrifying; and then there are evenings when you need to drive with your head out of the car in order to see. It happens, those two or three times, that at a certain point, in this strange fog, you see an indistinct shadow. You are driving at two miles an hour, you stop, and you reason about what you see. Because it is a predominantly agricultural region, you think, 'Oh, could it be a bull?' and then you begin to feel a chill even if the car has the heat on. 'It will ruin the car, even as slow as it is!' But it could be— again, in this agricultural area—a hay bale. And you stay right there. Suddenly, a gust of unexpected wind takes away the fog for a moment and you see a bale of hay! Why do we continue to say that doubts make us free? Doubts keep us suspended from reality! It is only when you are certain that you get involved. And sure, there will be clashes, and further searching, but this is good. Doubt suspends you, it places you on the side to look and see if it is true or not, but then you don't live, you aren't present within things."[12]

THE ONE WHO IS REACTIVE ASKS FOR FIRE AND GETS BURNED

The other great strategy that power uses to distance man from his heart is that of suggesting to him that the most effective way to face reality is his reactivity. And so, he never has the occasion to ask himself about reality, let alone about his own reactivity. It is the simplest way never to have a subject who can say "I" and oppose those who try to reduce the thirst for totality. "Two years ago, I went to Tampa, Florida, where there was this small group of GS.[13] They were kids, you can imagine, 14, 15 years old, and they listened to very strange music, a type of repetitive vomit—I don't know if you know what I'm talking about—that went on for hurs. It is a bestial thing. They call it 'trash music', which means music that you want

---

12. February 23, 1995.

13. "GS" (Gioventù Studentesca) is the educational proposal of Communion and Liberation specifically targeted to high school students. In the first years of the Movement (beginning in 1954), the life of CL coincided with GS: those were the years when Father Giussani taught religion at the Berchet High School in Milan.

to throw away, that is really like—I swear—vomit, belching. This is how they sing, get it? It makes an impression. Steadfast in the principle of education that 'an educator is with the ones he has to educate,'[14] that is, an educator is ahead of them in their issues, then is the first to slow down, I was with them. Then after a bit, I began to give them a few suggestions: 'I don't know, guys, but... Sting, for example...' That is, I tried to get closer to them a little bit. 'But no, you don't understand... of course you think like that!' I came back six months later, at Christmas—this had happened in June—and with great surprise the same kids were listening to the Beatles. They were all listening to the Beatles, and I was stunned: 'What, you guys are listening to the Beatles?' The same dreamy air: 'Beautiful!'... Afterwards, I understood that the album of the Beatles had come out! If you remember, in America they do 'remakes' and they launched a suffocating campaign, targeting all the kids, at school. The Beatles everywhere: the Beatles nude, the Beatles on bicycles, the Beatles on horseback, the Beatles on a walk, the Beatles on t-shirts, the Beatles on sunglasses, the Beatles on hats, the Beatles on everything, everything. The kids could not flee from the Beatles. In six months, their taste had changed. Unpredictable, absolutely unpredictable."[15]

There is a comfortable and manageable reactivity where the one who pays is the deepest part of you that is never consulted and, one reaction after another, it burns out. "Listen to a passage that I brought with me. An absolute solitude in which man feels the drama of his position, but defends himself like this:

> Once there lived a soldier-boy,
> quite brave, one can't be braver,
> but he was merely a toy
> for he was made of paper.
>
> He wished to alter everything,
> and be the whole world's helper,

---

14. This maxim, thrown out between the lines (I don't know where it came from; maybe he created it himself, at the moment), in reality was the principle of action in every educational undertaking of Enzo. He really "stayed" with us an extraordinary amount of time.

15. Summer vacation of the Bologna university students, August 13, 1997.

but he was puppet on a string,
a soldier made of paper.

He'd bravely go through fire and smoke,
he'd die for you. No vapor.
But he was just a laughing-stock,
a soldier made of paper.

You would mistrust him and deny
your secrets and your favor.
Why should you do it, really, why?
'cause he was made of paper.

He dreads the fire? Not at all!
One day he cut a caper
and died for nothing; after all,
he was a piece of paper.[16]

Such is the structure of the one who faces reality in a reactive way: he looks for fire and ends up burnt because he is a paper soldier, because reality grinds up his attempts."[17]

This progressive thinning of awareness is at the base of so many human and relational disasters that afflict human life both yesterday and today. "The desert that I know, that makes me sick, is the desert of affection that is around me, in the places where I am. We no longer love each other, in the true sense of the term. It is the estrangement of colleagues, where everything is determined by interests, by small and great private interests. The desert! It is the desert of affection, that is the thing that we suffer the most, then in the end we become cynical, but at the beginning we suffer. A desert of affection."[18] "In America, in the hospital, one asks you how you're doing and you don't even have time to answer before he has already left."[19]

---

16. Bulat Okudzhava, "Paper Soldier", translated by Alec Vagapov, https://ruverses.com/bulat-okudzhava/the-paper-soldier/6550/.

17. Florence, October 20, 1989.

18. Bologna, April 21, 1991.

19. Cesena, March 12, 1999.

But the medicine for this radical estrangement, for this prevalent cynicism, is worse than the sickness: "So we unburden ourselves to the right and to the left, we unburden ourselves as much as possible, because we are not able to face the problem. We have to unburden ourselves, maybe with some trip. This is the fashion! To go on a trip to unburden a little... and we return worse than before!"[20]

Values: a flag for power

In those years (above all in the years of *Mani Pulite*[21]) there was a huge discussion around values (a political party was even born!) and the thing was very delicate because, in the name of absolutizing some values at the expense of others, on the one hand, the Church was criticized for its incoherence, and on the other hand, she was invited to collaborate in the affirmation of common values, in order to build a more moral society. In short, there was an apparent benevolence in offering to Christianity a place in the common civic work, with the simple request, in exchange, that the Church close her eyes to "divisive" values (one of which was Jesus). On these themes, Enzo got (very) heated up: "Values exist only as a flag for power, which makes them turn wherever it wants, if they are not founded on an ontology, which is a difficult word that we use to say an objective point that anchors them to a fact. Otherwise, the value is, little by little, either affirmed or censured, according to the convenience of power."[22]

His most spectacular attacks were those of a conspiratorial stamp, those that he hurled against the "myths" of purity spread by the most beloved American films. "I will throw out a few things here. Excuse me, I do not claim to say anything dogmatic. I happened to say to a group of university students, those who are closest

---

20. Pesaro, April 30, 1999.
21. "*Mani Pulite*" ["Clean Hands"] (also called "*Tangentopoli*") is the name given to a series of judicial inquiries that, from February 1992, brought to light a widespread system of collusion between Italian politics and business.
22. Florence, May 6, 1989.

to me, around Christmas Eve or thereabouts, that in my opinion the greatest disaster of this society, with which the general Masonic line has taken power in hand, is Walt Disney. There was a moment of total silence. They all looked at me as if to say: 'Are you crazy?' And I said, 'No, this is real.' Walt Disney was a total disaster. It was the instrument of bourgeois, liberal-bourgeois, and Masonic education in society all over the world, that has easily managed to undermine Christian education little by little, contributing to what was already in act. Not only is there no Christmas without Walt Disney; so many human values of coexistence are made into absolutes by Walt Disney. A value without its own ontology cannot stand, because what remains in the heart? A nostalgic melancholy of what we see there described, because the heart cannot help desiring those things but, in essence, it is impossible to live them. How to live generosity, how to live altruism, how to live friendship, without their root?"[23] "Walt Disney has taken Christian values (generosity, justice, maternal love, solitude, and companionship... all the Catholic Christian values that did not exist before, except as a far, far description from certain human geniuses that had arisen in history prior to Christianity) and has taken them away from their ontology. And it became 'Try to be good,' 'Love each other,' 'Feel a feeling,'... etc. But without the ontology we are screwed! They have robbed us! The problem is this, don't you see?"[24]

Moralism is a sorry excuse for morality, and therefore it blocks true morality. Therefore, we fought against it, whether in the relationships among ourselves (correction) or in the critical work of denouncing public culture (*Mani Pulite*, for example). Moralism is also an optimal weapon for avoiding the heart of the question, the heart of man. "Four years ago, everyone spoke about peace. Now, peace is a phenomenon that is done by diplomacy, or some isolated march that doesn't have any impact—no relevance in the press, none at all. Honesty is a great headline. So, for a few values, we demand full coherence, while for others we even applaud their absence. On

---

23. Bologna, January 223, 1994.
24. Bologna, January 23, 1997.

the one hand, we are quick to condemn and, on the other hand, we are just as ready to justify ourselves. Moralism is a unilateral choice of values. Solidarity, ten years ago; peace, four years ago; now, honesty. I am not saying that within this battle there is not a desire for integrity and generosity. I am saying that this way brings with it not a morality but a moralism, an exaltation of one factor rather than another, guided in this, hand in hand, even directly, by those who form public opinion."[25]

One last aspect that struck Enzo a lot from the point of view of the morality of the youth was their immediate availability to do their "duty." Certainly, for one who went to high school in 1968, this was another symptom of the failed outcomes of the revolution. But it was, at the same time, a symptom of a structural weakness, because duty (lived badly) blunts the most incisive weapon of a young person: imagination. "I am not saying that the young person does not need to go to university; he should go. I am not saying he does not need to study, I am saying that now he needs to study, and seriously. But I say that we have to discover something so that they don't determine us like on an assembly line. In my opinion, this is the problem, because now you come out of high school and you have your daily duty as the highest thing in your life. And it is a duty without imagination. The ultimate duty without imagination."[26]

This way of facing human problems represents the exact opposite of the type of life that erupts when one has the (revolutionary) fortune of having the "encounter."

---

25. Bologna, October 17, 1993.
26. Bologna, October 1988.

4.

What the Heart Desires does Exist

THE WORD "ENCOUNTER" DESCRIBES THE HISTORICAL MOment when man (concrete man) becomes aware that what his heart has always desired, imagined, nervously pursued, all of this simply "exists." It is not the fruit of an effort, nor of a projection of desire; it arrives as a fact. It happens. Like a sunny day.[1] And through that fact the revolution happens: the certainty of a "good" destiny. Ultimately, this thing that is so simple is what our heart needs most (whether we know it or not, whether we admit it or not).

A GOOD DESIGN

How can we help the freshmen to begin something they do not know, and so overcome the threatening risks that college brings? This is a question for those who begin university, but it is also a question for anyone who lives; life is always a beginning, always uncertain. And here we come back to... Walt Disney! This time, though (in spite of him), he gave a prompt for a comparison which Enzo held dear: "When I was in America, I went to Disney World.

---

1. Father Giussani taught us the concept of "event" utilizing the beautiful verses of Albert Camus: "It is not with scruples that a man will become great. Greatness comes about, God willing, like a beautiful day." (A. Camus, *Taccuini* [*Notebooks*]. *III, 1951-1959,* Bompiani, Milan, 1992, p. 34.)

There is a ride that I remember very clearly, called Space Mountain. It is a large dome that one enters after walking down a long hallway. There are small pods shaped like missiles, and crazy things happen. There are lasers that make shapes and, suddenly, in front of you, meteorites that jump out at you, and it seems real—it is nothing to joke about. I don't think I am an impressionable child, but I swear to you that I had never seen anything like this. Anyway, before going inside, there is a long, very long, corridor, maybe a kilometer long (but they do it on purpose) leading to the dome. The warnings begin outside. The signs say: 'Anyone who has heart problems, anyone who is recovering from surgery, anyone who gets an upset stomach and vomits,' a whole series of warnings, 'we ask you not to enter,' because all these things will happen. Someone like me, seeing this, is even more tempted (I am vagotonic): let's go ahead, it seems like a joke. You go inside and, every 10-15 meters, it is the same warning, illustrated with all these little figures. When you are about to go in, suddenly, they project on the walls the faces of those who are taking their turn on the ride, and you see some hallucinated faces. Then, after these faces, you look around and there is a new warning: 'Now that you have seen the faces of these people... think about it.' Then you go inside and you climb aboard and this infernal ride begins. Now: what made it possible for me to go in there? What allowed me to face something that I did not know, something that was certainly very disconcerting, above all for me? Only one thing: the fact that I knew I would come out, that I was sure that it would go well. Look, even if they had told me that it was all a joke, that it was there just for effect, it would have been the same: I had to be sure that the outcome was good, that is, that I would come out. This is identical to the relationship with reality. The university, this new thing that you did not know, and that you do not know, that you are beginning, brings out what is always the case, but is not always so clear. When you get in line to register for classes, you recognize right away that not only is it a composite, essentially strange reality, that is, unknown, but it is also a kind of thing that can grind you up. They begin by telling you that 'you are a freshman,' you are a number.[2] They bring you here and there, you cannot even choose the class, you go into it with a ton of people who are totally different, each one nervous, without any connection with the others, careful not to make that connection. We can live this reality, we can accept to live this reality in a united way—without conforming ourselves, without giving up arms or losing some of our humanity—only if we understand that it is part of a good design for us. That is, only if we understand that all this strange and disconcerting thing ultimately has a meaning, and is part of a good plan. It is inside a good plan for you. It is not the enemy. It is not a stranger. It is strange, but as for its ultimate meaning, it is good for you. We have to understand this. Otherwise, in some way, we go inside and we just survive, that is, we lose ourselves. A total sadness. Or solitude."[3]

The historical fact that says to the world that reality is not the enemy, is not a stranger, that it is good for you, is called Christianity, the Christian announcement. We must recognize, first of all, before we are even in agreement or not, the nature and the importance of this news that runs through history from the year zero to today. "This is how reason functions, the structure of our humanity: it brings with itself all that it has learned until that moment. Suddenly, we stop in front of something like the Incarnation... a revolution. Is the concept clear? This happened, it is something amazing. I remember three or four years ago at the CLU Equipe,[4] some Buddhist monks came who were very religious, much more religious than us, all given over to their rule. At the moment of impact with us,

---

2. The Italian word for "freshmen," *matricola*, literally means the number of an item on a list or register.

3. Bologna, October 1988.

4. "CLU" (Communion and Liberation University) is the educational environment proposed by CL to university students. In addition to the educational instruments proper to the Movement as such, the CLU is characterized by a great variety of forms of presence in the environment (cultural as well as social and political) and by numerous opportunities for "shared life," connected for example to the necessity, for those who come from out of town, to share life in rented apartments. The "Equipe" is a moment of work proposed to the national leaders of the CLU that takes place at different times throughout the year, normally in Milan, but also in the mountains, on the occasion of summer vacations.

during the dialogue, this affirmation came out: 'God became man and is present here: this is our faith.' A Buddhist monk stood up and said, very honestly, 'I cannot believe this; for me it is too much.' This person grew up within a mentality that was cultivated for over 2,000 or 3,000 years which excluded this possibility for him. Now, suddenly, in front of such a shocking announcement that threw over everything he could think or that he could compare from his knowledge, he honestly answered: 'I cannot believe this.' The characteristic of what is in front of us, the claim of Christ, we can take it seriously, it is profoundly rational, because it puts itself forward as a fact in history. And, if it puts itself forward as a fact, reason cannot help but face it, even if it is not part of one's tradition. It puts itself forward as a fact, it happened, it is here; you cannot help but face it. You can speak up and oppose it to death, but you cannot help but face it, because reason, by its nature, in front of a fact, confronts it, demands its meaning."[5]

The announcement that what the heart desires exists, is a fact, an "event," as Father Giussani explained to us. It is an event that upsets the routine of daily life, the rules of the world: "Event means something that happens to me in life, and the 'I' takes on a new responsibility that makes it truly subsist, because there is, present, that to which one has to respond every day! One notices oneself in a way that he had never noticed before. Imagine that young guy that you were or that I was, 15, 16, 18 years old maybe—yes, fourth year of high school, when there was not even concern for the big graduation exam at the end of the fifth year—sufficiently intelligent to do well in the first quarter and to live off the income during the second, who plays sports, and his problem is getting up at five minutes before eight in the morning to get to school at eight, who throws on the first item of clothing he can find, quickly smooths out his hair and then out he goes. I knew this kid well, and if I close my eyes I see myself again... Suddenly, he encounters two beautiful blue eyes, big and deep, that he can never forget. These blue eyes are the property of a female figure who is particularly interesting. This

---

5. Bologna, June 23, 1991.

female figure, when asked, responds, "Yeah, sure." The next day, this guy wakes up at seven thirty in the morning. And at seven thirty in the morning, what does he do? He looks in the mirror to make sure he is well combed, and suddenly there is a sweater: 'Mom, does this match?' What happened? An event; this event provoked the 'I' to exist, to become aware of itself. The 'I' now consciously responds to someone and something, and life becomes more life, more possessed, more critical, more thought through! It is an event that makes the 'I' subsist! If it is Destiny that gives you freedom, if this Destiny becomes an event in life, it forces you to take responsibility, and every detail in your life becomes important! You begin to take yourself seriously!"[6]

"An event means something that happens: it is a father, a husband and wife, the husband goes home and the wife tells him, 'I'm pregnant.' It could have been or not have been, but now it is there. An event is something like this, that happens. So it is for you, so it is for the community: it could have been there or not have been there. You are all here, and it happened."[7] This was not just an interesting description. They were facts that we saw happen on a daily basis.

> What I remember most clearly is what happened after Enzo left. I got in line impatiently to reach the public telephone in the hall of the hotel and I made a phone call. I called my girlfriend in Milan and told her: "Today I found what I was looking for. From now on I will follow him." (Angelo Vato)

And the most surprising thing is that the same thing happened to those who met us who followed him.

The word "event" signals the method through which the unknown point, toward which the heart of every man tends, has chosen to make itself familiar. This word has great cultural value (because it signals objectively and literally a revolution) but, from the ontological point of view, it is not of a cultural nature. Father Giussani described it as an "encounter," a term that disorients us

---

6. Florence, November 12, 1992.
7. Bologna, June 26, 1986.

because of the disproportion between a fact that happens to us every day and what "that particular encounter" brings into the life of man: "Now, from this point of view, what wakes us up? Humanly, what allows us to say, 'Hey!'? A provocation. *Pro-voco*, [in Latin] 'to call out.' Something that calls you out. That forces you to say yes or no. And what provokes you? An idea? No. Because you can write down an idea and put it in a library, or set it aside in your mind. A discourse? Even less. What provokes us is a reality, a presence, whose dynamic is the only thing that wakes us up—that is, an encounter. The only way you can get out of this hibernation is not even just to grit your teeth and really want it, no. It is an encounter. There is someone who comes and says, 'Well, kids, there is more.' I am not saying, 'Leave what you are doing' (because I want *you* to do it, because it involves your responsibility!). But there is more. 'Are you with me? Can we see each other sometimes, can we keep alive this small light in our heart? We can't let our exams be the death of us. And you know how many times you will die. But if the encounter is repeated you will overcome it.' I remember when I took the physics exam; I really thought I was going to die. I gave everyone a warning... my parents were praying for me... it was really incredible. And yet, here I am. Because I had the courage to follow someone, to let myself be provoked by an encounter. I was not standing outside this mentality; I was totally in it. None of us is standing outside, we are all immersed in this reality. We need a provocation, an encounter, a reality that pulls us out, like one who says to you, 'Listen, are you studying medicine?'—'Yes'—'Do you know that some of us have thought about going to Ischia to study together?'—'To Ischia?'—'Yeah, three days'—'Wow!' And you come home and you do your usual things, but there is in the back of your mind, like a memory, something that does not allow you to die within the cage that you are already preparing. And this encounter, whether you want it or not, whether you planned it or not, already happened; we are here. Now it depends on how you are paying attention. It is not an alternative to what you have to do. Without an encounter that provokes you, you do not understand your function in the world, because others are assigning it to you. You do not understand your usefulness in the place where you are, because others determine it for you, an adequate doctor in the European common market."[8]

The information booth that we had for incoming freshmen, which we hosted in every faculty to welcome newly registered students, could therefore boast a continuity, a connection with what had happened 2,000 years earlier in Jerusalem, because it had the same effect, it generated the same fruit: "The greatest example of Zacchaeus, do you remember? I have always told you, I was there by the sycamore tree when I visited the Holy Land and I imagined the episode. I went under the sycamore; it is a stumpy big tree with a short, stocky trunk. Think about Zacchaeus, who went up there. (He was a mafioso and he went up not only because he wanted to see Christ, but because he had to stay away from people because, according to the Hebrew law, he was a sinner. If he was not three meters away, he would contaminate you. So he had to be far away. If he went down the tree, they would beat him up, because he was a recognized mafioso.) Christ passes underneath and looks at him, 'Zacchaeus, I am coming to your house!' Now imagine the people. Back then, it was like now. Imagine the people: 'Oh my! Even him!' In front of all those people, Jesus does not say, 'Listen Zacchaeus, now when you are all cleaned up (*Mani Pulite*), I will come to your house.' He says, 'I am coming to your house!' This is an embrace that does not have boundaries, that does not calculate. So, this poor Zacchaeus saw that what his heart desired (because he too desired beauty, justice, even though he betrayed it continually) existed. What do we need? What do people need, what do my children need, your children when you will have them, or if you will have them, what do they need? That there be a presence, people that make it possible for others to recognize that what the heart desires exists. Even if they betray it a thousand times, it exists. We need something like this."[9]

An encounter is therefore a human encounter. It is like all the other human encounters, from the point of view of the

---

8. Bologna, October 1988.
9. Bologna, January 23, 1994.

phenomenon, but it is distinguished from the others by a particular. This encounter makes you sense a unique and unmistakable depth through the perception that you are in front of "something with something inside it." It is an encounter like so many others, but one that opens a crack, a glimpse, not yet clear, of something within that is unique, exceptional. "Here, something happened (a telephone call, an invitation, a flyer, a booth), where there is something inside. And then it may happen that it is not like a flash of lightning in the dark that quickly disappears and everything becomes dark again. It is the curiosity for this something within that allows another human position to begin."[10]

> "Rossana, this is Enzo. I am coming to dinner at your house. Are you home?" And I worry right away about things to do, about friends who were absent. I would have wanted them all there, at least for coffee. "Enzo, yes, but I am by myself, my friends are not here." And he said, "So what? Are you there? I will be there at 7:30!" Two hours from now, an empty refrigerator. Enzo liked fish… With the friends who were there in the apartment and the yes of a friend I had just met from the apartment of the guys from ISEF, who knew how to cook fish, we were able to throw together a little supper worthy of the name. The center of the evening? That friend from Morciano di Romagna! The two of them had never even met, but Enzo talked with him the whole evening as if he had known him forever. (Rossana Gobbi)

The Spark: the fascination of correspondence

Catholic catechesis had been proposed to the majority of us, insisting first of all on the moral principles that moved directly to questions of conscience, without any mediation but, above all, without an attractive force that was capable of setting fire to the gunpowder of our humanity. In Father Giussani's proposal, the method was inverted: "'If you love me, you will keep my commandments.' He did

---

10. Bologna, October 1988.

not say, 'If you observe my commandments, you will love me,' which is what all the priests preach. Christian life is born from a fascination, not for all those things that we have to do or not do. Take this away from our experience and you will have participation in an institution, with that typical loss of the adult experience, wherein we participate in the institution, but private life is managed in its own way, that is, ultimately doing your own thing, sadly. It is in front of a presence we love that life is illuminated. The law makes us sad. In front of a presence we love, all of a sudden, we learn how to live."[11] This happened in Enzo's life, this illuminated his life, and this light was also reflected in our own attempts at realization. There was a fascination for a human accent that made present the same accent that had so struck the first friends of Jesus: "At the end, someone from the parish stands up and says, 'But these things, we are always telling them to each other; you have not said anything new. The only new thing you said, the only new thing that I understood, is the new accent with which you say these things.' I told him: 'Good, this is precisely the true problem, because if you try to change the accent of the words, you no longer understand the meaning.' So, this, in my opinion, is the true characteristic of the Movement: it is characterized by the accent of experience on the words we tell each other. It is as if our words were dense and full, full of experience, as if they narrated a full, humanly full experience."[12]

This new accent stood out first of all because it did not limit itself to raising questions. It also gave answers, *the* answer. Father Giussani made us notice many times that the insistence and clarity on the religious sense, on the heart of man that is a structure of questions, was made possible by the answer brought by the Christian event.[13] It is in front of the answer that man is able to understand what had always been his question, even though it was confused. "I sometimes go to Turin to help the community, and there was

---

11. Marche, June 10, 1997.

12. Bologna, October 28, 1987.

13. Cf. Luigi Giussani, *Qualcosa che viene prima* [*Something that Comes Before*], 30 Giorni, Rome, 1993.

a public meeting with Cardinal Saldarini and the university students. At a certain point, he stopped two or three of us after the meeting and made this comment: 'What impresses me is that you raise up questions in people, because then the people ask, "Who are these people? Why do they act like this?" The way you position yourselves, you raise up questions. Only, you have an additional characteristic that differentiates you from all the others that do this. That is, you are an answer, you bring an answer to the question that everyone has.' Now, it does not matter if this answer is welcomed or not. Christ came to His own, and His own did not receive Him. Yet He is the answer. This is what was given to me, to you, to all of us, to carry out as our supreme service. We have to be ourselves, we have to live what was given to us, so that it may be the answer to the question that everyone has, to the cry that everyone has."[14]

To be "the answer to the question that everyone has"... to bring this into the world becomes possible when the encounter makes it possible to live that particular type of experience that Father Giussani called "correspondence." Correspondence is a profound harmony you perceive between what is in front of you and what is in the depth of your person. It is only through correspondence that you can begin to "verify" the credibility of the one you have in front of you. "I always say that if Christianity were the Ten Commandments (as so many times we have been told), I would not be here. Because when life is decided mechanically by a law, one's only enthusiasm—is it true or not?—is to transgress that law. Because man cannot be defined by a law. By a love, he can! It is a presence to love, not a law to keep. It cannot be something from 2,000 years ago, which we read and say, 'The word of the Lord,' because no one falls in love with a word. Has anyone ever fallen in love with a word, or a book? Rather, we fall in love with a man, with a woman, and then, how dear their letters are to us! Or am I wrong? We fall in love with the presence who wrote the words. That presence, because of

---

14. Bologna, June 21, 1992.

whom those words are precious. That presence, because of whom that book is precious."[15]

Even though what we talk about is so much more "other" and different than man can imagine, this does not stop the visceral experience of correspondence, precisely because the urgency for this "other" is inscribed in our structure. Therefore, when it happens, it is (paradoxically) easy to recognize it, to notice it. "If your mother, when you were little, had come back from grocery shopping and said, 'You know what I saw on the corner?' 'What?' 'A strange house that in place of chimneys had long arms that put together the roof tiles, closed the windows, and washed the panes.' Anyone, you or I, would have looked at mom and said, 'Ah… nice story! And how does it end? Another fable!' Well, all our parents and all our educators spoke about Christ. This is something no less strange for a child… but no one ever rebelled. Never! Why? Because He corresponds. Because that man there, that one who promises and speaks, corresponds to the heart of man. He is far from what we imagine, but He corresponds; He seems far but he corresponds. This is what makes us consider deeply the answers that we give each other, as adults, as we have heard them given to us as children."[16] "Grace comes not to change human nature, but to clarify and fortify it. If a miracle destroyed the categories I normally use, those of my human nature, it would be an oddity, not a miracle."[17]

> Once, after a meeting of leaders where he and I were discussing what moves one's freedom, if it was anxiety or correspondence, he told me, "Look, Pietro, I am not able to make all these arguments like you, but go and read the last lines of "Decision for Existence."[18] They say this: "The path of the Lord is simple like it was for John and Andrew, for Simon and Phillip, who began to follow Christ, out of curiosity and desire. There is no other path, ultimately, than

---

15. Riccione, December 16, 1998.
16. Bologna, October 6, 1990.
17. Bologna, June 23, 1991.
18. In Luigi Giussani, *In Search of the Human Face*, Slant Books, 2025.

this desirous curiosity awakened by the presentiment of the truth."(Pietro Lorenzetti)

Prisca and Aquila

Whoever encounters a Christian encounters Christ. The event consists exactly in this, and in this it is differentiated from any other kind of human encounter, while remaining integrally human. "For this reason, what kind of attention and affection did Saint Paul have for every emergence of the Church, even the most particular! He felt everything so deeply! He greets, one by one, all the people in the community with such affection... it is something that doesn't have a comparison anywhere! 'Greet Priscilla and Aquila[wife and husband], my collaborators in Christ. They risked their necks to save my life. Greet also the Church that gathers in their house.'[19] How many could they have been, seven or eight? Their house! But he does not call them a little group, he calls them a Church. He uses the same word that he used to indicate the Church of Jerusalem, with which he indicated the Church. Every community, even the smallest, if it is authentic and if it is aware of being part of the universal Church, is an emergence of the universal Church. So let's look at this in the face: how many are in your fraternity[20]? Three, five, ten? But what difference exists in your life together, what attention for each other, what dignity there is in those relationships! 'Greet those two or three'—there is nothing like this anywhere else in the world!"[21]

---

19. *Romans* 16:4.

20. With the term "fraternity," Enzo is referring, in this case, to one of the many groups of adults that decided to adhere formally to the "Fraternity of Communion and Liberation." This is a lay association that, on February 11, 1982, was established as a juridical entity for the universal Church and declared an association of pontifical right by a decree of the Pontifical Council for the Laity. Those belonging to the Fraternity of Communion and Liberation normally gather together in small groups to help each other live the path indicated by the association.

21. Bologna, February 14, 1993.

Among the various phrases, I remember one in particular, at the end of the School of Community, at our house, we were six or seven, three Italians and four Parisians: "*Petite communauté, grand Paris!*"[22] Enzo was satisfied and enthusiastic about how the School of Community was going, even if we were only a ridiculously small number. In this little phrase of his we see all his trust, his hope, and the certainty of his faith in what he had encountered. He wanted to be within our French reality, without limiting himself to criticism. If he was there, in Paris, it was in order to be, through our teeny tiny community, the occasion for the great Paris to encounter Christ. (Alexandra Guerra)

Over time, in living together, the strangeness of the first encounter reveals its deep roots, the exceptionality of a person who died but is still present, as the Governor Festus candidly summed it up in the procedural case against Saint Paul: "His accusers... had some issues with him about their own religion and about a certain Jesus who had died, but whom Paul claimed was alive."[23] That's it, a simple disquisition on the facts of a man's death. A simple problem of calculation, because of which some people were ready to sacrifice their life. "And where is that man now? Because I have a need for Him now, just like they had a need for Him 2,000 years ago. Where is He? Excuse me, if He is real, He has to tell us where He is; we cannot say it ourselves. If I say, 'I don't know if that bottle of water is sweet or bitter,' and I unscrew the cap, I put my finger in it, I touch the water and say, 'It is sweet,' you tell me, 'You are crazy.' And you are right. Well, I 'tasted it' with my finger, didn't I? But I got the method wrong. To taste it, I have to drink it, because there are no taste buds in my finger. Why do we understand that Christ exists? Because we see something that exists by the effect that it provokes. It is a fundamental law. If we look out that window, and outside there is a tree that begins to rustle, we will say, 'It is windy!' But we do not hear it, we do not see it, nor do we talk to it; we are sure that the wind exists because we see its effect. Today, we see people that

---

22. "Small community, great Paris!"
23. *Acts* 25:18-19.

change in His name, just like 2,000 years ago. If He exists, He tells us how to relate to Him, because He is a reality. And He did give us the method: 'Where two or three are gathered in my name, I am present there.' He is present where people change in His name. It is called the Church. It's that simple. The rest is all arbitrary."[24]

"On the other hand, for us it is the same thing, because one who came here, an atheist who came here today, could not give a complete judgment on this assembly by telling us the number of heads that are here. He would have to admit that the only reason it was worth it to be here today is Christ, whom everyone says is dead—or whom everyone reduces to values—but who for us is alive today, here, just as He was then. It is the same identical thing for us. We are together, the Church exists, because we persist in saying that a man that everyone said was dead 2,000 years ago is alive today. Even among themselves they were afraid of saying it. It is the same identical thing that we experience when we hear it said to us, 'Christ risen is alive' here, now. The same identical thing. We feel that it is reasonable, but we are afraid even to pronounce it."[25]

"If Jesus is who He said He was, no time and no place can have any other center."[26] This was the true, distinctive sign of Enzo's personality, which put in second place all the spectacular (in every respect) aspects of his temperament. This was what, ultimately, Enzo left in the perception of those who encountered him, whether they came to terms with it or not:

> Thanks to the filial friendship with Father Giussani, Enzo fell in love with Christ and therefore his life was lived totally in relationship with Him. They were not words; we saw it. (Alfredina Pezzetta)

> I listened to him because of the mysterious passion that he put into communicating to us the only reason worth living for: a man who was present named Jesus. At the end

---

24. Riccione, December 16, 1998.
25. Florence, March 18, 1987.
26. Bologna, June 23, 1991.

of every encounter, I returned home with the desire to be a friend of that man. (Daniele Biondi)

One evening, the telephone rang and my grandma said, "It is the secretary of a doctor who is looking for you." Enzo invited me to meet him on the highway to go visit a friend in Reggio. I had to meet him at the Reggio toll booth in half an hour. I went to the meeting point. After a bit, a good while, a brown Fiat Croma approached, and Enzo was inside. "Get in. We're going to Ciccio Caprari's house." I said, "Okay, but I don't even know where he lives." "Really?! You are from Reggio and you don't know him?!" Somehow, he found the address, and we set out. When we arrived, we entered this beautiful country house with a barn attached and we met Ciccio and his family. We sat down at a table laden with salami, vegetable pie, Parmesan, Lambrusco, etc. Enzo introduced me to that family as dearest friends, and seeing how they treated each other, I understood that it was true. During the dinner we spoke about everything. I remember, among other things, the topic of milk quotas,[27] that at that time really set Enzo off. The way he was there struck me. To him, everything had a personal importance that was decisive, because for him, at the heart of every discussion, at the heart of every affection, at the heart of every relationship, at the heart of every circumstance, there was a precious and beloved friend, Jesus. He also treated me that way, as a friend. (Simone Mannocci)

He pushed the provocation and the discussion to a point that was exaggerated, and yet the kids came out, they matured thanks to this "rawness" of Enzo. But, above all, it struck me how, with this Socratic method, he brought everyone closer to Christ, he introduced everyone to the faith. He helped you to discover that you are made for Christ." (Father Primo Soldi)

---

27. This had to do with a European law that put a limit on the production of milk by each producer, beyond which there would be higher taxes, strongly disincentivizing production. Enzo, coming from a family of farmers and still having relatives who were farmers, had (clearly and radically) embraced the reasons for the protest, which generated very strong tensions in society at that time. I remember that, at a meeting of leaders of the CLU, during lunch he got into such a fight with Giancarlo Cesana on this topic that, in the end, he was the only one left in the room.

The wait was long for us because, as was obvious, we allowed all these meetings with people to run their course. When, finally, with a notable delay, Enzo welcomed us, shaking our hands, he told us, "I am struck by your humility and patience for having waited so long." We tried to downplay it, saying that that afternoon we did not have anything particular planned before returning to Cesena, and he, almost not hearing us and following his thoughts, said, "On the other hand, these kids have a great need of adults who can keep them company and I try, as best I can, however I can, to propose to them what I have learned: that in the sometimes turbulent path of life, we grow by following someone, who must not attach us to himself, but always bring us to Another, who for us has a specific name: Jesus Christ." (Raffaele Bisulli)

...He whom Paul insisted was alive

How does one become so certain, so in love with the presence of a dead man, who some claim is alive? How did Enzo do it? We have to accept a method of knowledge (we cannot know if a drink is sweet using the taste buds of our fingertips). We need another method, a very simple method, that we use every day of our life, above all to live the relationships that are most important for us, and to face daily life in its most basic and smallest aspects. "In our life together, in history, and in culture, we cannot avoid faith as a method of knowledge. So it is not something the priests have used to trick us; it is something that makes a person a person, finally, deep down! So you understand immediately that the bourgeois proverb, "To trust is good, not to trust is better," is truly a betrayal of man. Because the man who is a man all the way to his depth has only one characteristic: the capacity for relationship. We like people who have the capacity for relationship, and it is what we love most, and we say, 'Look what freedom he has in relationships, look what capacity for relationships he has.' This means that he has great faith! Whoever does not have faith exaggerates the instinct of defense, while man is made for relationship, for dialogue."[28]

Faith, therefore, is not to believe in something that is irrational, but to trust in a witness. It is not to turn off reason, but to rely on someone you can (indeed) trust to face even the things that your reason cannot know directly. Is this reasonable? In what conditions? "Take, for example, the case that you are in Verona, in Piazza Bra. You meet someone who is evidently beaten up and stumbling, who, clearly… has some problems, and he comes close to you. And you, like every good Christian, put your hand in your wallet knowing that alms help to pardon sins. You reach out to give something, but he tells you that he has to give you some bad news: 'Look, an hour ago Clinton died, they killed him. This is a total upheaval of society!' And you think, 'No! How am I going to manage? I am supposed to get married in two months! Now how am I going to manage when everything is changing like this? I will have to put the marriage up in the air; you never know with all of this social instability!' To believe a witness, who tells you something that you do not see, you have to be sure that the witness is credible."[29]

The witness lies at the center of the dynamic of faith as a method of knowledge. It is a dramatic matter, in any situation. Because whoever is in front of a witness is called to take a position (like what happened to me in front of Enzo), to choose one of two possibilities: "Is he crazy, a criminal, or are there signs that are not explained by this summary hypothesis, and that beg to be studied in depth, explained?" In short, in front of a witness, our most exciting and uncomfortable potentialities are always summoned, our freedom and morality, because a witness is always a challenge to our humanity. "In the university we have in Bologna, there are 1,400 kids that come regularly, and they fill the Cathedral every week, but why do you think they are there? You can say that maybe 10% of them are out of their minds, and I will concede it. I will even give you 20%…

---

28. February 23, 1995.
29. February 23, 1995.

But even only 50% of 1,400 kids, what are they there for, if it is not for a challenge to their humanity? Come on!"[30]

On this topic of the centrality of the witness in the dynamic of faith, Father Giussani had focused Enzo's educational method (following, in this, Jesus Himself). On the other hand, it is (or it should be) the hinge of every Catholic missionary action. There is an episode that many people know, and that I was able to document adequately only a few years ago: everyone knows that Enzo had written a book, probably with someone else and under a pseudonym (he made some quick references to it, here and there). It was a novel that had received "important recognition." Enzo told us that he and his friend presented themselves in turn to collect the prizes, and the people said, "But it was not him the other time! He didn't have a beard!" Naturally, none of us had ever believed the story, but the thing made both him and us laugh. A few years ago, a friend (someone very close to Enzo) forwarded to me a line contained in a novel written by one Antonio De Petro,[31] "Beyond life is the end."[32] In a dialogue between an angry bourgeois lady and a man who is very fascinating and deeply religious, the woman burst out and asked with a mocking irony, "And who do you think you are? Jesus von Nazareth?" The answer, if it was not written by Enzo, still describes magnificently his self-awareness and his temperament: "For me, God forbid, and praised be the devil. For you, it could be, ma'am. It could be." All those who met him were in front of this challenge and forced to give a judgment on that scandalous claim: "It could be."

This "mixture" of the divine in the human has always been a delicate topic and probably the fulcrum of all the great heresies born in Christianity. For us, the thing was quite simple: "What did we learn today? We learned something fantastic, that the supernatural is a human reality where Christ is present. The supernatural,

---

30. February 23, 1995.

31. This is a friend from Liguria, from the Movement of those years, who assures us that he is not the author of the novel.

32. Antonio De Petro, *Fuor della vita è il termine* [*Outside of Life Is the End*], Città Armoniosa, Reggio Emilia, 1982, p. 267.

not the strange thing beyond the clouds, is a human reality where Christ is present."[33]

IF I AM A CHRISTIAN IT IS ONLY BECAUSE IT IS THE BEST THING

Why did Enzo give himself to this human reality, he who, from the point of view of temperament, of his decisions, and of his capacity, would have been a cut above those who were a part of his companionship? In the encounter, Enzo discovered a whole series of dimensions that exalted the human well beyond what he had until then imagined and experienced. "If I am a Christian, it is only because, from the first moment of the experience I have met, it was the best thing! If not, it is not worth it. I have been in it because it was the best thing, humanly speaking! I would have had no other possibility of being here, because of how I was and how I lived. I always make a comparison and say that I want you to feel the challenge in its depths, to the point of almost irritating you, because otherwise we cannot understand. Like a plant that is more than a rock, it objectively participates in life, it is biologically more than the rock because it is more physiologically organized than the rock. Just like an animal is more than a plant, so, analogously, a human participates more in existence, organically, than the animal."[34] "I see Pussi—Pussi will forgive me—and Pussi is 99.9% an animal. He has an animal nature; but there is that 0.1% that is not reducible at all to the animal. So you are another nature. There is something else."[35] "And so, the Christian participates in being more than the others. I swear to you that I would not be in Christianity, if something like this was not clear to me. I wouldn't know what to do with Christianity, if it were all about just 'dos' and 'don'ts.'"[36]

---

33. Marche, February 23, 1997.
34. February 23, 1995.
35. Bologna, June 23, 1991.
36. February 23, 1995.

In Enzo, the encounter with Christianity opened up a horizon of human dimensions that before he simply imagined, desired, inordinately pursued. Now, one by one, they began to become clear and, above all, to make themselves accessible, even those that we normally try, more or less consciously, to avoid. One of the dimensions of the human that Christianity calls out to the height of its expressive potential is exactly what most excited Enzo: freedom. "Nature, used as a factor of salvation, is the highest that freedom can hope. Otherwise, we are, as Luther says, passive containers of the action of grace. Saint Ambrose says that you came into the world, you did not make the decision; however, to go to heaven without your "yes" is impossible. Amazing. We are not passive containers of the action of grace. There is a summit to reach for which freedom—the way we are made, this need for meaning and capacity to adhere—has to be used. Otherwise, I am out of here."[37] "The first decision is yes or no, and yes or no has the characteristic of not being a self-delusion, because otherwise you would find it weighing on you heavily; it would be insupportable. A coercive Christian morality is the most disgraceful thing in the world. It takes you away from things, and so you find yourself with this heaviness weighing on you."[38] The reason why Christianity exalts freedom is linked to the fact that without freedom the Christian fact cannot be "verified" by the one who encounters it. Christ always asks explicitly to be "recognized." "Because, if the beginning is an encounter, that is, a presence that enters powerfully in our life, the method for this thing to continue is the same. And the method is to become aware, to recognize that Presence."[39]

To recognize this Presence is a dynamic that paradoxically presents an aspect that is very simple and possible for anyone ("to look"), but that requires, for this reason, the right attitude, a simple attitude, the great re-conquering of "simplicity." "The Easter

---

37. Bologna, June 23, 1991.
38. Bologna, January 23, 1986.
39. Bologna, January 9. 1994.

poster[40] introduced a new term into Christian ascesis, our ascesis: that the challenge is 'to look.' If Christ is present, and He is not just words, and not books, and not moral precepts, but a Presence, our problem in life is not what we manage to change, nor what we have to give. It is that we have to accept to look at Him. The relationship with something present is to immediately look at it. It is not in the considerations that you can think; it is to look at it."[41] "We need this new humanity to be born, that, thank God, is not contained in any theory. It is born from the surprise of a small fact, which could have been confused with the rest of reality, but for someone who had a simple, needy heart, that fact became the key to change himself and the world."[42]

This simplicity was often highlighted by Father Giussani in different ways, as an essential condition for recognizing the absolute uniqueness of the Christian fact. Simplicity of heart is the only defense against prejudice and ideology (which he considered to be the bitterest enemies of Christianity). Enzo also underlined these things, in his own way. "There is a small village on a high mountain, a really high mountain, where the bus arrives only once a month, because there is always snow and it is a dirt road. But there is a group of people perched up there who cling to that place, mountain people who live there. Suddenly, the village doctor dies. A disaster, yes, because no other doctor wanted to go there, no one. They ask at the next village over and no one wants to go. They send requests to the whole region, here and there... Everyone says: 'No, no, no, I would rather be unemployed.' And so there is nothing to do, no one is going. At a certain point, they send a letter to the Head of State, and he makes a general appeal... no one! Total desperation. So what do they do? They cannot take it anymore and they write— in the end they make a virtue of necessity; it has always been like

---

40. Enzo is talking about a poster that each year is proposed by Communion and Liberation (originally in Lent and later also at Christmas) to offer a point of reflection and meditation on the two central liturgical periods of the Christian tradition.

41. Bologna, May 24, 1992.

42. Bologna, June 21, 1992.

this—some letters to Jesus Christ. 'At least, if He exists, He will respond,' they say, and in fact the letters reach Saint Peter, who says, 'I will go.' He asks someone to fill in for him, and then he goes to Christ: 'Excuse me, look, here is the situation. I have to go. Will you find me a substitute? Come on, put someone in my place and I will go down.' Jesus says, 'No, I will go! Something so impossible is really my job. I came into the world for this.' And so he decides to go. The announcement arrives in the village: 'Monday, three o'clock, new doctor.' At three, the doctor's office opens (the doctor is coming!) and he goes inside between the two lines of people, and sits down in his office. The mountain people have always been the kind of people who are not easily fooled: 'There is this guy here, who knows who he is, but we do not even know who he is...' So they send in the most severely disabled person in the village, they shove him inside and close the door. 'Now we will see how he manages!' The doctor says, 'How are you?'—'Uh, uh'—'Excuse me, but why do you talk like that? Can't you speak normally?'—'Yes, I can speak normally'—'But why are you in a wheelchair?'—'Ah, because I can't walk'—'Get up, why don't you?'—'Oh my, I can walk!'—'Then close that wheelchair and go.' So, he closes the wheelchair and leaves. 'Oh! So? Who is he?!'—everyone asks outside. 'Oh, calm down you guys,' responds the healed man. 'It is the usual cheap doctor from the public healthcare service... he didn't even bother to examine me!' Look what preconception does, you guys, what preconception does! When our students get engaged in the life of the university, like no one else does, others tell them, 'But you are the usual guys from CL. In the end, you will all join the DC.'[43] If there is a human factor in the Church, it means that Christ did not choose computers or angels to save the world. He chose people like me, like you. Which means that in the Church there must be the whole gamut of human sins! If not, it is not true that He chose humans. He chose a

---

43. *Democrazia Cristiana* (DC) was a political party of the center that for many years received the votes of a great number of Catholics in Italy. Founded in 1943, it remained active in government until 1994, breaking up after the scandals that emerged with the investigations of *Mani Pulite*.

computer. Preconception is the only thing opposed to faith. It destroys the possibility of growth, and this is the problem."[44]

Preconception is not disastrous in itself (being in itself inevitable), but it becomes so when it persists in front of a reality that says the opposite. It crystallizes in this way into ideology, which keeps us from taking into consideration anything that does not enter into our mental, social, and cultural schemes. "Mary Magdalene was the prostitute of that area, and everybody knew her. Everyone knew her; she was one of those whose name everyone knew. 'Ah... me too, me too.' Everyone. In Modena, there is one I know. Her name is Gina. When Gina walks by, everybody says, 'Eeeh!' It was exactly like this. So think about it: she went there, knowing perfectly well how everyone was looking at her, including the disciples. She went there because she needed Christ. And she was the only one who went to his feet with the gaze of someone in need. Think about all the others, the elbows they gave each other: 'Oh, look, look, there she is! Look, look who He's with... He doesn't even know she is a prostitute, look!' But this one looked at him as one in need, and Christ looked at her, noticing her correct attitude. We do not have this gaze because we are self-sufficient, we are all set, we try to be all set."[45]

"This one looked at him as one in need." Here is the key to everything. To understand the Christian fact requires an exclusive use of the heart according to its true nature, which is that of entreaty. Father Giussani explained it as the synthesis of the Gospel's concern, "poverty of spirit." Enzo had started using this criterion to "evaluate" people, to put the "great ones" in their place. Who is the greatest? "The first great one that I know is named Simeon. Simeon... We have to imagine it a little, because otherwise we don't understand. Simeon was a priest of the Temple, an old man, one of the oldest. The Temple was the place where the Hebrew mentality was born. Therefore, it was the place of power, and more than just civil power, because it had control of consciences. Well, he was

---

44. February 23, 1995.
45. Bologna, April 21, 1991.

one of those, the oldest. This man, immersed in the power and the dominant mentality, kept in his heart an expectation so pure that, against the entire dominant mentality, he recognized the salvation of the world in a child! It is something that gives me chills just thinking about it. In a child, the most laughable thing that exists, the most easy to eliminate, the least effective. It is incredible! Do you think this man Simeon didn't have to fight for this? That his expectation was simply a conviction of his, something that he thought up? Could it have survived in an environment where everyone was expecting a liberator who would correspond to their social categories? The political liberator, the social liberator, that's what the Messiah had to be! Simeon needs what that child is; he needs a presence who does not make proclamations, but who saves his life and stands out as a new personality that has never found an equal in history. That man says the same beautiful prayer that we recite each time we pray Night Prayer: '*Nunc dimittis servum tuum, Domine...*' 'Now let your servant go in peace, Lord, for my eyes have seen your salvation.' Anyone... the great ones... the great politicians, the great leaders of the people... salvation: a baby! Come on!"[46]

The thing that struck us and provoked us was the definite perception that he was not speaking about stories from another time, but that the same thing was happening in the same exact terms in our day, in the relationships among us. "What has happened to us? What is this community? A baby! In the same way. What is this group of people compared to those with power in their hands, who direct public opinion? What are we, if not this baby? Because salvation is given to be recognized in a place like this. It is the same identical thing: to recognize in something laughable (look at your faces!) the salvation of the world. Accepting this, a new history begins. Not accepting this, there is no Christianity. An angel. Come on, an angel, are you kidding?! It could have been taken for a vision, something imagined. What happened to us? A telephone call, a flyer, is it not the same thing? An invitation to come here; is it not

---

46. Bologna, April 21, 1991.

the same thing? Well, that woman, Mary, believed that angel, and a new history began."[47]

IT WAS LIKE LIFE EXPANDED

The encounter produces a revolution. When the encounter happens, what happens can only be evoked in some way by using analogies. "I remember that I had a major crush on a girl, one of those memorable things that you never forget. I never was able to study at night because I said that I heard the silence. Those two months, I studied without problems even at night. It was like life had expanded, the usual things had another meaning. It is like this. It is a distant comparison with what happens when an encounter like this takes hold of a person, moves her to a hope for herself, something different, something greater. You see, it is something much more, much more than falling in love, like I described. It is a distant comparison, because it happens like this. One has a new desire for everything. It is as if he discovered within himself a principle, a bubbling fountain that makes him encounter everything. His interests expand, his courage in relationships is freed, his horizon of affection expands. It is like a new point of reference, radically, ultimately new in our thought, in our affection. Imagine, you guys, that there was a strange people, in a certain place on earth, that had always lived in the shadow of the evening, that is, at night, because the sun never was able to illuminate them. They had always lived like certain shrimp, I think, that live in caves, that always live in darkness. Just imagine that there was a people like this, that has always lived like this. And how did they possess things? How did they possess themselves, things, the desk, the usual things—friends, structures, houses? By groping around, because they did not have infrared rays in their eyes. Everyone was like this. Imagine that, all of a sudden, the darkness is pierced and the light appears. The usual things (those that they had always possessed by groping around, trying to give them a shape, a connection, a definitiveness, imagining

---

47. Bologna, April 21, 1991.

it) acquire another substance. They are invested, transformed by another finality, another relationship, another type of position. This is comparable to what happens in an encounter like this. It is like the child who, in the arms of his mother, feels that he belongs totally to that person, and insofar as he belongs to that person he feels secure. Something greater is everything that is at the root of my way of thinking, my way of feeling. We abandon ourselves to this and then everything that we have around us acquires a new light. It is the experience of belonging to something; it is belonging. The relationship that I have with Widmer who sang before, with Manlio who I see sitting here, with Mescolini and with others, with Guido, with Davide, is this type of relationship."[48]

It was dizzying just to imagine that there could be a line that connected falling in love, shrimp, a child in the arms of its mother, and the companionship of us there with him. The encounter and its continuity marked a sure path for the "certainty," the existential certainty, the dimension that we all aspire to and that we had come to doubt was even possible.

One of the aspects that most struck us was the almost immediate outcome of this encounter, which was the unity of the person. "It is only in the encounter that the unity between the heart and reason is accomplished for the person."[49] The friend that shared with Enzo all those years of leadership since the beginning, Giancarlo Cesana, the friend Enzo perhaps loved best, remembers precisely this aspect that distinguished him from others:

> About Enzo, more than a phrase or an episode of life, what struck me was him, above all now that I ask myself what the exceptional event of his process of beatification means for me. With him, I shared much without ever thinking about a "finale" like this. Enzo was such a unique person for three reasons, that represent also the central aspects of the education of Communion and Liberation: unity of life, in Christ everything holds together, we do not need to forget or separate anything of family, work, free time; intelligence

---

48. Bologna, November 23, 1989.
49. Bologna, November 23, 1989.

proceeds from affective energy, from attachment, in more demanding words, from love for the person and reality; and life is belonging to God, that is, Christ in the companionship (the community) in which we are called. Everything is faced and decided together. (Giancarlo Cesana)

The expansion of life in all its dimensions was the most exciting and unquestionable fruit of that encounter. It was the fruit that, if it made us go to bed remembering that we were "useless servants" (maybe after a day of incredible successes), equally made us begin each day with this elementary certainty: "I could have not been here, and I am here. Am I, yes or yes, a living gift?"[50]

---

50. Pesaro, April 6, 1998.

5.

We Need to Not be Alone

ONE THING THAT ENZO CONTINUALLY REPEATED, A CONstant refrain in the background, was the phrase: "We need to not be alone." For him, for us, Christianity was a companionship. Father Giussani looked at us like this, as friends. It was not a series of passionate homilies, not deep reflections or coherent moral systems that were particularly effective. It was friendship. The then-rector and president of the University of Munich, Nikolaus Lobkowicz, encountering our communities of university students, described us in this way: "Traveling the world, I have seen that among all the movements you are the only ones for whom friendship is a virtue."[1] This definition was so spot on that Father Giussani, in those years, repeated it everywhere. Enzo was for us the eruption of a friendship that was at the same time totalizing and demanding. It was the definitive overcoming of a deep solitude that suffocates the person and blocks the Christian experience. On the other hand, Giussani was in love with the verses of Eliot that speak about this communal root of Christianity: "What life have you if you have not life together? / There is no life that is not in community, / And no community not lived in praise of God. / Even the anchorite who meditates alone, /

---

1. Luigi Giussani. *Alla ricerca del volto umano: Esercizi della Fraternità di Comunione e Liberazione* [*In Search of the Human Face: Exercises of the Fraternity of Communion and Liberation*], Litterae Communionis-Tracce, 1996 (7), p. 9 (translation: ours).

For whom the days and nights repeat the praise of God, / Prays for the Church, the Body of Christ incarnate."²

Solitude is the pain whose meaning you do not understand

"I always tell the story of the great Father Gnocchi. At the end of the last war, in these parts (the front passed by here as well), there were unexploded mines, bombs, and the like, and little kids often played with these things, and then they blew up and it was a disaster—children ripped apart, mutilated, etc. Father Gnocchi started the Institute for Mutilated Little Ones to welcome these children when they were abandoned and alone. He built something wonderful. The idea came to him because one day he was visiting a small hospital in the country by chance, and met a child who was undergoing his fourteenth operation. The child was 10 years old, maybe 12. It was impossible to tell his age; he was full of scars and his face was marked by the reconstructive surgeries, and that very next morning he had to have yet another operation. And Father Gnocchi, having pity and above all moved by this shell of wounds and pain, sat down on the little bed and said slowly, softly, 'When they have done such damage to you and when you are hurting like this, what do you think about?' And the little one was stuck, looking at him with that face, and told him, 'Nothing.' This is the most moving image of what solitude means that I can think of. Because solitude is precisely the pain whose meaning you cannot understand, and you are alone in your pain. Like when my parents made me stay inside on Sunday afternoon and all the others were playing outside. Everything annoyed me, nothing made sense. Solitude means impotence. We are like slaves."³

Enzo told us constantly about the risk of a life lived in solitude, because it can become for some even the aim of their life.

---

2. T.S. Eliot, *Choruses from "The Rock,"* https://www.poetrynook.com/poem/choruses-ôç£the-rockôçø#google_vignette.

3. Riccione, December 16, 1998.

He always told us about his notorious nerdy friend, who lived an upright life and then, suddenly, was destroyed by a trivial event. "I said, 'Oh, look, a vulnerable nerd. Incredible!' But think about it for a moment: all it takes is a feeling gone wrong, a feeling that can happen to anyone... (Maybe now we are so indifferent that we manage to control these feelings. Once, maybe, we were more passionate. Today, we change our loves so often... there is no problem!) But think about some other thing, a disgrace in the family, a particular problem, something that happens... there. The position of one who has to face by himself the problem of a strange and difficult reality, something not his own, is so unstable that he is swept away, he can be swept away in a moment. Either he is so indifferent to himself and to the world that he is able to repress every little thing that can wound him, or sooner or later something happens that can sweep him away. We cannot just grit our teeth and bear it."[4]

This was not just a recommendation. Solitude is a nasty beast for many reasons, but what makes it so devastating is when it becomes an objection to the embrace of the companionship, that is, the embrace of Christ. "Once I was the doctor on call, and I was at home with the pocket radio. At half past midnight, I heard the doorbell ring. I was reading, trying to kill some time, and the doorbell rings. I opened the door, and it was a dear friend from the Movement, with her face all distressed. I said, 'What are you doing here at half past midnight?' She was a little indecisive, she seemed a bit off, so I said, 'Come on in.' I tried to offer her something, a cookie, whatever I had there, but I understood that it was not a cookie she needed, so I said, 'What's going on? Spit it out,' because she is a really concrete type of person, a true iron-clad Emilian. She looked me in the face and said, 'Listen, Enzo, after all these years that we have worked together and have discovered a friendship like this, you have to explain something to me.' I said, 'Yeah, if I can... it's past midnight... if I can, I will, for sure.' 'Okay, what does it mean for you to live for Christ, what does it mean that Christ exists?' I looked at her and said, 'All this at half past midnight, after a day like

---

4. Bologna, October 1988.

this? Are we crazy?' Then I understood that she was not joking, so I pulled my thoughts together and said, 'Look, for me Christ means only one thing: that I am no longer alone.' She looked at me and understood, because she is intelligent, and then, her face having reacquired her right features, she left: 'I'll be going now. Ciao.' Beautiful. This is the point. It is like a companionship that you carry with you. You are no longer alone; it is like an expansion of the self... Like a mother is expanded by the baby inside her, so we too are expanded in this companionship."[5]

This companionship was what Enzo had sought (without knowing it) as the place where he could truly "put his heart into what he did." He understood it after the encounter, above all in facing decisions that would be hard to make alone. "We are not able to put our hearts into what we do; we cannot hold on, because after a while reality is difficult and the heart gives way, and after a bit one begins to complain or defend oneself. We need to not be alone. We need to not be alone! That is why I took the phone and sought out Giussani. I had the luck of reaching him, and I said, 'Excuse me, Giussani, if I call you at night like this. I am not asking you to resolve any technical questions or to tell me what to do, because the facts are clear. But if I had not found you, I would have had to search for someone else because—I'm not sure if I'm getting this wrong or not—but I need a comparison, a help, a comfort. A comfort, even simply a comfort, because I am afraid, I am uneasy.' He replied, 'You are not wrong; it is right for you to call. Because all the scientific certainty in the world cannot give you the confidence to try, just like it cannot give you confidence in life.[6] We need a memory of a living relationship. Otherwise, we cannot go beyond what we can measure, what we can do.'"[7]

---

5. Bologna, November 23, 1989.

6. This conversation refers to an extremely risky surgery that Enzo was about to perform on a dear friend whom Father Giussani had entrusted to him. It was a last-ditch attempt to save her life, after all the other doctors, including Enzo's superiors, had judged her inoperable. Against all odds, the surgery was successful.

7. Rimini, December 12, 1998.

"The real problem is here: we need a place that supports us. Without belonging—i.e., without something to which we belong, to which we can refer, and for which your 'I' is not just a scattered 'I', drifting off the road, but someone who has roots in faces, in people—we cannot manage. This here is the definitive point: whether we are doctors or not."[8]

Enzo told us this on every occasion, even in facing together the most intimate aspects of life:

> "This is why the most important thing in life is not to be alone and not to have the wrong friends. Hierro, don't forget this: in life we can commit errors in the choice of a school, of a job, of a girlfriend; we can commit errors in everything! But we cannot make an error in our choice of true friends." (Hierro Fanego)

This dimension of "not being alone" was not an abstract principle. It coincided with something concrete, as it was central for our vocation, that is, for our salvation. With a simple and concrete word, a "companionship." "We need the companionship! My God, how true this is! Because we cannot manage alone..."[9]

It takes at least two

What is a true companionship? What is the Christian companionship? We learned it with the method that is most fitting to our human structure: by living it. And we understood the value of what we were living through repeated moments of reflection, a reflection on experience.

"I discovered that I needed the companionship. I pity certain adults now who don't feel this need anymore because either they have understood everything, or they have to build a family and a profession... I pity them because they are already screwed. I began to feel (even I, who thought of myself as half a Rambo) the need of the companionship as a help, because on my own I could not

---

8. Cesena, March 12, 1999.
9. Florence, September 5, 1998.

manage and I felt it. From that moment, I understood that there was a path, and this gave me the peace and the tranquility to go out there and break a leg."[10]

The insistence of Father Giussani on going on vacation together, and in the mountains, was not only because of the amazing spectacle of the magnificence of God's works, but perhaps more because of being able to live that same spectacle in a way that was capable of exalting it: to live it together, following. And so, it became easier "to go out there and break a leg":

> I was a kind of "stick in the mud" when Enzo arrived there to lead us on the hike to the mountain peak. That day, leaning on a big boulder, he explained in detail how we had to go up the mountain. I, way in the back, listened as if it had nothing to do with me. I was sure that I would never make it up, because of the pain in my joints. Enzo's unmistakable look reached me right where I was, and invited me to try. I threw out some excuse, but Enzo said, 'We will help each other.' This is how it was! I made the ascent, while for the descent I was forced to go on his shoulders. With one sure step after another, we went down into the valley. Many times afterward I remembered this, because what has always kept me moving was a gaze on my person that makes me free, even to let myself sometimes be carried on the shoulders of Another.(Nadia Bertelli)

> I met him for the first time on a vacation of the university students of CL at Santa Caterina Valfurva. I was 18 years old, I was going through a time of low self-esteem, I came face to face with my limits and was not able to bear them. All around me, even in the Christian community, I received at most a 'pat on the back,' and *from a distance*. I remember that Enzo brought us to Mount Cevedale, an ascent of over five hours, of which the last two were on a glacier. Since I was obviously overweight and often didn't have the right equipment, on vacations I was often excluded, even by Christian groups, from the more challenging trips. I wore tennis shoes, and many of us didn't even have sunglasses or sunscreen to protect ourselves against the "mirror" effect of the sun on

---

10. Colfosco, September 2, 1987.

the glacier... But he wanted me close to him, and when he saw that I was marking time, he encouraged me in his energetic and hopeful way: "Come on, let's go! We can do it!" (Gabriele Donati)

The companionship is the "form" of the event, it is "public," it "makes itself clear." "Giussani told the story of someone who was very good at sailing. He passed the competition exam and he got into the Amerigo Vespucci, a sailing ship school for training future officers of the Italian Navy. It was a terrifying environment. In this environment, which was very far from every grace of God, one day while he was there swabbing the deck, he heard another who was cleaning the deck singing: '*Ho un amico grande grande*' ['I have a great, great friend'].[11] So he made friends with that guy. This was enough to begin to cause trouble on the Amerigo Vespucci, because those two were already something else. But up until that moment, what had happened? He sang, 'I have a great, great friend,' and that's it. One could say to him, 'Who knows what song is that?!' Right? But in that moment, the problem began. The problem on that ship was those two, presenting a different, new reality. Start by getting together. This is a witness! If one wants to cause a ruckus, we cause a ruckus together; if one is having a hard time, we help each other. But we need to stay together. This is the newness that witnesses objectively to the presence of Christ, and so we need to move like this: the fundamental characteristic is to be together. Christianity cannot be lived like a personal, spiritualistic interpretation. This is a pietistic and sentimental devastation of Christianity. Go and read the whole *Acts of the Apostles* and find me a reference to the fact of this purely individual problem. Being together implies the individual problem as well, but isolating this from the task of a visible witness to Christ, we cause the disaster that there is now. In order for there to be a Church, we need at least two. Two! You and him."[12]

---

11. This is a verse from a song written by Claudio Chieffo (1945-2007), a singer and songwriter from Forlì whose songs have accompanied and marked the communal life and the liturgies of Communion and Liberation.

12. Bologna, November 8, 1992.

The communal dimension is a cornerstone of the charism entrusted to Father Giussani, who insisted continually on the necessity of learning this from anyone, even from those who are not Christian, even from those who are opposed to Christianity. It is so important that he invited us to learn it even from our "enemies." "He came there and, the first few times he went to class, he came out and found that there were always the same group of kids gathered in the hallway, during the break, and they were talking animatedly among themselves. He was struck and said, 'Who are those guys?' 'They are the communists,' the students responded. Now he understood what had happened in the Church. It was not that people in the Church were not trying to be Christian, but it lacked the characteristic of visibility, which meant it lacked the fundamental characteristic of what was and what has always been and what will always be the experience of the Church: for people to be together. Everyone was Christian, but what was lacking was the constitutive factor of visibility. Therefore, it was as if the reality of the Church were not there. Without this, it is as if the Church does not exist."[13] "In order to be present, we need this 'togetherness,' which is the first thing that strikes people. Christ knew this, and so he sent them out two by two. And Christ said, 'Our Father,' when he prayed."[14]

The Church is "the togetherness of people." There was, though, a quality of this being together that we needed to be reminded of constantly: "If you do not seek Christ in the companionship, my friends, and therefore, if the companionship is not the most precious and most beautiful instrument to walk toward what explains life, there is no other way: sooner or later there will be a tremendous disappointment. There is no other way. The companionship, instead, as the instrument by which we discover what is truly among us and that decides the tone and the truth of life... then yes, you cannot be let down. Even if everyone became Muslims, you would start over again to rebuild it, because it is essential to understand

---

13. Florence, March 18, 1987.
14. Florence, March 18, 1987.

what has converted your life."¹⁵ There began to form on the horizon of our enthusiastic consciences the demanding and sacrificial experience of the "sign," that is, of something that works as long as you do not impede its proper dynamism. "Don't stop at the sign," we often heard repeated and we repeated ourselves, "even if it is the most beautiful sign that has ever happened to you, because over time you will suffocate it." To be together was not an end point, but the condition for making the great journey: "Therefore, to live the Church means 'to be with.' It is only in this way that we can create the condition for the Spirit to act."¹⁶

We understood that we were entering the thorny field of "morality." Even to us this word sounded unpleasant, but we began to speak about it, and above all to correct our bad shots, like one who lets his picture be drawn by the person he loves. "We were in Verona, at an Equipe of the CLU. The companionship had become something fantastic. Cesana, Nori, me, Vittadini, Luigino, Intiglietta, Simone... Wow! The enthusiasm! Because then we would see each other, we would meet up afterward, and the time after the event became more important than the time of the actual event. We would meet up to drink together and tell each other everything. It was really wonderful. We decided with Giussani to start to observe silence at 11:45 p.m. We waited for Giussani to leave and then... Yay! Let's go out! And down goes the beer and down goes the rest. A beautiful little evening of telling each other everything, tossing out a little bullshit, a little gossip, and at 2 a.m. we returned home. As we came in, Giussani was there... in his pajamas! Waiting for us! (Someone had played the spy, and boy did he pay for it then, and is paying for it still. Because there are things one never forgets!) Anyway, Giussani was waiting there, and we looked around at each other, and he said to us, 'Before I am able to go to bed, I have to tell you something. Come here. Now you will answer me please: What right do you have to do this? Tell me what right you have, what do you have more than the others that you do this? Tell me!' Naturally,

---

15. Bologna, June 26, 1986.
16. Florence, May 8, 1993.

there was a general panic. The only one who tried to diffuse the situation was Cesana, and in the back with me he said, 'Listen Enzo, we have to tell him at least that we have more children than the others. Come on, otherwise...' And then Giussani concluded by saying, 'Okay, I understand: the problem you don't understand is essentially moral. Therefore, I want to begin speaking about this topic from now on, and we will see each other in Milan, because I have to tell you what I think of you wretches.' Keep in mind that we were the companionship that had revolutionized the Movement, and it was that companionship that had made all this mess."[17]

What kind of a ending can we expect from that story? What normally happens when a priest says to those caught in the act that he wants to talk about "morality"? Can we expect something more than the classic useless lecture? "It was the first days of January, and I was on vacation, a ski week with the CLU from Bologna. I came down from the mountains, and he gave me an appointment at 8 a.m. in Milan, on Via Martinengo. I came down, arriving 15 minutes early, and he was out in front, walking back and forth. So I make myself comfortable, park the car, get out, and say, 'Oh ciao, how is it going?' He says, 'Listen, please'—when he begins like that...—'there is an idea, an idea that I have understood, that if we do not understand it right now we will be swept away. I just got back from Spain and I understood this idea. All the facts that have happened, all the difficulties we have had... if we do not understand this idea, we will be swept away.' I say, 'Yes, now let's go inside and discuss it.' He says, 'No, no! Here, outside'—it was terribly cold—'here, outside!' Because he's the type to burn the moment, he cannot wait a minute. So, walking back and forth, in the freezing cold of winter, he began to tell me his idea, and essentially it was this: 'Enzo, look, I understand that we are leaning on values more than on Christ. It is a problem of morality. If we do not discover this, everything will be swept away.' I looked at him—I had understood nothing—and said, 'Oh, yes, yes.' When one talks like that... He understood right away that I had not grasped anything he said, and

---

17. Summer vacation of the Florence CLU, 1987.

so he went on, 'Okay, we will talk about it again.' And he went on to speak of something else. But there was a great intuition; it would be the beginning of a change in the story of the Movement. We had stopped feeling the companionship as something that makes Christ present to us, something we ultimately have to respond to! And he explained it to us like this: 'You are children of your time. What does your time do? Ask yourselves and go out into the street and stop the first person you meet and ask him what intentions he has in life. You will find no one, either among us or among the others outside, who tells you coldly that he has bad intentions; everyone has good intentions. What does our time do? It keeps those good intentions from becoming a work! No one takes those intentions as a working hypothesis for himself, so that they become a work, that is, a morality. By not turning those intentions into a working hypothesis, we sweep away the possibility for a true subject to exist. We need the companionship, with all its good intentions, to become a work. You have to take a position in front of Christ. You have to say yes or no to Him, here and now, within this companionship. And it is a permanent responsibility, not just once; it is a choice that you make moment by moment. And this is called morality! Morality does not mean to be coherent and never make mistakes, but to say yes to this Presence. Because then, even when you make a mistake, you return. Even when you make a mistake, you don't get discouraged, and the ideal is there within the things you are responding to.' This was crazy—another revolution! That I, being with my friends, had ultimately to respond to Christ!"[18]

Therefore, we do not enter into the companionship just to sit down and relax. We need to struggle, to keep vigil, like the one who accepts putting all that he is into play in the companionship: "If you do not exercise your freedom, which means 'intelligence' (*intus legere*, 'to read within,' that is, to understand what reality carries) and 'affectivity' (that is, the will to attach yourself to what reality brings, and not just to what you see) after a little you say, 'Okay, they

---

18. Summer vacation of the Florence CLU, 1987.

are just like everyone else… they talk and talk, but then they act just like everyone else.'"[19]

Intelligence of what reality carries, and affection… Enzo used these directives with us in a way that was anything but rhetorical; it immediately became a proposal, something decisive and sure.

> Shortly thereafter, there was an assembly where he invited us to reflect on why it was worth it to walk the path of Christian experience. I felt a sudden racing of my heart, raised my hand, went to the microphone, and said, "I would like to know of what flesh the world is made. I am here for this." Enzo was bent over his notes. A little surprised at such an unusual response, he lifted his head, looked me in the eyes with his piercing gaze, a little incredulous, as if to ask me, "Are you really interested in this?" and said to me, "I'm in."
> (Manlio Gessaroli)

Companionship immediately became knowing how to "keep company." "Companionship means to feel deep down with the people you have in front of you a unity for our destiny, as Mother Teresa of Calcutta said, for Christ. This is the point that is lacking, so much so that we can have everything and still be profoundly unhappy."[20]

> After the thousandth disappointment in love (the thousandth not because I had experienced disappointments from different people, but because the same person had refused me many times), I had a bad idea: to ask Enzo's secretary if I could talk to him. My question was as simple as it was naïve: "Why can't I have what I most desire in the world?" The telephone rang and Daniela passed me to Enzo and, just like that (I think I was almost in tears), I asked my question of Enzo. His answer was serious and cold: "Paglia… that's not what we are friends for." Obviously, at that time (but also now) the answer seemed cold and distant, even if it called me right away back to an idea of relationship that either had something true within it (the true reason we were friends) or he was really crazy. That phrase, so disproportionate to the

---

19. Bologna, October 1988.
20. Sicily, November 21, 1997.

problem I posed, pronounced with such certainty, clarified immediately the level of relationship that Enzo asked of me and others, and offered me a challenge and a road to verify if the reason we were friends was truly, even experientially, greater than my desire for that girl to love me back. (Andrea Pagliarani)

The communal dimension lived in this way in those years already then aroused suspicion, jealousy, spite—today maybe even more than back then. Enzo understood the reasons for the suspicion: "This is difficult for us, because we live in a time of a terrible mistrust about this 'togetherness,' a mistrust about everything that has a solid identity, that is specific in an identity, that is visible in a precise face. We can be together in tolerance, in solidarity, in protest... but together in identity, no! Gestures of generosity, protests, okay, but the next moment each person is on his own. That, instead, the life of one, plus one, plus one, may be defined by belonging to a companionship... that 'we', that being in a group can sometimes risk becoming closed. How many times have we heard this accusation brought against us: "You are a ghetto, a sect." But to live this communal Christian identity as a ghetto happens only because of ignorance and by a total betrayal of its real content. In the ghetto mentality, I defend my power and I am always suspicious of anyone who could come near me. It was what I felt the first time I met the Movement; they kept me at a distance because they thought I was a spy for something else. I had to say, 'Take me with you; I am not going to do anything bad.' If I am "inside" because of the true nature of what was born, who can say: 'You are outside!'? This is the only reality I know in the whole universe that has this openness, the only thing!"[21]

A beautiful intuition by Enzo corrects so many dangerous deviations that touch on the theme of the divine Presence in the companionship, deviations that have been a countersign against the history of the Church even up until our day. Modernity seems to have brought back an ancient heresy, giving it space, and so

---

21. Bologna, November 8, 1992.

"suddenly the God 'among' us became the God 'in' us, that one feels, that one venerates on his own, in his conscience, and reduces it to the terms that he feels, that he thinks, that he imagines, that he expects. But God is 'among' us, not 'in' us like a feeling! This is the most terrible reduction of the presence of God, and therefore it makes unity impossible. Because everyone makes an end out of oneself. *'Tot capita tot sententiae*' ['As many men, so many opinions']. Unity is possible only if there is something outside of us from which we all come, so your difference from me is safeguarded, your characteristics that are different from mine are safeguarded, and yet we are together. Each difference is exalted, is useful, important, and builds up; each capacity is useful, important, and builds up, because we are already together from the beginning, not because we all agree in the end, or because we all understand each other in the end, or because we try to put ourselves together!"[22]

IF THAT STUFF DOESN'T BECOME FRIENDSHIP, WHAT IS THE POINT OF IT?

"Pay attention: the word companionship can become external to us, because it is still something detached from the self. It would be better to say 'the event of friendship,' because it is like the blade of freedom, which cuts cleanly into the problem. "The event of friendship," as love for the destiny of another: friendship is the mutual willing of the destiny of another. We are together for destiny, we walk toward destiny. And it is something that is so human, so humanly evident as positivity, so humanly desirable, humanly necessary that one would have to do violence to oneself to keep from having it. Instead, what normally happens? We guard ourselves from each other; each approaches the other guarding himself from the other, fearing the other."[23]

Enzo Piccinini was for us a "dearest friend" because he lived friendship "as a virtue," as the peak of humanity, and indicated to

---

22. Bologna, March 24, 1992.
23. Bologna, October 6, 1990.

us, time after time, where that friendship was happening among us, calling our attention now to the group of the medical students, now the literature group, then the group of CUSL[24] or of CP[25], of jurisprudence... It was always a surprise because the people he indicated were not exactly "exemplary" in every way. In a certain period, we were invited to observe what was happening in the science department, the group of "Jano's friends,"about which he even spoke to Father Giussani. It was difficult to distinguish that group from a bunch of flower children who had just of late returned from Woodstock, after having lost the way because of the fumes of alcohol. And yet, "they were friends," and therefore people to watch. This was the method:

> At a certain point, Enzo said, "There is no organizational method that is going to work in order to meet the kids. You need to love them. Like him (pointing to me with his finger), who has a sensibility that every one of us here dreams of!" I followed the eyes that looked at me, embarrassed and surprised (I had no idea what my sensibility was, let alone that of others!). (Paolino Casadei)

Enzo had also lived his "flower child" period, and something of it had remained in his sensibility. But he did not subtract anything of his experience from correction and confrontation with the Christian encounter:

---

24. "CUSL" (*Cooperativa Universitaria Studio Lavoro* [University Cooperative of Study and Work]) is an association of university students born within CL in various Italian cities in the 1970s, that had as its aim the offering of services expressly devised for those who live the experience of study in the university. Initially, it was dedicated to the production and editing of lecture notes and to photocopy services. It then expanded its activities to other sectors, such as agreements with local shops for discounts or special group prices, the management of university classrooms and study rooms, etc.

25. "CP" (*Cattolici Popolari* [Catholics of the People]) is the name chosen, again in the 1970s, by some students who, starting from the experience of CL education in the faith, freely chose to get involved in "university politics." From this came the constitution of "lists" for candidates in the academic organs which, at various levels, involved representatives of the students.

January 1989, Borca di Cadore. The first thing that made Enzo strangely likeable to me was the fact that he had us sing twice "In this world of thieves" by Venditti, only because at a certain point the song says, "There is still a group of friends that never surrenders." (Simone Zanotti)

There were so many aspects that struck us about Enzo. What "convinced" us, though, was his passion for friendship, the awareness and the exercise of friendship as the only adequate road to "conviction," that is, literally, of "connection" with Christ. "Once, I brought with me to Bologna a 14-year-old girl who needed to go to the dentist. Because I had to go to a meeting, I didn't know where to "park" her, so I sent her to my friends from CUSL. While I was at the meeting, every now and then I asked myself, 'What did I do? They are adults, and at CUSL they are printing, writing, who knows what that girl is going to do... she will hate me.' After the meeting, I went to pick her up. I said, 'Sorry, how did it go?' And she replied, 'Listen, Enzo, I was struck by something that I had never seen.' 'What's that?' 'How they were such friends with each other. You know, they tell each other things...' —that girl attended a classical high school and in class she was not very used to having relationships like this—'...and then they help each other with money, they tell each other amazing things. Even with me they were great.' She was struck by a type of friendship. There was no longer any difference of age, because the true human need that we have is only one thing: true relationships."[26]

The "Enzo method" was this: a tenacity and a risk in friendship, as the most evident sign of the originality of the Christian event:

> We were in the car and I asked Enzo, "How can we help our friends get interested in our Christian experience?" He answered, "What arouses curiosity and desire for our experience is not what we say; it is not what we do. It is this level of enthusiastic friendship, whose only motive and reason for being together is Christ." (Hierro Fanego)

---

26. Bologna, October 5, 1988.

We Need to Not be Alone

For this reason, what most saddened Enzo was the fact of throwing away the unique, unrepeatable occasion for a friendship that lived up to its name. "We have spent five years working with the freshmen. We have been here, some two, some three, some four years together, but what distance there still is among us! What a difference there is between being here, together, and feeling that we are friends! What a difference there is! We need to get over this distance. And so we need to grasp the root, that root of evil that continues to make us keep our distance. That root that continues to allow only what you think or see, for which reason it is impossible to embrace the other unless he is like you expect him to be."[27]

So many perceived through him that it was possible to "embrace the other," even if he is not "like you expect him to be." This powerful embrace was perceived even physically on first impact and (another miracle) it was contagious:

> When Enzo came to Bari, once, while he hugged me, I thought, "No one has ever hugged me like this!" More than once since then, over the years, I have heard people say to me, "Give me one of your hugs." But I know that what they were talking about was not one of my hugs; it is the echo of Enzo's embrace that they feel and want. And it is not the embrace of Enzo that we feel and want, it is the embrace of Jesus. (Achille Fonzone)

> When I was 24 years old, I needed help from Enzo for my dad's health problem and I came to the hospital in Bologna. After a bit, Enzo arrived and as soon as he saw me he hugged me. Well, that was the most significant hug of my life. I was expecting a warm greeting, that was Enzo's style, maybe a pat on the back, a few jokes… Instead, Enzo surprised me with an embrace that never ended. He crushed me and held me tight in an embrace for a very long time; it lasted at least a good minute. The hug was not accompanied by anything else. He didn't say a word during that minute. Through Enzo, I received the embrace of Jesus Christ and the certainty of the truth of the relationship with him and with all other men and women. Since then, I have surprised

---

27. Bologna, November 21, 1985.

myself by doing again instinctively the same gesture with others (let's hope so!), so much has that embrace become for me the way to demonstrate the friendship that unites us. (Alessandro Cartoni)

Enzo was aware that friendship is the most original point of Christian experience, and that the culture of the world is nothing but a dangerous and confused imitation of this dizzying experience. "This is what we have to discover today: what is able to overcome this malaise that makes us still distant from each other? Sure, we are together, we go skiing together, we date each other, we go to school together, we do everything… but we have still not overcome this distance in our life together. We don't feel that we are a part of each other like friendship requires."[28]

This "feeling a part of each other" was like a prayer to someone who could make this thing happen, that seemed so impossible in itself, a prayer to the Mystery. "It is as if there was a Presence here (not totally clear yet), full of the Mystery (we do not understand it very well), that connected us with a possibility of a friendship that we have never heard of. There is in the air a promise of friendship, a vibration that is a promise of friendship, a new relationship. At any rate, I don't know if I would still be here, had they only described it to me. It was precisely because of a relationship, of a familiarity with someone, that certain steps, which at first sight seemed absurd to me, little by little revealed their underlying reason. In short, what is the content of this encounter? A new hope, a promise of a different, new friendship, for which I—who was walking without even understanding how to walk, without even recognizing what it meant to walk, that is, I was walking a bit haphazardly—put myself in motion, and even someone like me made the first step, and now I am here. This is the least intellectual way possible for our humanity to be really set in motion."[29]

The least intellectual way to be a source of friendship was the elementary way of making certain "gestures." Enzo was truly very

---

28. Bologna, November 21, 1985.
29. Bologna, November 23, 1989.

creative in this; he was always at the limit of reasonableness, of exaggeration:

> I came from Pesaro, after having studied in Milan, and I was hoping for everything from that meeting of leaders on Tuesdays. I escaped from the office where I worked with my father, toward 5:30 p.m., and raced to Modena on the train. At the station, Enzo, whom I had only just met, picked me up, and we ran up to Milan in his car to split the costs of the trip. That Tuesday, November 23, the Taro River was swollen with a torrential rain, and the waters carried away the railway bridge of the Milan–Bologna line. We heard it on the radio when we were returning from Milan after the meeting. So in Modena, Enzo insisted on coming down with me to the train station and going to the ticket window. My train had been diverted to Fornovo, like all the others. It had to cross the river there and then return to Modena. How long? No one knew. Some hours. "Okay," I say, "Enzo, thanks, you can go. I will wait for the train." It was 11.30 at night. "Don't speak of it," Enzo says, "I'll wait with you." "Enzo," I objected, "it is useless to waste time here, with me. You at least can go to work tomorrow." He did not allow me to insist: "We never leave our friends in difficulty." The train arrived at 4:30 in the morning. And he did not move until he saw me get on that train. (Marco Montagna)

This tenacious faithfulness was also present in his personal relationships, and it was exactly the same in the educational responsibilities he shared with us younger people:

> At that time, we were looking for someone to help us live what we were hearing from Father Giussani, and we took the opportunity to ask Enzo the question that was close to our hearts: "Is there someone who can help us 'live' in daily life the words we are hearing from Father Giussani that are setting our hearts on fire?" Enzo took us seriously, spoke with Father Giussani, and on his suggestion began a faithful friendship with us. For more than two years, he came to meet us punctually every two weeks. (Giuseppe Capaccioni)

Enzo did not claim that this intuition was "his." He was a source of friendship because he was the "object" of a friendship, in which he wanted us to participate, as a gift to recognize and welcome. "We just sang, 'Truly God is great,' but the sign of the greatness of God is your friendship. It is something truly singular, but more than singular, it is miraculous, precisely because only God can make it. Only His presence, that we love, want, desire, beg for, can generate the sense of unity that among some of you is already evident."[30]

Therefore, there was an appeal that was constantly repeated and touched the heights of our humanity, of our affective capacity: "Everyone has to get interested in friendship. When you fall in love, you understand what it is: if that stuff does not become friendship, what do you do with it, how long does it last? As long as there is an inclination? What is the use, then? Is it a game? Because compared to something serious, the game has this characteristic, which is that it doesn't have a future. Love without friendship does not have a future."[31] We will have to come back to these dizzying words, but we at least have to stop for a second and register the blow: "love," the love for one's woman ("that stuff") reaches its summit in friendship ("otherwise, what is the point of it?"). "Love without friendship does not have a future." We were all kids at an age when we were making fundamental decisions for our vocations. Few of us understood these words, and many misunderstood them. Others used them as an alibi.

The friendship among us was the motive of a deep fascination and, at the same time, of envy that could even end in hatred. Among the "uncomfortable" aspects of our style there was the question of "preference" (obtuse people call it a circle of "little bosses,"[32] and even the little bosses are often obtuse). Starting from the

---

30. Folgarida, August 6, 1991.

31. Sicily, November 21, 1997.

32. A small number of students were chosen by the adult leader of a CLU community to share this responsibility. In turn, these students might choose others to help them "guide" their respective groups (e.g. the medical students, the literature students, etc.).

consideration that God is the first to prefer, we too exercised this practice to the full, with all those limits that God, of course, does not have. But, in fact, this preference objectively works, because it generates true personalities:

> I discovered what life awaits, because ultimately that is what life is: to be loved to the point of preference. To live is to be preferred by God, and we are fulfilled when we recognize this. But we need an embrace like Enzo's to recognize it. Preference is the experience of the most objective thing there is—that God prefers me. (Achille Fonzone)

> When you were with him, you felt super-preferred: he looked at you, welcomed you, was interested even in the details of your questions like no one ever was before. In 1996, my boyfriend, now my husband, had left me. We were together almost six years, close to graduating and to the possibility of a definitive commitment. I was destroyed, but Enzo offered a companionship that was both affectionate and powerful. I had the "luck" to be there during a period when Enzo was kept home for a forced rest (he had had knee surgery). One day, Widmer accompanied me to his house and we stayed there talking for a long time in the living room. He even offered me a *crème brûlée* that he bragged that he had made himself! I felt preferred. My private matters interested him, so that he even took care of my pain, kept me company so tenderly (and he was definitely not the tender type!) that he even gave me a homemade dessert. He was interested that I should re-center myself on what really counts and what can really satisfy our desire and sustain a romantic relationship over time. He never let me stray on this point. Another time, I waited for hours outside his operating room to annoy him with my love-related sorrows. When he came out he was visibly tired and his face was clouded. When he saw me, I thought he would send me away and instead he stopped there and listened to me. (Francesca Bisulli)

Preference is an extraordinary energy; it has to be corrected, like everything human, to understand its origin and aim. But whether we want it or not, God, in the Old and New Testaments, has preferences: "It is God who gathers that particular people, and those He gathers are "His." And He calls us "among", because God's mode of action is preference, like the entire powerfully human process of love."[33] It is, therefore, a mysterious dynamism, that reaches the Mystery, "like the entire powerfully human process of love." The challenge is not to tone down the "injustice" of preference, but to understand its aim and to correct it in service of this.

> The beginning was rather turbulent, I think, because of a mutual prejudice about our characters and about how we lived our responsibility in the Movement. When he came the first time to the School of Community he said, "We two have to become friends." And this friendship happened, because, as he said once, "we are not able on our own to be friends, but God has given us this possibility. Friendship is a miracle, which means it doesn't have to be a worry." (Paola Olivelli)

"We have to become friends"—it was a strange kind of preference. I remember the episode when Father Giussani stopped the car he was riding in, got out, and, running (!), came up to Piccinini's car, knocked on the window and said, "You and Father Giacomo Tantardini[34] have to become friends!"

Christian preference is the affectionate acceptance of one whom God indicates to you as an inevitable step toward your destiny. "They came together through the relationship they had with Christ and, therefore, men and women found themselves together, pagan and Jew, and they went outside the confines of a nation, of an ethnicity, they embraced all those who accepted the name of Christ as true for their life. It was a unity founded on the fact of God, that is, Christ. 'All of you are one in Christ Jesus.' And so, a new community arose in history."[35] The little bosses who were not obtuse

---

33. Bologna, February 14, 1993.

34. Father Giacomo Tantardini (1946-2012), educated at the seminary of Venegono, met Father Giussani in the 1970s. He moved to Rome as the leader of the local community of Communion and Liberation. He also collaborated on the weekly magazine *Il Sabato* and with the magazine *30 Giorni* directed from 1993 by Giulio Andreotti.

35. Bologna, February 14, 1993.

understood this when they were preferred or when they preferred and so, things went miraculously well.

> We were not compatible with each other. I was very much in awe of Enzo and I was not able to put two words together with him, and then I was not even able to play soccer... But we had to "build the Movement" and this was my desire, and this was his certainty. (Massimo Savini)

Obtuseness is the opposite of openness, the opposite of preference: "In every relationship there is a preference. The problem is whether this preference opens you up or closes you, whether this preference exalts the need for truth that you are, instead of closing it, and this means that there is a place for everyone."[36] "To give you an idea of what I am saying... If in some way this companionship is a preference that you exercise (because you choose friends to walk with you toward Christ in a definitive way), this companionship should open you to the world, to everything."[37]

Preference is openness, and it is also "responsibility."

> Then Enzo speaks and very simply says, "For me, the greatest thing that has happened this year is the friendship between those two." He then points to me and my friend Berna. We shrink into a corner, in a mix of confused feelings, between shame, embarrassment, and a certain undeniable pride. Every true preference always implies a responsibility. He was so clear that everything plays out in a total, invasive, definitive, uncomfortable, human, and therefore limited friendship, like what he proposed to us, that he indicated a glimpse of what was being born between us, in front of everyone. He underlined the path, the beginning between us, and at the same time he called us to be true to the reason why it was given to us, that is, to bear fruit. (Isacco Neri)

Enzo was a person who had strong preferences, and very intense ones. He always exercised preference as a risk and an expression of freedom, and at the same time as an ascetic form of obedience. He

---

36. Bologna, February 14, 1993.
37. Marche, February 23, 1997.

did it in his style, a bit like in a Stallone or a Schwarzenegger film (we saw all of those movies together!):

> Courmayeur 1989. The winter vacation of the university students of CL from Bologna. I had just converted. I was 21 years old. One evening, at the end of the *frizzi*[38] that I did with another two people, Enzo ran up to me and said, "That's it! From now on you will be with me! We'll see each other upstairs later." (Flavio Gerardi)

We have to go to the root

The dynamic of preference and the experience of a friendship on which to "lean" one's own existence seem only the typical and legitimate dreams of adolescence; afterward, things reveal themselves for what they are. Enzo could not get on board with this. On the contrary. We remember well the example of the invitation he made, as a young teaching assistant, to his professor, an expert surgeon, to a CL assembly led by Enzo himself: "The meeting was over and he got up to leave. I met him, out of breath, at the door and asked him 'Professor, how did it go?' I was a little afraid. He looked at me with a gloomy face and said, 'These are all beautiful things. Only, they are for kids! Life has left its mark on me. I have had to make compromises, and I have to make them. These are the enthusiasms of kids. They are all very true… but they are for kids!' I swear to you that my world crumbled, and he was the first to go. How can it be that something is true for kids and that's it? Something true is as true for the one who is five years old as it is for the one who is 90. If it's true, it's true! How can one give in to this?"[39] It is not a banal observation. Today, so many of those who gave their youth for that exciting experience justify their cynicism exactly in this way, considering it an illusion of adolescence. This is a historical revisionism that most of the time justifies the decay of every real human passion.

---

38. "Frizzi" refers to skits that highlight and make fun of the most ridiculous moments of a CL vacation.

39. Florence, November 12, 1992.

In any case, the desire to live a friendship and to be the object of a preference does not simply characterize one phase of life; it is life's constant aspiration, dodging and resisting the thousands of inevitable disappointments. For this reason, Father Giussani had an intuition that was full of consequences for the development of the experience that we had met in the university: it was necessary that the one who lived the type of friendship through which he encountered Christ not be forced to interrupt it when he became an adult. Giussani had, therefore, the intuition of the Fraternity of Communion and Liberation, the intuition of an "adult friendship." "Why was it born? From this intuition: we have to go to the root, because the root is the truest and most decisive part of the trunk, because a trunk without its root is blown away. The root is the response you have to give to Christ. This new morality made us capable of things that we could never have imagined, as, for example, the fact that a friendship like the Fraternity (which was possible, we thought, only for monks) became possible for people like us, people with families. Something 'forever.'"[40]

"The wager we made in entering the Fraternity, what was it? A forever friendship, a forever commitment. I would like to ask any one of you: 'Excuse me, my friend, are you capable of promising that you will be my friend forever?' No one would be able to do it. And so why do we make this wager, founded on your freedom, without structures and without convent walls to keep you in? It is the recognition of this Presence as the reason for living that makes me overcome, all at once, in action, every difficulty, every problem, my temperament, our different histories, what I feel, what I don't feel, my opinion, my instincts."[41]

"The Fraternity is made up of people who recognize each other as friends and gather periodically to recall the memory, to recall the fact that Christ is present. In the Fraternity, we begin to see if life is distracted, if it is betrayed; if life is helped and if it is moral or immoral. It is a friendship like this. It is a group. Christ had 12 friends,

---

40. Summer vacation of the Florence CLU, 1987.
41. Marche, October 22, 1995.

and with them He saved the world. The Fraternity too is a group. There were 12 apostles; there are 12, 15, 25, 30 of us... (after 30 it begins to become difficult to be familiar with each other). But, from a certain point of view, there can be as many as we want, we can even have 100 people (though I have my doubts), provided we call each other back to this intensity. Therefore, we can form whatever group we want, but we have to do it."[42]

And we did form a Fraternity, with him. The purpose became more and more clear, step by step, in action, even if the methods had to be built responsibly, a bit like explorers (our group was closer to a 100 than 12). And we helped each other to correct our aim.

> We met up in the crypt, on the place where the Saints Vitale and Agricola were martyred, on Via San Vitale in Bologna, a little before the church closed. A song together, then he said some words, always provoking us to go deep in our personal relationship with Christ, an *Angelus*, and then we left. He did not want to stop to chat. He wanted that moment to remain impressed on each of us. Every two or three times, we had an assembly. It was the content of his education and he immediately shared it with us, who were just entering adult life, as the greatest charity he could give us. An essential moment, even in its content, one that fixed itself indelibly within us and accompanied our days. (Raffaello Vignali)

The Fraternity is like a home. "When is it that we call something a home? My home. A home is where I go and things are not against me, but for me. That is, I can relax. Now, the fact that our companionship is a home is a wonderful thing because even just thinking that there is another person, another freedom, is a wonderful thing, understood correctly! So we need to avoid errors on this. The home is not just a way to make our life comfortable. The Fraternity is not the Fraternity because there are no problems within. We all love each other, we all have the same ideas, we never argue, nothing ever happens, no one betrays, we are all great friends, we help each other, etc., etc. No, no, no! What is that? A

---

42. Marche, October 22, 1995.

mushroom patch! What is it? It's a little gross, a little sticky. The home is something fantastic, Lucia, because I can be with you, whom I have never seen. This concept of home is the opposite of the absence of problems; the opposite, therefore, of settling into a comfortable life (I have a place where I am all set). Here, I have a place where I am dramatically in motion. The home is true as long as it makes life more dramatic. And the more it makes life dramatic, the more life opens itself, the more it goes beyond appearances and overcomes the slavery of the mood. There is nothing more contrary to the Catholic-Christian experience than the idea of settling into a comfortable life. Therefore, these small homes bring you to that ultimate home, which is our companionship, which persuades us of the definitive companionship of Christ."[43]

The Fraternity is a place of adult friendship where the exaggerations and the underestimations of the individual get corrected, where we collaborate in the building up of the Church in the world, where we pray and forgive—that is, where we put problems in their proper place. "And those fraternities that do not love each other... come on! Sure, we have to examine ourselves, but it cannot be that this is the relationship of fraternity or the relationship among us... the betrayal of someone. Come on, what newness is there?"[44] "The Fraternity is a friendship. Therefore, it is necessary that there be a place where one can say at some point, 'I have a problem,' or, 'I don't understand,' or, 'I don't have any money,' or, 'How do I manage with my father?' or, 'In my opinion the Movement...' That there be a place where one can say these things with the desire to be corrected, with the desire to explain the trouble one is in, and to call the others, one's friends, for help. The help of a place like this, a place of adults, is the most beautiful thing in the world, the truest and the most intense, so that we don't drown in our own juice, so we break through our balance sheets. And then, the spectacle is born of a people that is different from the others. They are glimpses of a people, because now it seems that we have understood, and a minute later

---

43. March, February 23, 1997.
44. Porto San Giorgio, February 28, 1999.

everything crashes down. They are glimpses of a people, flashes, but they remain forever. Anyone, seeing us, will be forced to say, 'Hold on a second, and yet something is there!' In any case, they will not be able to remain indifferent."[45]

Glimpses, flashes of a people. This was the way of living that Father Giussani in every occasion wanted to become ours: a people *sui generis*, of its own kind, as John Paul II defined it at the Meeting of Rimini.[46] "For a whole year, Father Giussani has been underlining the essential question of the people and the 'I.' There is a genetic relationship between the 'I' and the people: without belonging we do not stand on our own two feet, we do not live, what we do is not true. The symbol of this belonging that even defines the expressiveness of the person is Russian folk singing. Giussani always underlined this for us. I remember the difficulty we kids had, when he had us listen to this for the first time at CLU, because it seemed so hard to understand and to listen to! Then, we understood its key point (but it is always like this with things: there is a key point that we need, to enter into it): it was the example of what belonging means, a belonging that even changes our personal expression. Russian folk singing, if you listen to it, is exceptional. It is a single voice and there are hundreds of choir members... It is incredible! It is the example of what we are saying, of what a people means for us, our experience of community, what it means to belong, that defines even our sensibility, even our personal expression. Otherwise, it is not true; otherwise, it is just participation. Think about being here... whether it is only a participation, or if it is the awareness that I am you, you are me, even that you are more me than me..."[47]

---

45. Marche, October 22, 1995.

46. The "Meeting for Friendship Among Peoples" is a gathering held each year in Rimini since 1980, the year in which some of those belonging to Communion and Liberation decided to propose publicly "all that which is beautiful and good in the culture of the time." Starting from the "ineradicable and objective factor that unites all people: the desire for happiness, for goodness, for truth, for justice, that abides in the heart of each person and that therefore lies beneath the value of every diversity," the Meeting became, over the years, a central event in the cultural, civil, and even political life of Italy and at an international level.

47. Porto San Giorgio, February 28, 1999.

To participate in this people there is one unique, great, realistic, and freeing moral indication: "A companionship that helps you to betray as little as possible. You will betray, don't worry, you will betray; betrayal comes by itself. The challenge is to betray as little as possible."[48] "Let us help each other to betray as little as possible."[49]

---

48. Marche, June 10, 1997.
49. Marche, February 23, 1997.

6.

You Are Good as You Are

ONE UNIQUE, GREAT, REALISTIC, AND FREEING MORAL INDIcation is to betray as little as possible. This did not mean, "Everything is okay." It meant, "Everything can be offered." And so, you can no longer use the pretext of your limitations to return to your solitude—this is false humility. You cannot wait to be worthy in order to put yourself in motion. The encounter with Christ frees us from our limitations, not in the sense that it cancels them, but in the sense that it embraces them and puts us back on the road, just as we are, without waiting to be better but in hope of being better. Enzo repeated to us often that we have to shorten more and more the time that passes between the fall and the getting up. This is the most convincing sign of the power of mercy.

For a young person, to hear someone say "You are good as you are" is the beginning of the revolution. The revolution began for us just as it had begun for Enzo.

MAN IS "SOMEONE" WHEN HE IS "SOMEONE FOR SOMEONE"[1]

"We need an esteem for ourselves, and this is possible only if we are esteemed, esteemed at our origins. The discovery of being created is

---

1. Pesaro, April 30, 1999.

this extreme positivity in our life, the discovery of one who wants us like this, just as we are. It doesn't matter if your character is not the character you would like. Let it go, because you are unique, unrepeatable; you are wanted and loved. What more do you want? Give your contribution freely! Those who are like that are capable of friendships. Otherwise, we are only capable of friendships, that is, of relationships, 'under certain conditions,' always! Instead, the one who is esteemed at the origin, it doesn't matter what he does, it doesn't matter if he succeeds or not, it doesn't matter if the others respond to him, if the others value him, because the esteem and self-worth that he has is original! You understand then… this definition of friendship is fundamental, it smashes all the incrustations of our fortune-cookie psychology… It smashes everything. You discover that you are made, and more, that there is Someone who makes you in this moment; you are wanted then as now. Discover this, please! It is like falling in love forever!"[2]

"It is not a question of ability, of your capacity to do something, of having understood who knows what, because this certainty is given by a summons; that is, someone who wanted us and loved us so much that he put us here together, over-valuing each of us (me first of all). Over-valuing us, over-esteeming us. Here lies all our strength. You who think that you are worse than everyone else, you who have a thousand doubts, who would not want to be here… even you! This is the newness of the world."[3] In effect, to perceive ourselves esteemed in this way is truly the newness of the world. It is an over-esteem that is not born of what one is able or not able to do; a gratuitous esteem, for the simple fact that we exist. It was incredible to see the change in the friends who began to live with us, even those who did not have the "fundamentals." Within a context that gives value to the person, the person can bear fruit. "Sixty percent of young people go to a psychologist. Of course they do—we don't help them to esteem themselves!"[4]

---

2. Sicily, November 21, 1997.

3. Bologna, January 23, 1994.

4. Pesaro, April 6, 1998.

Clearly, it was not enough to say the right words. It was not the discourses (even if, re-reading them, they are very beautiful) that made possible this re-awakening of our humanity. It was the fact that we constantly rediscovered the necessary energies to embrace the other (the great sacrifice), those same energies that came from being embraced. "And so it is beautiful to hear Jesus Christ say, *'Even the hairs of your head are counted.'* Listen, there is no expression more beautiful that indicates love for a person: even the hairs of your head are counted. Do you understand?"[5] "In 300 million years there will not be anyone like you, and for thousands of years there has never been anyone like you."[6] "What you can give, no one else can give in your place, because He thought of you from the beginning."[7]

To be loved: this is the great revolution. Normally this love lasts only a little while, and that is the problem. If the motive for love is instrumental, once the objective is reached, the dance is over. The problem is being able to live this certainty with continuity. "It happened to me many times during an assembly with young people (I walked with thousands of them). At the end of the assembly the usual young girl comes up and says to you that what was said is very beautiful, but it is not true, things are not this way. She says, 'I came into the community because everyone said that it was beautiful—great discussions, great things—and I discovered that you are like everyone else.' Thank God! You are quiet because you understand that it is a dramatic moment for her, whereas for you these are things you know well. You listen to her and stay there. She says, 'You see, the leader... the figure of the leader... and we are all following behind him, chasing after him with three meters of our tongue out, and we never understand anything. There are privileges. But what is this?... No one pays attention to me... Is this a community? At the beginning I was happy, but now I'm not.' What do you say to her? The most you can say: 'Look, even for me it was like this, then over

---

5. Bologna, November 23, 1989.
6. Pesaro, April 30, 1999.
7. Bologna, November 21, 1985.

time you get used to it, little by little. If at the beginning something struck you, it cannot have all disappeared because, if it struck you, it remains. We need to try to understand, to see. Get someone to help you with this.' While you speak, you look at her and understand that you are not touching anything. She gets even more surprised and steps away more, she becomes distant, and even tells you, 'Everyone has already told me that!' So I feel totally disarmed. At the end you say, 'Say a prayer to the Virgin. Then we'll meet again. But this is the path.' Two months go by, you do the usual assembly every other month, and, at the end of the assembly, the young girl returns and you say to yourself, 'No, no... now what do I do?' I don't know what to say, because I imagine that she is going to say the same things. She stands in front of me and suddenly a big smile appears and she says, 'Piccinini, you were right. The community is beautiful; I am so happy! Now I understand what you said about how beautiful this is! It was my problem, but now I feel like I belong. The leaders too... what a beautiful relationship. I am so happy!' Now you have a doubt, and you ask, 'Did you find a boyfriend?' And she says, 'Yes.' What did this girl find? She found someone who says to her, 'You are good for me the way you are; I love you just as you are; you are useful just as you are.' She found someone for whom she feels useful, accepted, wanted, loved. This is the analogy of one who finds himself created, discovers that he is created. There is Someone who loved us one by one and continues to love us one by one."[8]

"We are the fruit of Someone's tenderness. How I want to help you understand this! And so, what can your problems be? The example of mutual love is a distant analogy. In front of the fact that you are useful, just as you are, that character that you wish was different, that temperament, that hair, that nose, those eyes, that shyness... You are useful just as you are, because Another has loved you and loves you as you are. And so, the whole problem is to discover and to love the One who has loved you!"[9]

---

8. Sicily, November 21, 1997.
9. Colfosco, September 2, 1987.

> The relationship with Enzo touched personally the thing that was most fragile in me: my self-esteem. I finally felt treated as a woman, respected and loved in my deepest self. And from there came a total revolution in my life. I found capacities that I never thought I had. Enzo made the deepest part of myself flourish, the most secret part, that needed so badly to be understood. (Cristina Chiocchio)

Falling in love is a distant analogy... This esteem can be perceived even in the most tragic situations of existence. Its power can revolutionize the circumstances that seem most hopeless: "I remember a few experiences that were among the most atrocious of my life. One was with a man who came from the lowlands of Emilia like me, so you can imagine. The sick who come from Romagna always come with 10 other people, as do those from Veneto, and those from Marche, the same... Those who come from Emilia come alone. So sad. Alone with their sickness! They are used to this, but it is dramatic. So I went to his house a few times until, at a certain point, the end came. His relatives called me and said, 'Doctor, we don't know how to tell him. Can you tell him?' I went there and sent everybody out. I went to his side and said, 'Listen, things are at such a point that anything can happen. You need to be prepared. The moment has come for us to repeat everything that we were taught, even when we were children.' So he looked at me and said, 'Now I understand. We are...'—there was some condensation on the ceiling, and drops were coming down—'...we are like those drops there: as long as there is a thread of water, we exist. When someone decides to cut the thread, we no longer exist.' I said, 'Only one thing allows us to accept this: that the One who holds that thread loves us. To return to Him is to return home!' He went to Confession and to Communion. He asked for it. It was an extraordinary thing. But that is how it is."[10]

"To be someone for someone"—this is not just a wise reflection. For Enzo, for us, it was the recognition of a fact that had happened to our person, and because of this fact "dignity does

---

10. Pesaro, April 30, 1999.

not depend any more on the high fives you get from those around you, on the consensus you have around you, on someone who says, 'Good job,' but everything depends on the fact that you understand that there is someone who loves you, and in serving him, my God, what a change!"[11] This someone could be written with a capital "S," but the capital "S" works through the apparently casual action of one or more lower-case "s"es. This "election," this "preference" that, starting from the Mystery, reaches the creature through other creatures, is a question that is not banal, not easy to digest. "A mystery of election" Father Giussani defined it, describing it like this: "It is through Abraham, who is a man descending from Adam... It is through Abraham. Not through Ham, Shem, or anybody else: through Abraham! It could have been Lot, who was Abraham's nephew; he was there close by! God could have been off by half a millimeter! On these observations depends the value of heaven and earth, depends the value of the heat of the sun or the color of the sea!"[12] He could have been half a millimeter off... but He took you. And you, with the same apparent casualness, will reach someone else. From here comes our enthusiasm for life, the value of the heat of the sun or the value of the color of the sea.

I have not found among the available transcriptions the wonderful description that Enzo made about this dynamic, and therefore I will report it "ad-lib," sure that I am not being too inaccurate, given the impression that it made on me almost 40 years ago. Enzo was very fond of the Canticle (*Isaiah* 49:14-16) of the second psalm for Saturday Morning Prayer. Here, Isaiah describes the disappointment and lament of the people of Israel who feel abandoned, forgotten by their Lord. At that point, God intervenes in a decisive manner, asking His people if it were ever possible for a mother to forget her suckling child, to have no compassion for the son of her womb. Then, as if recognizing that... in reality... yes, even a mother can forget her son, but the Lord loves with a unique love: He will

---

11. Colfosco, September 2, 1987.

12. Luigi Giussani, "The Mystery of Election," *Traces*, March 2001, http://archivio.traces-cl.com/Mar2001/ptn.htm.

never forget. And here was the detail that really excited Enzo. To help us understand that there are things so important that they cannot be forgotten, Isaiah uses this simple and powerful image: "See, I have written your name on the palms of my hands." Many times Enzo gave us this example, more or less with these words: "When we had a test in class, during high school, and the teacher wouldn't let anything get by (not even the famous little notes rolled up in the most unthinkable parts of the body), I remember that I wrote on the palm of my hand (so as to peek at them at the right moment), the most important things, those that let me solve the problems. Just think: God wrote my name on the palm of His hand! He wrote the name of each of us on the palm of His hand! Do you realize what kind of esteem He has in every moment for each of us?"

Where did this certainty of preference and esteem come from? It came from the fact that someone had physically written his name on the palm of his hand and that this someone (Father Giussani) was the concrete instrument of the love of Someone:

> One evening, leaving the headquarters of CL very late, one of us asked Enzo if Father Giussani would one day become a saint. Going down the stairs, Enzo stopped and answered in his plucky way, "I don't know if he will become a saint, but I know that he changed me! Christ changed my life!" (Daniele Biondi)

"What decided my life was the gaze of mercy he had on me. I was not that kind of guy. Not only before I met the Movement; even in the Movement I wasn't that kind of guy. Whoever knew me before—there are two or three of them who always come to visit me and tell me, 'We still can't believe that you have changed'—knows that I was such a thug, so inflexible, so dogmatic, a tough one who struggled to believe. And yet, it happened. I changed. The source of the change was not immediately a work I made on myself in a certain way. It was a gaze of mercy on me that happened. This embrace, that you discover for your whole life, is what allows you to be in the world as a permanently open question, as a prayer. I need mercy like the air I breathe."[13]

The Church opens its doors in the morning and prostitutes and saints come in

> "This guy too"—Enzo said, turning to me who was sitting next to him during a School of Community—"has a dual nature" (explaining the dual nature of Christ, true God and true man). "He too, who is 80-to-90% animal," he said, laughing, "has a 10% that is good." I understood in time what he wanted to demonstrate: my very nature, together with my limits, my instinctiveness, my sin, participated, if looked at loyally, in the redemption that Christ was accomplishing. And so, nothing, literally nothing, could become a scandal, an impediment to Christ embracing me and me looking to Him, following Him in his concrete, physical companionship of the Movement and of the whole Church. (Beppe Serafini)

"My friend, you are good as you are! Someone has thought of you, Someone who is greater than everything we have here. And to understand this brings an immense gratitude. It is useful to have a nose like this, a mouth like this, these feelings, these crises. It is all useful, my friend."[14]

> What dominated our life together was never the absence of contradictions, or our coherence, but the possibility of a constant starting over, which he synthesized like this: "Whoever we are, whatever we have done up until five minutes ago, we can begin again, now, now, here." (Manlio Gessaroli)

"Therefore, I want to tell you not to worry, the fact that you feel many kilometers away is not an objection, nor is your understanding that your daily life is so far from being lived as saved, that

---

13. Summer vacation of the Marche university students, August 15, 1997.
14. Bologna, November 21, 1985.

is, lived with this fact that has happened within every moment. Of course!"[15] "This is the faith that moves the world, that moves mountains, that takes away the mountains of your shyness, of your indecision, because you are great just as you are. You are within a larger horizon."[16]

A little more than 20 years old. A soccer field, a game among university students, in the summer, people cheering on the bleachers... With the megaphone in hand, together with a handful of my classmates, I led—or better, I whipped up—the choirs in favor of our team, with expressions worse than those of the worst hooligans that were original, engaging, and effective for a part of the public, but rather less agreeable to the rest, who were cheering for the same side, but would have preferred more elegant rhymes. I was very harshly reprimanded at the end of the game by the present authorities, with the accusation that I had scandalized some of the "new" people who, profoundly upset by the vulgarity of the tones, had stopped cheering and left. The whole was argued by the above-mentioned authorities with wisdom, using the lexicon of the latest chapters of the School of Community. I had failed terribly, for sure, maybe—I thought, while I heard the somber chastisements—"I" was a mistake. A dark atmosphere, interrupted later by: "Come, Enzo wants to meet you." He was not interested in the vulgar language of the megaphone; he wanted to meet the one who had caused all that uproar. A person who did not ask you to be different than you were, but who pushed you to go to the depth of what you were, to give the best of yourself and your energies. In a few words, "I" was not a mistake. He loved me just the way I was, and he brought out of me the energy and the will to give the best of myself. And to do it he pointed to how he acted, with his vitality that was so engaging, so immediately perceptible by anyone who came across him even for a little bit. He had met Jesus, truly, and he followed Him ardently in a companionship of friends. It was CL. (Assuntina Morresi)

---

15. Bologna, January 23, 1986.
16. Bologna, November 21, 1985.

"And so, take courage! Take courage because it is a path, not a finish line. It is a road, not a finish line. We are all on it. Everyone, from the one who has taken one step to the one who has taken a hundred."[17] "The most beautiful definition I have ever heard of the Church, existentially speaking, I read in a book of Marshall (*To Every Man a Penny*[18]) when at a certain point he defines the Church like this: 'The Church is like a cathedral. In the morning it opens its doors and the prostitutes and saints come in.' Because the criterion of the Church is this: to be in the Church, to stay in it. There is no other criterion to 'screen,' to select,"[19] "there is no aptitude test on the basis of which you come in or stay out."[20] "Everyone, everyone can come in, because its content is the adventure of the connection with Christ, and that's it. You are not asked to be a certain way or to think in another way; you are asked to accept this connection, this link."[21]

"So it is clear that the problem is that in a situation anything can happen; because God chose men like me and you and did not choose angels, anything can happen! Inevitably, within our companionship, we should expect all the rottenness that we see in the great facts of the world. If not, what kind of humanity would it be? Christ chose the human to be present; he did not choose Caselli[22] only. He chose many others, including Caselli. He did not choose perfection; he chose the human being with all his drama. So it is clear how anything can happen."[23]

Anything can happen. And we saw everything in the community. We did not pretend or close our eyes. To say, "You are good

---

17. Bologna, January 23, 1997.
18. Bruce Marshall, *To Every Man a Penny*, Houghton Mifflin, 1949.
19. Florence, March 18,1987.
20. Ravenna, May 23, 1999.
21. Florence, March 18, 1987.
22. Gian Carlo Caselli is an ex-magistrate responsible for important investigations against terrorism and the mafia. At that time, he had started a case against Giulio Andreotti. He was the symbol of the moral coherence that had become the most exalted social virtue during *Mani Pulite*.
23. Summer vacation of the Marche university students, August 15, 1997.

as you are" either hides a brazen lie, or is the fruit of an action that overcomes and embraces every inevitable mortal limit of human action.[24] "And so you were imagining this man who said He was God... the son of a shop owner (like the pharmacist of Riccione). The son of a shop owner who says He is God, and the people follow Him. Many had begun to follow Him because, at a certain point, they saw that this man did extraordinary things. Someone had a hand like this... zap, all set! And another guy was like this... zap, all set. 'My son is sick'... zap, healed! In the end, the people followed Him in floods. They brought Him the sick, their relatives, an avalanche of suffering people! 'I cannot see!'—'Receive your sight.' And there was this flood of people who followed Him a bit confusedly. Imagine that paralytic who was healed. A fantastic episode. Jesus is already known, there is a large crowd of people pressing around Him, one brings an uncle, one brings Him a man with Parkinson's. Everyone is crowding all around, and He is in this little house, and the people huddle around him. The stretcher-bearers arrive late with the paralytic and they try to enter, but with that stretcher they can't get in. This stretcher is also very bulky! What do they see? They were intelligent stretcher-bearers, quick thinkers. They see that the house is without a solid roof, it has a straw roof. 'Let's lower him down from the roof!' And what do they do? They drop the paralytic down from the roof. Imagine Christ, engaged in a discussion, who sees this guy coming down... Now He had seen everything. This guy comes down and everyone says, 'Oh, let's see what he does! What a spectacular way to come in!' But this one says, 'Your sins are forgiven.' 'What's that? He's not going to heal him?' It was a let down. But those who were humanly intelligent understood (after having spent a bit of time with Him) that He operated at the level of true humanity. Therefore, as we understand clearly, there is a moral pain that is much heavier than a physical pain or a physical limitation. This is so true that we can be happy without a leg, and in total crisis with both. So, 'Your sins are forgiven' means: 'All

---

24. A phrase that, in this regard, Father Giussani read to us often was from Ibsen: "Tell me, God, in death's abyss / is no fleck of hoped-for bliss / earned by man's will?" Henrik Ibsen, *Brand*, Act V, 1775-1777.

your evil no longer exists. That is, it exists, but it doesn't have power anymore. It doesn't have power! It does not have the ultimate power in your life.' That one can say this... Whoever is humanly intelligent understands that it is the greatest thing that can happen to you, that your evil may no longer have all the moral weight that brings you down, with a dogged shame, that brings you to your knees. 'Your sins are forgiven.'"[25]

"It was my first question... While before I had an idea, and this idea had to work, and with this idea I used everything and everyone, the premonition of the presence of the Mystery makes it so that the evil I do does not stop me anymore, because the Mystery remains and is not canceled by the evil I do. Everything rests on this, my friends. Without this, all the rest is forced, even the commitment we put into achieving things and even the rituals in which we participate."[26]

> Telling him about a discussion I had with a person from the community, after having listened to my story, he said, "I understand. You are 99% right. And what do you do with your clearly valid arguments if, looking at her and walking with her, you don't look at that miserable 1%? Your relationship will always be based on power. What do you win, if affirming Christ does not pass through your abandoning yourself to that miserable 1%? Sooner or later it will happen that you abandon yourself." (Beppe Serafini)

> It happened in 1993: my girlfriend (today she is my wife and mother of our four children) got pregnant and the thing was, as you can understand, especially back then, a great upheaval. He came up to me in his usual way, 10 centimeters from my face, and he began with a firm and "strong" rebuke that he finished by saying, "I would like to give you a punch in the nose and..." Then, making as if to go away, he turned around and told me, "Antonio! Let me point this out! Remember! Sin is always the beginning of a great hope!" He was, for us, the "unrelenting means" (as he said) of the experience of God's mercy. (Antonio Vittiglio)

---

25. Riccione, December 16, 1998.
26. Florence, November 12, 1992.

> It was a time of tension within the CLU community in my city. I happened to tell some joke to someone else from the Movement. For me it was a joke that didn't have any value, but apparently he felt offended. It was taken so seriously that it had to be discussed at a dinner with the small group of leaders and Enzo. In front of the many considerations of these people on the gravity of the matter, at a certain point, I said, "Okay, I was wrong!" Immediately Enzo intervened, giving value to my admission in a way I didn't expect, in a way that I think no one of all the others there present expected. He said with his typical energy—unfortunately I don't remember the exact words—that to admit our errors is an action that indicates a true and strong humanity. This matter closed and we moved on to another. I have never again been afraid of my errors, nor of having to admit them in front of others, above all in front of myself. Every time that life has put me in front of an error or an incapacity, my mind returns to that evening and Enzo's 'pardon.'" (Francesco Vignaroli)

This was the rule among us, even and above all among those of us who shared the responsibility of guiding the community. Correction was the rule, and pardon was certain when the error was recognized. Paradoxically, the admission of one's error was the objective to achieve, and we were helped in this, in order to become aware of the grace of forgiveness:

> We reacted instinctively, without thinking, and Enzo was very angry. But when I arrived at Via Martinengo, without saying anything, he hugged me and pressed me tight. (Domenico Viola)

From here, and from here only, was born an original, new way of facing our limits with a very particular attitude, aware of the gravity of the thing and, at the same time, invaded by that almost unjustifiable feeling that Father Giussani loved to call "naïve boldness."[27] "This realism that we have in our own regard is a false realism. Not because the data you observe, that you grasp about yourself, are not

---

27. Luigi Giussani, Stefano Alberto, Javier Prades, *Generating Traces in the History of the World*, translated by Patrick Stevenson, McGill-Queen's University Press, 2010, p. 99.

real. Certainly, they are very real. You are so cold in your analysis. But reality is greater than this. You know how to sum up what you manage or don't manage to do. You are ruthless, but reality is greater than you."[28] It is that boldness that allows you to conclude (and not with a light heart) that "at 70 years of age, as Giussani always says, even the list of your sins is a hymn of joy. Not bad!"[29]

We were in a place where one can be present with all his limits—not "being comfortable" with his limits (even less with his sins), but perceiving that it is enough to have a sincere affection that makes those limits the field in which the Lord can demonstrate His unique power. Therefore, moralism was truly out of the question. "If I consisted of the balance sheet of my life, I would have to hide myself behind the last one of you (those who know me know this is true). This is why it is an embrace that makes me start, that gives me the courage to put myself in play, that makes me feel that I was esteemed more than I thought I was worth."[30] "Then, in the end, there are those here in the community who steal just like everyone else. You say, 'Oh, then, what is this crap?' It doesn't matter. Come on! When they told me, in America, one the first times, 'The Pope, that is, the Vatican, with all its money, with the IOR,[31] even he steals...'—'I don't care about that at all!'—'But how can you not care? What are you? Are you Catholic?'—'I am a Catholic with all the frills, I know what I must love, and you can all go to hell!' In America, there was the problem of priests who got married, and then... 'If the Pope got married?' I say, 'I don't care about that at all!'—'How can you not care?' Because I know what I must love, and all that stuff doesn't matter to me at all. Life is like this. Our life is like this. Therefore they hate us. We are indomitable. We sin, but

---

28. Bologna, November 21, 1985.

29. Marche, June 10, 1997.

30. Marche, October 22, 1995.

31. IOR is the *Istituto per le Opere Religiose* (Institute for the Works of Religion), an entity of the Holy See charged with the management of assets for the charitable works of the Vatican. At the time, it was at the center of financial scandals.

we do it differently than the others... because we sin while looking at Christ!"[32]

"You understand at 23, 25 years of age... you intuit that what you have is 'sown by truth.' Your betrayal, that thing that makes you go to bed with remorse and that twists your stomach because you did not want to do what you did, that thing for which you wasted your time, that thing you were excited about and then you lost the thread and you don't know how to recover it, that thing for which it seems that the world crushes you and the injustice is too heavy... that thing is sown by truth. Do you understand? The impetus of youth within a thing like that is more than a new birth!"[33]

Many of us know the words with which Enzo concluded his testimony in front of more than 7,000 students, five months before he died: "The gusto of life is not denied to the one who makes a mistake, but to the one who does not have a sense of the infinite, of destiny, of the ideal, of the Mystery present, because then the problem is not 'to make a mistake' or 'not to make a mistake.' The gusto of life is not denied to the one who makes a mistake; it is denied to the one who does not have a connection with the Destiny that makes everything, with the Mystery present."[34]

And besides, why are you afraid of your temperament?

Enzo was a "temperamental man." This went swimmingly for those who found a certain empathy with him, and a bit worse for those who perceived, on the contrary, a visceral incompatibility. There was, though, a common thread between these opposites: from whatever pole you started, you were forced to come to terms with something that was "underneath." It was that something underneath that rendered the fascination of that temperament continuous and

---

32. Bologna, January 23, 1997.
33. Florence, May 6, 1989.
34. Rimini, December 12, 1998.

his invasiveness "bearable," creating constant occasions for reciprocal correction, even (at what cost!) for him.

"'And besides, why are you afraid of your temperament?' [Father Giussani had asked him]. You see, this was a liberation! 'Why are you afraid of your temperament? If God made you like this, you serve Him with what you are!'"[35] It was very illuminating for me, some time ago, to read a letter written by Enzo when he was 19 years old. His awareness of the problem had already matured. "I monopolized the situation and, later, the discussion took on a single track, centered on what I had said. Therefore, as often happens in these cases, it was not at all constructive."[36] In effect, this trait accompanied him for quite some time. He joked a little about it, but he also felt its weight:

> He started and finished every conversation; no one contradicted him. To me, it was like being at the theater to watch a movie where the hero is also the director, producer, costume designer, and screenwriter. (Andrea Alberti)

The friendship with Father Giussani, as we have seen, had meant a great upheaval at this level as well, "after the encounter that had transformed even some traits of his temperament, while it had exalted others."[37]

In front of the event one encounters, each person responds with his own temperament that (in following) will become a treasure for the community, for the Church, and for the world. "The reasonable attitude, in front of this fact that has happened, has two faces. The first: 'I will spend my whole life to understand what has happened to me' (it is a temperament in search). The second: 'I'm diving in: what am I waiting for?' (it is my temperament). But both these temperaments have as their principle of action the fact that has happened. My temperament: 'I will dive in... If I find a correspondence, I jump in, and every man for himself!' But the seriousness of the position of searching is equal to the impetus of

---

35. Rimini, December 12, 1998.
36. July 27, 1970.
37. Luigi Giussani, "That Surge of Life." *Traces*, June 2000.

my temperament; it is exactly identical. What decides the matter is that 'it has happened to me.'"[38]

There are so many episodes connected to this aspect of Enzo's personality. Whoever met him was immediately struck, to the point of embarrassment, by his way of presenting himself, capable of touching all the extremes of human expression, even those that would normally be incompatible. A kaleidoscope of opposites. Some were scandalized, others let themselves be questioned. I was convinced in time that nothing was left to chance. Every gesture was willed, in service of the one who was in front of him, even the most apparently or effectively instinctive gesture. The strategies did not always work, in the end, as is the risk of every daring project. But Enzo wanted to give "his all" to everyone.

> He was a child with his innocence and spontaneity, with his smile, his gaze that embraces you as if to ask for forgiveness, that tone of voice that made itself sweeter to help you understand that he understood you, even if he thought differently about something... (Alexandra Guerra)

> He had a tough character. He was often rough in his ways, always attacking. Everything was a challenge. Friendship with him was a constant struggle, but with such enthusiasm...! (Gianpiero Di Febbo)

> Everyone told me that he was a great guy, but I couldn't stand him. I didn't like the certainty with which he expressed opinions that were absolutely debatable, and neither did I like the harsh way he related to my friends and me. He seemed always on the verge of a fight. Always raising questions, asking the reason for everything, pressing. I was never able to enjoy a dinner, a game of soccer, or simply a walk, in peace. That's the word; Enzo was certainly not a man of peace. (Andrea Alberti)

> In terms of food, he had a strong predilection for a restaurant in Villa Verucchio that cooked only bluefish (anchovies, sardines, scallops, grey mullet). All strong flavors. In

---

38. Marche, February 23, 1997.

everything, Enzo could not stand anything mild. (Mimmo Pirozzi)

He came to my parents' house for dinner and ate and drank enthusiastically. Above all, he liked those strong flavors that normally regular palates taste out of courtesy for the host; he wanted all of them. (Giovanni Cesana)

At the beginning of every academic year, we organized an event for the freshmen, a kind of introduction to the university. It was an event that Enzo always took special care of, because he guided it in his role as a university professor. By random circumstances I found myself introducing Enzo, because I was a representative of the students. That day, Enzo was terribly late, well beyond the 15 minutes we normally wait for professors, and we were waiting for him nervously in a packed theater. When he arrived, about 45 minutes after the appointed time, he was simply furious. We discovered afterwards that he was coming from Piacenza, where he had performed an extremely difficult surgery. There had been additional complications, and the outcome had been different from the one hoped for. He went up the stairs of the stage and sat down in a rush, not at the place reserved for him, but at mine. I adapted and tried to swap our "name tags." He stopped me and made a gesture for me to hurry up and begin. I introduced him in the driest way possible, and he began a beautiful talk in which, 'disguised' as institutional indications, he gave the freshmen reasons to verify their vocation in their university studies, and proposed an experience of fullness not limited to classes, in that period of life that is so special. All that angry energy was instantly transformed into a passionate outburst of welcome and attention to the destiny of those young people that he didn't even know. (Andrea Prosperi)

We were doing School of Community with him and, at a certain point, he asked us, "How do we recognize Christ? For you, how is it? Where is Christ accompanying you now? Give me examples." An hour of babbling attempts at an answer began, and after each attempt Enzo pushed us further: "That's not it, that's not it." At the end of that hour, without a conclusion or a hint of an answer, he said his goodbyes and, among the general bewilderment, told us, "Let's take this up again when I return in two weeks." In the following days, while waiting for him to come back, in front of even the tiniest fact that happened, we were asking, "Is it Him?" I don't remember what he told us when he came back... (Giuseppe Capaccioni)

Gesticulating, he would tell us about the latest film he had seen. I would go to see it at the theater because I was curious, and I always came out a bit disappointed, because his story had been so much more exciting than the actual film. (Giovanni Cesana)

The intimacy I had with him was so intense that at moments I had to distance myself because I couldn't handle it. (Aureliano Palmeri)

His gestures were directed to his friends in such a way that they had a "beyond," an "after" within, and they placed in the soul of the recipient a message that only time would unveil. Gestures and words like "prophecies," inserted into the apparent banality of the day, because he already had this "beyond" in his eyes. (Cristina Rossi)

I was by instinct not at all attracted by that bizarre exuberance. His only register was "absolute," without "ifs" and without "buts." Instead, I was a specialist in "if" and "but." Enzo had an unsustainable intensity of life, and I left the meetings and outings with him physically exhausted. Moreover, his educational method had a privileged instrument: soccer games, a tribal practice whose profound meaning escapes me even today. Basically, nothing about him was made for me. Maybe for this reason it was easy to pay attention to where he wanted to guide us, much more than the way he guided us. That intensity of life was not the fruit of his character, it was a search for meaning, in every instant, and it was without compromises. (Andrea Prosperi)

That night on vacation, eating the cured meats offered by Franjo, and playing cards, something I didn't know how to do, he called me a fool (deep down that's what I thought about myself; he only put it in front of me). The morning after, at 7:30, long before Morning Prayer, he was waiting for me on a stool at the coffee bar with two cups of macchiato, bent over as if he had a cramp, and asked my forgiveness... and the more I told him, "No, you're right. That's how I am," the more he repeated, "No, Pietro, no: it wasn't right, and you are not like that." (Pietro Lorenzetti)

January 5, 1993, a freshman in the faculty of medicine. I was speaking at a table about my high school graduation exam, and how I had made a bold comparison between pop singer Francesco Guccini and the nineteenth-century poet Giacomo Leopardi. I had not yet said anything else, not even a comment, I had only introduced the topic... "What a stupid thesis. How can you compare Guccini to Leopardi? They ought to have rejected you, for sure..." He had not even understood what I was saying. He could not have understood. I had not said anything yet. "How can you make that judgment if you haven't even heard what I was saying? Who do you think you are? You know who you are, Enzo? The typical CL guy with the truth in your pocket, that is what you are, and if no one has ever told you that, I'm telling you now!" His closest friends stopped Enzo from jumping over the table. He sat down and told me, "Go away, I don't want to see you anymore." We were in the outskirts of Modena, and on the way there I had broken my girlfriend's Citroen Visa, that was now going only on one cylinder and was making an infernal racket. I said, "That's right, I'm going, I'm going right now." (Andrea Alberti)

All of us older ones present remember the scene even today. It was a bit like in the army: "Punish one to educate a hundred." The tragi-comic aspect was that another freshman, in a silence that we could cut, raised his hand naively and asked, "Enzo, excuse me. What do I do?"—"What do you mean?"—"I am in the car with him."—"You get out of here too!"

We left from Modena on one cylinder and arrived in Cesena almost at 3:00 in the morning on January 6. For a year, I didn't speak to him, and I didn't even want to see the group of people who would remind me of him. Then I changed a lot, and maybe he changed even more than I had—and the one who changes as an adult always amazes me, even now! When I found out that he had died, I went home crying. My father already knew about it. I give him a very sad greeting, hugged him, and started to leave for Bologna. He stopped me and said, "Before you go, you have to know something. Do you remember six years ago, when you were a freshman and you argued with Enzo?" To myself I asked how he could know that fact, something I had never told him... "That night, he called me at 2 a.m. on the house phone. You were not yet home. At first, I was scared. Then he told me, 'Listen, Arturo, this evening I had a fight with your son. I was reactionary. It is not okay, but I am working on it. Anyway, I am sorry, but not because he got mad. That will pass. I am sorry if my behavior will distance him from the Movement, from our experience. I won't be in touch for a while, but I will be following him. Forgive me; I am working on it. I will not leave him. The fight today must not distance him. For this, I would never forgive myself. Good night, and sorry for the late call.'" And that is what he did, he did not leave me. (Andrea Alberti)

I as well, being often close to Enzo, made note of this perennial battle to bend his own temperament toward the great task, and when the ardent struggle failed, he was pained, literally discouraged. A visit to two of the many cities he followed: first stop, Tuscany, and then Umbria. It was a particular lunch, a kind of summit meeting for local and national leaders to resolve "frictions" of a generically "educational" character. Enzo was very tired (he had probably been in the operating room before we set out). His way of resolving the friction was sharp, harsh, summary, and effective: after receiving the insult (a bit heavy, it must be admitted), he got on his feet and gave the detractor a big slap in the face, from one side of the table to the other. There! Resolved. The slap reverberated chillingly off the Renaissance vaulted ceilings of the room. And then, only silence and the frozen embarrassment of the guests (priests, politicians, businessmen, students...) incapable of any movement (some still with a pastry in their mouth, stuck in their locked jaws). With the friction resolved in this manner, we got back in the car and he, driving, visibly downcast, said to me: "Widmer, look, it's not right.

I know that it is not okay, and I always do it again. I should not act like that. One should never act like that. Remember that, please."

On another trip, this time to Turin, an unfortunate driver did not let Enzo pass in the third lane of the highway, the fastest lane. We were behind him (and as always running late), flashing our headlights. The poor soul, who thought he was already going too fast, loses his nerve, puts his foot on the brake (something you shouldn't do), and forces us to brake dangerously in the third lane. At that point (I should have expected it), downshift, illegal pass on the right, get back in the third lane and... we stopped. We were not going slow; we parked the car. In the third lane. Enzo got out of the car, walked toward the car of the unfortunate man, put his face up to the glass, and simply shouted an extremely loud "Ahhhhhh" (like King Kong) that made the windows tremble. He did not say anything else, got back in the car, and we set out again. We were on a mission, and this could be considered an archaic and elementary method of road education.

At a graduation dinner that closed an extraordinary period of "historic" friendship and responsibility shared entirely for many intense years, we managed to have a fight at the table (on his initiative) in one of the most "in" restaurants of Bologna, Battibecco. Little by little, the other clients left and, little by little, we also got up and left, while we were still shouting at each other. The guy we were celebrating remained sadly alone to pay the bill (and a very high bill it was).

Enzo was all this.

> I saw him for the last time in 1999, in May, at Monte Cusna. Enzo's usual force was relaxed in a tenderness that struck me and moved me deeply. It was his farewell. (Simone Mannocci)

This tenderness, this ultimate and hard-won self-irony in front of his temperament (which even he found intrusive) was the flowering of an awareness, as much given as won: "Let our coherence be the continual taking up again of this faithfulness, because it is similar to the image of the child who makes a mistake and starts again. Our coherence is the image of a child who, in front of his parents, makes a mistake and starts again, because his parents do not stop being his parents when the child makes a mistake."[39] "We do not need to make some kind of effort to become this or that person. You are already chosen, my friend, you are here. What more do you want?"[40]

LET US INVADE THE MOVEMENT WITH HUMANITY!

For us, the encounter with Enzo brought with it the amazed discovery that "everything" that is human, every aspect, gains in being placed in the Christian companionship. And that, vice versa, this same companionship gains in being invaded by our humanity. "The first invitation is this: let us invade the Movement with humanity! Mine and yours. Let us begin to put into play here what we are. This is the way to have an experience, an experience that takes away your doubts, my doubts, my perplexity, my nervousness. Our communities have to be invaded by humanity, mine and yours. All that I am. We already have religious practices, and in abundance. There is a gaze of mercy, my friend, on you, because of which you are here. All that we are waiting for is the commitment of your life, and the only way to understand this gaze is this. What are your doubts? What do you want to cut away from your life? Come inside, my friend! Play out your life all the way. This will make you understand everything."[41]

"As we go on maturing, we are a spectacle to ourselves,"[42] Giussani told us, not because we become better, but because, in the Christian companionship, we see dimensions of our humanity explode that before were not even imaginable. "If I had to compare my life, how it developed (there is a law of physics that says that the horizon changes when the point of observation changes), I would

---

39. Bologna, June 21, 1992.
40. Bologna, January 23, 1986.
41. Marche, August 15, 1997.
42. Luigi Giussani. *Generating Traces in the History of the World*, p. 98.

use this metaphor: my life is like a hot-air balloon. The more I go, the higher I go, the more I engage myself, the more I am within this life, the more I discover aspects of humanity that before were impossible—the capacity for faithfulness, for friendship, for loyalty, for starting over, for overcoming difficulties—that I had never even thought of before."[43]

The fundamental aspect of humanity, what is perhaps at the root of every other aspect, is certainly the discovery of the "person," of the person's unique and irreducible value. From this awareness (registered before it was even understood) derived, or better matured, a way of being in relationship, of treating each other that was the real reason for the wonder of those who came across our companionship. "The great Francis Xavier, when he met Ignatius of Loyola for the first time at the Sorbonne in Paris, had gone with his henchmen (he was a real trouble maker) to try to break up a public conference in the square. While they were all hidden behind a column, ready to jump out, Ignatius of Loyola began with this phrase: 'What is it worth if you have everything and lose yourselves?' A phrase like this is incredible! Tell me if there can be a phrase that can describe better than this the value of the person, of each person: you are worth 99... the one who is lost is worth 99."[44] "Search in all the religions of the world, in all the philosophies of the world, in all the thoughts of all the philosophers and intellectuals of the world, search for an idea of the person that is so definite, and with which we can fall in love, as Christ's idea of the person, Christ who died for you, for each of us, one by one! He thought that we were more important than Himself. Find me another one like this! For this reason, we can say that Einstein, a microcephalic, and a person with Down syndrome have the same dignity. This is the origin."[45]

> He had the effect of making me understand that I was important—not special or weird (even if he told me that

---

43. Rimini, December 12, 1998.
44. Florence, 1987.
45. Summer vacation of the Marche university students, August 15, 1997.

once, in the middle of the General Assembly of the CLU at the Fossolo Theater). (Paola Belletti)

Even today I still do not understand what Enzo saw in me that moved him to trust me with such a great responsibility. I think it was his constant way of challenging people and their freedom, pushing and provoking a reaction. (Francesco Cerini)

He looked at you always as an *opus dei* [work of God], he was excited about your singularity and saw in you already the fruit of that seed which the Lord had planted within and of which you had not yet become aware. (Maila Quaglia)

Already at the beginning of my Christian story, he had seen something within me and had asked the young friends I had just met to go visit me at the seaside ("Otherwise, we'll lose her!"). And I, annoyed and surprised, found them in front of me at the Adriano Campground of Punta Marina, near Ravenna. That was all it took, it was done! Love had taken hold of me. (Cristina Rossi)

During his time in the university, my son did not study much and was very passionate about music. He played concerts, met singers and important musical groups, and so in CLU he was a rare bird and was not always accepted. He was even sometimes looked at with suspicion and pushed to the margins. Little by little, he distanced himself from the community. The last time he went to the CLU Exercises[46] in December 1998, even though he didn't want to. When he returned, I asked him what had struck him the most and he told me, "The testimony of Enzo Piccinini." And so, once when Enzo came to our community for an assembly, I introduced my son to him, explaining to him for a moment who he was and what he liked to do in life. Enzo told him, "I too

---

46. The "Spiritual Exercises" are an annual gathering that every part of the Movement (GS, CLU, Fraternity, Memores Domini) proposes as a common moment of reflection and prayer. They normally last three days. The CLU Exercises take place at the beginning of December.

played in a small band[47] when I was young, and I loved it! You know that the music world is a difficult world, sometimes disordered... so be careful, and bring your testimony there as well." My son told him that the day after he was going to have an important concert in a city. Two nights later, Enzo called me on my cell at 11:30 p.m. to find out how the concert went. It reminded me of how when Father Giussani followed a person, he followed him all the way, and when he had that person in front of him, that person was everything for him. I saw the same thing in Enzo. (Mario Dupuis)

I remember so many discussions about individual people, about the relationships that were formed in the student apartments, about the young people's families... There was an attention to the millimeter, one by one. "We have to get down to the psychology," he often told us, as a way of indicating the extent of the embrace we had taken on. All the way to the psychology meant to the point of putting ourselves in the shoes of the other, and to the point of understanding when our support was insufficient, to the point of finding a psychologist who was "human" (I remember that back then it was old Dr. Reggiani in Modena), to whom we sent those who needed medical support.

Where did this attention come from? It was not principally due to a particular inclination to do good (that was not quite in Enzo's character). It was rather the inevitable consequence of an "ontological" awareness. "So what is the value of my person? The greatness of my person is that I am a relationship with the Mystery who makes all things. And the Mystery who makes all things became incarnate, became Christ, and this Christ became this companionship. Here

---

47. Enzo's band was called "The Rebels" (not by chance). On the drums: Enzo Piccinini. As with other things, no one believed this story. Once, coming down from the summit of Monte Cusna, we stopped to eat at an out-of-the-way restaurant in the Emilian Appennines. At a certain point the owner, while he was serving us the first course, looked at Enzo and exclaimed, "You're Enzo Piccinini!" This did not amaze us at first as Enzo had begun to be well known, because of his work and because of his responsibility in the Movement. But this time was different: "When I was a kid, you guys were my idols. I followed you everywhere, and I came to all your concerts... And I remember that you were the first one to wear those shirts with flowers that came from America, with those long collars...!"

is the discovery of the absolute value of the person, so that we say woe to the person who harms a child, who gives scandal. The person is relationship with the infinite! The kingdom of heaven is me. The kingdom of heaven is a person, is the pearl of great price, is the treasure. My life is this supreme good, because it is a relationship with the Eternal."[48]

This awareness became in Enzo a particular "way" of treating the person. This made all the difference, above all in his work.

> Enzo Piccinini had a unique characteristic that I saw grow over time and mature in his human and professional path, a characteristic that originated from his deep and radical faith: the care of the person. To take care of the person was, for Enzo, to identify the qualities and the deep needs, the questions and all that characterized in an absolutely personal way the path of each person toward their own happiness. His human and also professional relationships were never formal or "technical." (Fabio Catani)

> I was hospitalized on August 2, 1991, and had my operation on August 6. From the first day in the hospital, I was welcomed and followed by the whole group of doctors on Piccinini's team with such attention and passion that I always say I wish the same dedication to all those who are forced to stay at a hospital. I need to specify that it was not a special attention given only to me, but it was like that for everyone. In the room next to me, there was a man from Rimini who had been operated on a couple of days before, and he was constantly giving thanks for the way Enzo and his coworkers took care of him and his family. (Mimmo Pirozzi)

> I was hit by a sickness that had been affecting my immune system for three years. I had to decide where to get care, and he told me, "When you decide between Padua and Bologna, you call me." I called him and told him it would be Bologna. In half an hour, he found a family to host me and he found me a job. I was full of fear; at that time, life expectancy for my condition was very short. I have lived for 33 years since then. Today, I am married, I have grown up and I experience

---

48. Florence, 1987.

so much love, but I remember Enzo's gaze when he hugged me and said (because my defenses at the beginning were nothing), "Now you are in a tunnel, but later you will come out and the sun will be shining…" I still now in certain situations tell myself this same thing, and I look at the sky, and his gaze accompanies me in my life."(Anonymous contribution)

"It doesn't matter if he is from Kosovo or if he is Serbian; he has value. He has value because he exists. So, dignity happens within a relationship, a relationship with that which makes every instant, every fragment, every expression, eternal. Therefore, each person is untouchable, and this is true from the beginning to the end, from when we begin as two cells to when the old man is decrepit and can no longer reason and is a human larva, like my dad was, with my mom who was there assisting him for years. It's incredible when I think about it! Alzheimer's for years! It's dignity, you understand? It is ultimately a dignity. And it doesn't matter what you do—it is an absolute, true dignity. But then, if this is the case, how beautiful that phrase of the Bible becomes, how great when it says, 'I have loved you with an eternal love, for this reason I have attracted you to me, having compassion on your nothingness!'"[49] [50]

> Once, he was invited to the GS vacation. I was in the back of the room. And I remained there. I did not go to say hi to him. He was surrounded by a whole host of kids who were asking him questions, and at that time I still did not feel a part of them. Returning home, the day after the end of the vacation, the telephone rang (there was only the land line in the house in those days). My mom answered and yelled up the stairs: "It's Enzo on the phone." Enzo who? Him? The guy who eats with gusto and speaks with gusto and gets you all excited when he tells a story? What does he want with an insignificant little guy like me? He had seen me in the back of the room. He wanted to know what I thought about what he had said, about the questions that were asked, about the vacation, about GS, about everything. I was a part of them. (Giovanni Cesana)

---

49. cf. *Jeremiah* 31:3.
50. Pesaro, April 30, 1999.

7.

That Naive Boldness that Characterizes Us

ON THE OCCASION OF THE 40TH ANNIVERSARY OF THE MOVEment of Communion and Liberation (1994), Father Giussani wrote a message to all the members using these words to describe the heart of our experience, the gift we were given: "As we go on maturing, we are a spectacle for ourselves and, God willing, for others, too. A spectacle, that is, of limitation and betrayal, and therefore of humiliation, and at the same time of inexhaustible certainty in the power of Grace that is given us and is renewed every morning. This gives us the naïve boldness that characterizes us, for which every day of our life is conceived as an offering to God, so that the Church may exist in our bodies and souls through the materiality of our existence."[1]

The encounter with the companionship of Christ generates a boldness within material existence. It is difficult to describe in a few pages the "fever of life," the creativity, the openness to risk that our daily friendship made possible and, in some way, a duty, because there was no aspect of life that did not provoke a response, which was necessarily and tentatively "new" because it aimed at a totally new objective. And for this Enzo was always the first in line.

---

1. Luigi Giussani. *Generating Traces in the History of the World*, pp. 98-99.

That Naive Boldness that Characterizes Us

I WAS A HIPPY

In the last years of his earthly life, time seemed to be a "relative" dimension for Enzo. In an epoch when technology did not yet allow one to be connected 24/7 (we had only just moved on from the pager to the cellphone), it seemed that Piccinini had found the secret of ubiquity. He could manage, on the same day, to be present in places that were very far away from each other. In one day he might exit the operating room, to arrive at the summit of Mount Cusna, and then to hold an assembly in some city on the Adriatic coast.

In particular, he spent a lot of time with us to go see beautiful things (in nature and culture)—beautiful because we enjoyed them together. And he even had his own methodological theory, which was that the outing should be "brief, intense, and university-style." It was not about doing things quickly (even if we went very fast) but about making the time spent together full and without disintegration (intense and curated), because, being a limited resource, time was precious. Even in this, the encounter with Christianity had impacted his character, rounding out the edges: "I was a hippy. If there is an animalistic type, it is the hippy, at least in my time (later... did hippies become more poetic? I don't know). I went around half of Italy, I saw the most beautiful places and I slept in barns (I showed them my ID, they gave me a bowl of soup, and I slept in the barn). Then there were meetings in various places, and I spent a summer like this. I came home hating my fellow human beings. I was so free! Let's leave aside the outcome of the matter, but I remember as if it were yesterday that, when I met the Movement, all those places I had seen, where I had lived like a gypsy, I re-evaluated them all. Later, I brought others from the community to those places, with an interest that at the time I couldn't have imagined; I had overlooked those places in my search for freedom."[2]

Enzo rarely traveled alone; a trip (like everything else) was for him an occasion to share. He often brought along someone who needed to talk to him and other times a person he wanted to know

---

2. Florence, March 18, 1987.

better because he had been struck by something particular about him. In these cases, one got in the car and did not know where he would be in three or four hours (somewhere between Turin and Taranto) and what time he would return home. Other times, he brought with him two or three cars of friends, taking advantage of "visits" to the local communities for which he was responsible.

> I remember in particular when he came for three days to tour Umbria with some university friends from Bologna. (Giovanni Proietti)

I was a freshman that year: three days between Perugia, Todi, Gubbio, and Assisi to meet friends, to discuss things with them, with the inevitable soccer game and tasting of local food (truffles remained on the palate and in the mind).

Other times, he brought us to see the places of his youth, each one with some specific characteristic connected to his story, each one a bit strange. We went many times to visit Mantua, which he really loved. It is a sad and beautiful city, its castle, the water lilies at Martiri di Belfiore, the *sbrisolona* (an almond crumble cake) and the *risot al puntel* (a pork chop over a plate of white rice that you "obligatorily" eat with your hands using the meat as a spoon). Then Venice (the carnival), Modena (*tigelle*, a type of flat bread filled with cheese, cold cuts, or other things, and the cathedral), Munich (Oktoberfest and rivers of beer), Rome (with a stop at the restaurant I Quattro Mori), Busseto (Giuseppe Verdi and the donkey stew)... all brief, intense, university-style visits. Culture all around.

Another category of our trips together were the "pilgrimages," which I intentionally put in quotation marks because it would be difficult for any outside observer to define them as such. They were more like treasure hunts or obstacle courses to arrive at points where the Mystery (more and more familiar to us) had given signs of Himself. One memorable pilgrimage was a one-day round trip to La Salette, an out-of-the-way place in the French Alps that can be reached by going up the Monginevro Pass. Along the way, of course, so many things happened: one of us was without his ID (at the time there was a border checkpoint there) and so he had to get

That Naive Boldness that Characterizes Us

out of the car and cross the border on foot, traversing a ski slope. We picked him up, set out again, and it began to snow. A French man flashed his lights at us (at us...!), passed us, and then slid into a ditch, looking at us from the window, until he stopped against a tree. We laughed, "He didn't get hurt." Then we went on, and all we could see was mountains, without any other signs of life except, at a certain point along the road, huge dark statues of the crying Virgin, standing guard at the unattainable sanctuary. The Virgin Mary appeared there in the 1800s. But this was not a "classical" apparition. The Mother of the Savior, Our Lady of Help, showed herself to two kids in that place, "crying" in anguish because she was not able to hold back divine judgment on the unfaithfulness of men. The future story of these two kids is equally disturbing and the whole thing clearly made an impression on me. Enzo loved it.

Another pilgrimage was to Lourdes. Classic. But with Enzo nothing remained within the lines. We received a message from his secretary: meet up at 11p.m. at the train station in Modena. Okay, we'll be there. I was in my first years at the university, but I had already understood that Enzo's rhythms were different. "We will drink something together at his house," I thought. I did think that the place where we were meeting up was strange, but by then strange was the norm. We met up there and we realized that there were quite a few of us (about 15). Enzo arrived and said, "Okay, we'll make three crews." He looked around and saw that our fleet of cars was rather poor: his Fiat Croma, a Ford Fiesta, and a Fiat Ritmo. "Okay, you go ahead. I'll close the group." One of us, at this point, asked naively, "Where are we going?" "To Lourdes," Enzo answers, as if it was something obvious—after all, everyone leaves at 11 p.m. from the station in Modena to go to Lourdes and return the following night.

It is difficult to forget so many episodes of that "pilgrimage," even after 40 years. Again, some of us had not brought IDs (to be fair, we didn't need them to go have a drink in Modena). Therefore, we prepared a shared strategy to cross the border at Ventimiglia: "It is very simple," Enzo says, "no one is checking at this hour. Simply, we keep some distance between us so as not to attract attention, and pass at a slower speed. Don't attract attention, so as not arouse suspicion, and everything will go smoothly." The Ritmo passes; no problem. It slips into the tunnel just past the border. The Fiesta (we soon discover, because we arrived last) must have had some problems, and had to change the agreed-upon strategy all of a sudden. We found it, in fact, right at the border, with six or seven people around, performing strange operations on the car. We get closer and ask what's going on (pretending not to know them). They told us that they had gotten out to use the restroom, and the last one had closed the door and left the keys inside. Therefore, the border agents had come out of their cubicle and were helping them to pry open the door without breaking the rear window of the car, while the others were pulling on the door, and still others were trying to hook the safety lock lever with a metal wire... In short, a great combined effort with the police. In the meantime, the Ritmo, upon not seeing us, had thought they also needed to change their strategy, in the most logical way: retrace their steps by driving in reverse (with double arrows, for safety reasons) through the long tunnel that divided them from the great gathering on the border. So much for "Let's not draw attention to ourselves." We thanked the police for their kindness and said goodbye.

First stop, Carcassonne: an amazing city. We were not, though, able to appreciate culture in those conditions. We instead opted for a soccer game on the irresistible green grass that surrounds the imposing medieval walls. Then we set out again. Clearly, no one had thought about a change of clothes... We finally arrived in Lourdes (close to Spain). We visited the grotto and made it in time to catch the last Mass of the afternoon (I didn't even see the famous baths). It was brief, intense, and university-style. "What are we doing?" "We are going back," Enzo answers. "I have to work tomorrow." It felt like being in the 1985 movie *Fandango*. The evening fell, and Enzo said to Luca Rossi, "I'm a bit tired" (he had driven for close to 20 hours). "You drive a little. Go towards Italy." He woke up around two in the morning and saw a sign: "Paris, 250 km." We had taken a bit of a detour... He got back behind the wheel, cursing. "We are having a problem with the Fiesta," they informed us. In short, the alternator had broken and therefore the battery was not recharging and the lights were becoming more and more dim. What should we do? "Let's do this: we'll go in front, the Ritmo in the back, and the Fiesta in the middle, so that no one sees it." Hundreds of kilometers in the dark with the Fiesta becoming more and more invisible. We passed through Ventimiglia again (it was easier to get back into our country without papers than to get out of it) and, a little after sunrise, on one of the tallest highway overpasses in the Savona area, I saw from the rearview mirror that the Fiesta had pulled over and broken down in the emergency lane. Heroic—it had given its all. I told Enzo. He asks, "Are we in Italy?" "Yes," I answer. "Good." And we proceeded. We lived like that. Everything okay.

The real classic, though, was the hike up Mount Cusna. Every year in May, without fail, we set out to climb it. Enzo was very fond of this peak. It was at 2,000 meters of elevation, right between Modena and Reggio, next to its bigger and more famous brother Mount Cimone. An old friend had a house in Febbio, at the foot of the mountain, and often in his youth Enzo had spent his days off there. Now it was a liturgy that we repeated every year (and often many times in the same month) that included, in order (a bit like in a *Fantozzi* movie): meet at the North Modena toll booth at 5:30 a.m. Stop at the Piccadilly café in Villa Minozzo for a breakfast of vegetable pie and beer (garlic and hops that then come back up from the stomach while we hike; but the liturgy cannot be revised). Take a road that calling it a dirt road is a euphemism, since it is also the bed of a creek that has water only when the snows melt, on whose boulders we left several cracked oil pans from the undercarriage of our cars, that would break off in this rough terrain. Then walk for about an hour and a half to arrive to the cross on the summit, with an extraordinary panorama from which one can see the snow-covered Alps, and the regions of Veneto, Lombardy, Emilia Romagna, Tuscany, Liguria, as well as (according to Enzo) two seas, the Adriatic to the east and the Tyrrhenian to the west. We never saw the seas, and so we made fun of him (but a local shepherd, one year, told us it was true, and we did believe him). Finally, we descend and stop at the pond of the Zamboni refuge, full of easy-to-catch fish. There, the trout were so hungry that they would bite even if you used as bait the dandelions from the shore, and then they ended up on the grill.

It was an event where the different generations of students from Bologna crossed paths, and above all an occasion to see of what stuff the freshmen were made. Sometimes, after the hike, we stopped to visit the spectacular medieval Canossian church in Toano; sometimes we took the opportunity to play a game of soccer (with snow boots) followed by Mass in the small church of Febbio. The pastor was so happy to see so many young people, and he started conversations during the homily, asking questions to Rondoni who, leaning against a column, was snoring loudly.

That last year, at lunch on the grass field of the Zamboni refuge, we spoke with Enzo about the boiling political moment. For the first time, the city of Bologna could change color. He told us that the best way to give a decisive blow to the communists (it was like a scene out of the Peppone and Don Camillo books) was to attempt the assassination of Guazzaloca (the candidate for the center-right). It was "demonstrated by psycho-social theories" that the candidate who undergoes an assassination attempt in an election year increases his votes. Therefore, the plan was simple: blow up the car of the candidate on our list. Enzo responded to the worried or derisive looks on our faces, "Let's do this: next week, you buy the newspaper and look at the first page of the *Resto del Carlino*. You don't have to do anything. I will do it all. I can do it." We did not know if he could do it (maybe he could); we did not know if he would have done it (I would say no). It happened that Guazza did win the election on June 13, 1999. We did not celebrate. Enzo did not live to see that event. That was the last time I saw him, driving away in a rush with his Audi A4, Sunday May 23, 1999, three days before his death. He had dropped us off at a gas station before

Modena, because he had to run to lead an assembly of the Movement in Ravenna. After the Cusna.

Read this!

Enzo had always loved to read. In his last years, his free time was drastically reduced, forcing him to prioritize many things. Even his passion for his favorite soccer team, Inter Milan, was changed, less "stadium-like." Not finding the time to read, though, cost him a lot, above all because even that youthful passion was transformed in the encounter with Giussani. "I met Father Giussani years ago. He had noticed my restlessness, because I always felt out of place around believers. I remember that he asked me if I liked to read. 'I always have,' I answered, because it was an old passion. He asked me if I would agree to read some books. I did not know that this would be the way he would help me to grow."[3]

"In that period, he had taken me to heart. I still don't know why, because I was so far from what he loved. The first thing he did, to rebuild my human fabric that had been destroyed, was to give me books, as a gesture of friendship. I stole many from him, and every now and then he still remembers this, and gets really mad... One of the first books he gave me was Bruce Marshall's *To Every Man a Penny*.[4] Because it was about priests and the Church, I read one of every 15 pages, skipping whole passages, because it seemed to me abstruse and far from any of my interests. But I didn't know that I had to give an account of the book. The next time Giussani saw me, he asked me what I thought about it. 'Did you read it?' 'Yes.' (What should I have said?) 'And what did you think about it?' I didn't want to look bad, and also I had to give an agreeable answer, acceptable for a priest. Therefore, I gave a bit of an artificial response, that I thought sounded beautiful: 'This book taught me how to pray.' Giussani answered with a thunderous laugh, because it was clearly a big fib, and he must have read it openly in my face (I

---

3. Bologna, June 1995.
4. Florence, March 18, 1987.

had taken on a composed air...). Then he looked at me attentively and said, 'Excuse me, but this is the kind of book you can read on the beach!' I began to understand that it is better to be religious than clever, because otherwise one always loses—religious, that is, true. These books were the beginning of a real formation for me."[5]

Since then, Enzo had made this mode of education his own:

> Eighteen years old... Enzo came to meet me suddenly, for no reason. In the heart of an ordinary afternoon. I only remember Enzo's gesture of opening a book liberally covered with paper to hide the title and the author, and, reading aloud, for me, "Love and hurry do not go together. Love is measured by patience..."[6] I still do not understand today why he visited me like that, why he read those pages. But isn't this the irresistible sweetness of friendship? The connection with us, the content of our dialogue or the events were not always made explicit; explanations were not always given. There broke out among us kids a race, some on their own, others together, to discover the hidden source of those words that we felt were an integral part of that world that Enzo was showing us—another level of things, of living, of being, by which we were irresistibly attracted, which in some way was inaccessible to us, but whose existence we would never doubt. What unleashed our longing to know was the urgency of knowing some hidden side of Enzo's soul, and of that Truth that he carried within him as a perpetual seal. (Cristina Rossi)

> One evening, he told me that Father Giussani had given him some novels to read, which they would later discuss together. And so, our evenings were spent speaking about the books he had read. One after the other, including *Saints Go to Hell* by Gilbert Cesbron, *Ilia and Alberto* by Angelo Gatti, *Lavallière* by Maria Sticco, *Valentina Velier* by Bonaventura Tecchi. Some of them he didn't lend out... "Otherwise you won't return them to me." Many of them were impossible to find, because the dominant culture had buried them. He didn't want to reveal the title of his favorite book ("It

---

5. Turin, November 19, 1994.
6. Oscar Milosz, *Miguel Manara*, Human Adventure Books, 2016.

describes me too much") but he gave a hint, the final line: "We need to stop thinking that we are active in love," and so began the search of the used book stalls. Only two years ago I managed to find what Enzo told me was an absolute masterpiece, *Hearken Unto the Voice* by Franz Werfel. These books have accompanied me since then and they have been the greatest education to see the other with empathy. (Raffaello Vignali)

On various occasions, Enzo held public presentations of these texts, and many transcriptions have already been published.[7] I remember very well some passages of a book that he loved so much, that he had presented at a Happening[8] of Youth in the Margherita Gardens in Bologna, *Letters on Pain* by Emmanuel Mounier. In particular, a phrase from that amazing text seems to describe Enzo's profound nature perfectly: "The only thing that counts is the divine restlessness of dissatisfied souls."[9] Enzo was a dissatisfied soul, full of divine restlessness, that restlessness that led him to say, "There is nothing more anti-Christian than the one who tries to settle into a comfortable life."[10] His life was a continual dialogue with these fiery words of Mounier: "See, it is absolutely necessary that we give a meaning to our life: the tour de force that consists in impressing upon it the seal of the Infinite,"[11] "the divine restlessness of the one who gets up in the morning and it is as if the things that he sees and has known for 10, 20 years, someone had given them to him in that

---

7. Enzo Piccinini, *Il fuoco sotto la cenere* [*The Fire Under the Ashes*], Società Editrice Fiorentina, Florence, 2018.

8. The "Youth Happening" was a festival at the end of the academic year (June/July) in which the students of the CLU shared publicly a moment of "end-of-school goodbyes," with popular and cultural events and shows. They took place in several Italian cities, and often reached very significant proportions in the large universities, involving tens of thousands of people.

9. Emmanuel Mounier, *Lettere sul dolore. Uno sguardo sul mistero della sofferenza* [*Letters on Pain. A Gaze on the Mystery of Suffering*], Rizzoli, Milan, 1995, p. 23 (translation: ours).

10. Bologna, June 1995.

11. Mounier, op. cit., p. 23 (translation: ours).

moment."[12] It was a constant battle, for him and for those who were close to him, a battle for a truth that is never painless, that never coincides with even our most pure intentions. "We need an eruption of deep and burning lava to come and melt the motionless flood of our days. And this lava is called truth. The heart and the truth never proceed in harmony. At this point, we have to return to the true nature of affection; it does not consist in being happy together, but in being more together. It is a truth that hurts, a sacrifice that hurts, a struggle that hurts."[13]

Reading Mounier, Enzo had understood what it truly means to love. In front of the silent gaze of a daughter in a coma since the age of two, up until her death at 16, the French philosopher had loved this "host" with an unbounded love: "The only thing that remained was to be silent in front of this new mystery, that little by little has pervaded us with its joy. Maybe someone should envy us for this uncertain paternity, this unexpressed dialogue, more beautiful than any children's game."[14] Reading these words, Enzo commented, "She never called her parents dad and mom!" And then, "This should be the normal relationship with our children."[15]

Another book that he particularly loved, maybe because it described in a very raw way the environment where he worked, was *Bodies and Souls* by Maxence Van der Meersch.[16] A particular passage had struck him, and perhaps not by chance it had to do again with the relationship with children: "It is strange—he thought—how we can instill and develop in a creature we love a virtue and a purity that we do not possess ourselves!"[17] A phrase that certainly scandalizes the conformist who rails about moral incoherence, about scandal. Instead, Enzo vigorously shared this attitude as the only alternative to moralism: "He teaches the daughter exactly the

---

12. Bologna, June 1995.
13. Mounier, op. cit., pp. 93-94 (translation: ours).
14. Ibid., pp. 66 and 68.
15. Bologna, June 1995.
16. Pellegrini & Cudahay, 1948.
17. Translation: ours.

opposite of what the father does. Why? This is also what we do with our children. Only if one loves, does he say what is true, even if he is not capable of living it. If one were tied to coherence alone, he would not be capable of an action like this."[18]

There is a book, however, that few people know. It tells a story that, in retrospect, is maybe the most exact and moving image of Enzo's earthly existence, with a finale that is totally different:

> At a certain point he stopped and asked me, "Do you like to read?" I answered yes and he told me, "Read this," and handed me *Pagans* by Ferenc Herczeg. (Raffaello Vignali)

This is a novel from 1902, a great success in its time. Then it disappeared. It tells of a dramatic historical period in the *puszta* of Hungary, marked by a bloody rebellion of the indigenous population (the pagans) against the kingdom of the Christians. The protagonist is a young religious (Màrton) who is sent on mission to attempt to convince the rebels to stop the bloodshed. It is the bishop Gerardo who orders this, a man of great authority, who has for the young man a particular, strong predilection, a "preference." In sending him into enemy territory, the bishop sends the young man a message (he is a religious, but with a "wild" nature, barely restrained): "Tell my child Màrton that Gerardo wants him to pick the fig from the thorn and the grapes from the hawthorn." An enigmatic and prophetic phrase: the total trust of a man in another man, the courage of risk, of betting on the pure freedom of the other, the prophecy of a greatness, hidden and almost impossible, that is waiting only to emerge.

The young man sets out and crosses, unarmed, the region that is in revolt, until he arrives, after various misadventures, at the camp of the enemy, led by a fierce female warrior. A detail of the young man's attitude as he approaches torture reveals an unexpected and unforeseeable truth to the pagans: Màrton is one of them; in fact, he is the son of their last king, the great Thonuzòba, defeated by the Christians, who had raised his young heir after he had become

---

18. Palermo, November 5, 1997.

an orphan. Here is where the "wild" temperament of Màrton, or better Alpàr (the name received from his father), came from. Full of wonder, the whole rebellious population prostrates itself at the feet of the young man. And here, Alpàr returns to be the pagan he was, falls in love with the female warrior, abandons his religious habit, and puts himself at the head of the rebels. In a short time, he puts the entire region under sword and fire with an unheard-of furor, almost wiping out any sign of Christian culture, until he receives the news that the bishop Gerardo has also been killed. In short, a total victory. I remember that Enzo told us about these pages to make us understand the deepest root of the exceptionality of the Christian fact, the reason why the gates of hell will not prevail against it. Alpàr was sure of having wiped out everything; behind him, everything was destroyed. But something happened: "Having abandoned the helm, he turned with wonder to the temple. The bells rang as for a feast, and their sound was surpassed by the devout song of thousands and thousands of voices. In the heart of the country that had become once again pagan and free, there echoed the hymn of faith in Christ! How come?"

This was the aspect that struck Enzo: the most powerful sign of the permanence of Christ in history is not even the civilization that is born from it (and that can be destroyed), but the people who, simply, "get together again," in the name of a fact, of a presence that has conquered their hearts. This is what power is terrified of: the reemergence of a social reality that gathers around an exceptional presence. Turning back to admire the work of his destruction, the desolate earth, Alpàr sees on the horizon defeated men start walking, one by one, gathering around the temple, around the ideal; he sees a people reborn from its ashes.

I like to see Enzo as a man who was made the object of a visceral and prophetic preference, but this time fulfilled: "Tell my child Màrton that Gerardo wants him to pick the fig from the thorn and the grapes from the hawthorn." It is this that Father Giussani saw flourish in Enzo—he waited patiently for the fig from the bramble and the grape from the thorn: "The encounter had transformed even some traits of his temperament, while it had exalted others."[19] Because Enzo, to this preference, answered yes.

IT WAS AS IF WE WERE PLAYING IN THE CHAMPIONS LEAGUE FINAL!

Soccer games were not just soccer games. As in every other thing, after the encounter they had taken on another depth, another objective. They were the most striking example of how both old and new meet each other in Christianity, how they live together, fertilize each other and clash in a battle that is not always victorious. A game was therefore all at once a competition, competitiveness, a proof of strength and authority, an education in the faith, a valorization, a humiliation, a spectacle of friendship and of scandal, a work of art and a primitive rite:

> I remember the endless soccer games to which he always invited me. I remember one in particular, in October 1982, in a field near Settecani (Modena). It was raining non-stop (I don't know how he knew that I had an almost ancestral predilection for soccer in the rain) in this field without lines, with two rusty goal posts. It was a game that lasted perhaps more than two hours... (Gabriele Donati)

There was a tradition that I had witnessed ever since my first years in the university, that mixed sacred and profane in a rather naive way. At the end of every *Via Crucis* (Way of the Cross procession) on Good Friday, after a whole day spent walking in prayer, in a gesture of the highest spiritual and aesthetic value, there was the unmissable game between university students and adults, while we waited till midnight to break the fast. There was never a time when things didn't come to blows. I was a freshman (I still remember it) and the game ended early because Enzo and Licio (who was at the time the leader of the university students) would not stop kicking

---

19. Luigi Giussani, "That Surge of Life." *Traces*, June (2000), http://archivio.traces-cl.com/archive/2000/giugno/surge.html.

each other violently in the butt. I do admit that, little by little, things got better, very slowly.

In the educational method of authority (an essential foundation in the pedagogy of CL), the role of referee was symbolically and methodologically very delicate. Therefore, no one wanted to be the referee when Enzo was on the field. The thing got resolved easily, by giving him the role of referee as player-referee. It was the only way not to end up fighting or endangering the safety of a third party. Still, it gave rise to unbelievable scenes. The games, for example, did not end until Enzo's team got at least to a tie (hours!) and when things didn't work out, he would whistle for a penalty kick for a foul committed at midfield (it was the category of the *"fallaccio,"* a mean, ugly foul).

In one game, in an August heatwave at the seminary in Rimini, after a sumptuous fish lunch, on the cross of a corner kick, Icio rushed forward to head the ball, but his full stomach reacted to the excessive force, rejecting the fish stew he had just ingested. It all happened in perfect synchrony, ball and vomit flying together toward the goal. The goalie obviously got out of the way, and it was a goal. Enzo canceled the goal for… "obstruction."

In one game between doctors and nurses from Sant'Orsola Hospital, the nurses had rejected the rule of the player-referee (understandably: they were laymen), and contacted a professional referee, complete with uniform, whistle, and cards. Ten minutes into the game, Enzo expelled the referee. A rematch is set, after clarifying the rules: 10 minutes into that game, Enzo is expelled, and dutifully leaves the field. He then begins, from the sidelines, a heavy action of "moral suasion," made up of constant and personal insults at the referee: "You don't have balls!" And so that we would understand that it was nothing personal, that it was simply scientific evidence, he adds, "I am a doctor, I know these things. I am telling you this as a doctor!" It was a diagnosis. I don't think that rematch reached the end either.

The game often became a theater in which drama and high educational principles were mixed together without well-defined borders. Through soccer, we tested the fiber of the freshmen, their capacity for resistance, resilience, endurance, talent. If someone knew how to play soccer, he could pass to the next level, because this talent was already a sign of potential openness to the faith: intelligence, spirituality, and temperament were "given attention" with care to choose the people from whom we would ask responsibility, the people with whom we would connect ourselves totally. Sometimes, when someone was not strong on the field, we needed to look for other, more challenging ways to bring them out. Young Beppe was invited to a soccer game and was put on Enzo's team. Having demonstrated that he was no Maradona, after his third bad pass the game was halted. Enzo pointed to him with his hand, without looking at him, and asked us, "And who invited this one?" Silence and frost; the truth was problematic, threatening a semantic short circuit. The unfortunate guy answered, "Enzo, you invited me!" Ice. Enzo did not like to say, "I was wrong" (but he did invite him!). It was something that came out of him when it was absolutely inevitable or obvious (a bit like Fonzie from *Happy Days*).[20] And there... the brilliant intuition broke out: "But you know you are terrible at soccer. You should have never accepted!" The educational principle was saved, and a great friendship was born.

The soccer field was a bit like the testing arena, the metaphor of earthly life and also of the next one:

> He asked me, "Can you imagine, Iano, that when we are in heaven we will play a soccer game without ever getting tired?" (Aureliano Palmeri)

Soccer was a puzzle piece, made to interact with the others that, a bit at a time (with much patience), were placed together to form the great image, as Father Giussani often reminded us,

---

20. This American television series was very popular even in Italy in the 1980s. One of the protagonists, Arthur Fonzarelli (Fonzi), was a heartbreaker capable of any undertaking, except that of admitting his own errors.

repeating a phrase from Romano Guardini: "In the experience of a great love, all that happens becomes an event inside that love."[21]

> There were two things planned for that evening, soccer and dinner together. I remember perfectly a very, very contested game, characterized by an energy that, for me, was absolutely over the top. That is, I have a competitive spirit, but in that game, it was as if we were playing in the Champions League final! After the game, we all went to the headquarters of CL and ate dinner together. With the same intensity, we entered into a discussion. I saw, for the first time, an intensity that didn't just have to do with "pieces" of life, but with everything. That evening, for example, I saw it in playing soccer and eating dinner (and a bit later, I would see it in commenting on a work of art, in writing a flyer, in discussing politics, in helping each other study, etc.). (Tommaso Agasisti)

Soccer also was part of the educational method, even an integral aspect of it. I remember a summer game on the French border, the university students of Bologna against those from Genoa (more than 1,000 cheering against 120). At a certain point, a foul was committed on me (who at the time was the head of the CLU in Bologna, but at the same time had been sent by Enzo to follow the community of Genoa). The tension rose to such a point (we were losing 1 to 0), that the Bologna fans came threateningly onto the field. At that point, the young leader of the Genoa community decided to call off all his players and leave (one of them was even a young boxer...). The game did not end well. It was not a pretty sight. I called Enzo and told him about the episode. He said, "You have to tell Alessandro that the community is not his property, that if he wants to lead, he has to follow, and so certain decisions he has to take to you. Otherwise, he can make his own movement. If he does not understand this, we won't go there anymore." After two days, Alessandro and Father Mimmo drove 150 kilometers on mountain roads to speak with me (what a vacation!) and they invited me to

---

21. Romano Guardini, *L'essenza del cristianesimo* [*The Essence of Christianity*], Morcelliana, Brescia, 1980, p. 12 (translation: ours).

lead their final assembly (another 150 kilometers across the mountains). From there was born one of the most meaningful friendships of our life.

"A spectacle, in other words, of limitation and betrayal, and therefore of humiliation, and at the same time of inexhaustible certainty in the power of Grace that is given us."[22] Even soccer, over time, became part of this spectacle. Licio, the one who traded kicks in the butt with Enzo after the *Via Crucis* (that too was not a pretty sight...) speaks of his encounter on the soccer field 10 years after that infamous scene. He was ready to start again from where he had left off. But something had changed:

> I had decided to play on the opposite team, and kick Enzo the whole game. When I arrived in the locker room, he came to me and wanted me at all costs to play with him. I didn't want to, because to play with Enzo was a nauseating procession of passes to him who had to score (his teaching on dependence). But he insisted; he wanted me on the attack with him, and he passed me an infinite number of balls, sending me toward the goal in every way. (Licio Argelli)

> We had argued that day, animatedly, because we were not part of a lukewarm story and the questions were all burning. If you don't have a sense of the game (like those games played to the last breath on the soccer field), you don't know anything about what the CL Movement and the faith are. (Davide Rondoni)

We raced to sit next to him
Just like for soccer, so also for the lunches and dinners there was a change in the way of conceiving them. They were an occasion of true "communion" (which, among other things, speaking in Christian terms, was born precisely around a table). Dinners and lunches, often dedicated to concrete issues to face, were always attentively thought out as a moment in which the concrete (the problems connected to responsibility, the welcome of new arrivals, the desire to

---

22. Luigi Giussani, *Generating Traces in the History of the World*, pp. 98-99.

be together, and, not least, our hunger to satisfy) was linked to its ultimate meaning.

> His trips to Turin always followed the same "liturgy": he arrived in his Fiat Croma, and already during the trip he called one or another of us to know how life was going. We always gathered at the Italia '61 location, and from there we went to a field we had reserved for the soccer game. There came out on the field his vehemence in the game, the humanity of kids who were discovering Enzo's fascinating humanity. There was then a dinner during which he told us about himself, about his friendship with Father Giussani, about his work, about his travels, and when he got back in the car around midnight he began to call the kids again. (Father Primo Soldi)

I remember that in 1985, as a freshman, I participated in one of these "liturgies." Enzo, Macio (who, at the time, was the president of CUSL), and I got in the car for Turin, for a soccer game and dinner. A very taxing dinner for me because already at the appetizer we were drinking Barolo. I was not so used to that; the more the time passed at the table, the more happy I was and the less I remembered what was being said. After a rather heavy first and second course (the raw minced meat had been marinated in lemon since the day before, together with some devilish alcoholic mixture), something not so dangerous was eventually served: a watermelon cut in squares inside its rind. "Finally," I thought to myself, "something harmless." And I dove in headlong, not realizing that the transparent liquid in which the squares were immersed was not a syrup, but grappa. And obviously the dinner closed with a nice glass of whiskey. Everyone was very happy. This was the first time I went out with Enzo and I looked at Father Primo and said, "And aren't you, a priest, ashamed of yourself?!" What a great first introduction! Then, absolute darkness. I don't remember any topics of the surely interesting dinner. I remember only that after a few hours I woke up, lying down on the back seat of the car, and I heard Enzo say to Macio, "It is late. You guys come sleep at my house in Modena." This I remember. We entered an apartment that was already very crowded (he had four kids) and Enzo peeked into the bedrooms, just as he had described to Father Giussani.

We met each other in that apartment so many times at such improbable hours, and every time we arrived at his house, he and his wife Fiorisa always prepared something, like nuts, salami, or cheese, and when they were able, a plate of pasta, or some food donated by his patients (often from the south). Always. Even when he went out with the university students (the leaders or the freshmen), we often went out to dinner, and he had a special way of handling the check: "For those who can, 5,000 lire. For those who can't, whatever you have." He often contributed what was lacking.

To optimize time, then, the meeting with the leaders of the university community of Bologna, the "little group" (more or less the number of the Apostles) was always Monday at lunch, to set up the week. Since we couldn't afford to go out to lunch, the secretary had taken charge of preparing something to eat. With 2,000 or 3,000 lire we could get by, and communion tasted better.

Around the table it is always simpler to perceive the implication of the words spoken. Father Giussani had taught us in this way: "The person we come across becomes an encounter if we find him engaged in a 'different' way—with a difference that attracts us—in the things everyone does. If, that is, as he speaks, eats, and drinks, he makes a qualitative difference perceivable, and offers it to our existence, causing us to go away struck by the fact that eating and drinking have an absolute meaning, and a word spoken in fun has an eternal value."[23] And this is what happened for us:

> We were together for public meetings, diaconias,[24] various gatherings, but above all we went to dinner together. The moment of the dinner was the most anticipated. We raced to

---

23. Luigi Giussani, *Generating Traces in the History of the World*, pp. 18-19.

24. The "diaconia" is a service to the life of the communities of Communion and Liberation. It is made up of "leaders" who are invited to make the educational experience of the Movement more accessible to everyone, and who would accept the invitation according to their free availability. Local, national, and international diaconias were created to serve this aim, as were specific diaconias for every educational environment (e.g., adults, university students, and high school students).

sit next to him, to be able to hear him speak (the best place was always in front of him, so you could look him in the face). We asked him about everything—literally, everything, from the life of the CLU to national and international politics, recommendations for books to read and films to watch, and then personal questions, the life of every day. (Assuntina Morresi)

At the table, naturally, we spoke about big things and little things, without any break in continuity or intensity.

> The dinner on the topic of girlfriends went forward and turned into "Who is the hottest girl today?" And there was no contest, as Enzo imposed on us... Sofia Loren... (Luigi Tabanelli)[25]

The well-deserved "rest"

Vacation was the moment when Enzo dedicated himself totally to his family, and "took a break." But his concept of vacation is not exactly what is normally meant by the term. He usually took advantage of the hospitality offered by many friends who invited him all over Italy, preferably near the sea in the south, which allowed him on the one hand not to break the family bank (never very full) and on the other hand to live even this "off time" in the context of friends.

As I said, his "off time" was *sui generis*, for many reasons:

> He was on vacation in Sicily, as a guest, on the first floor of my family's villa in San Vito Lo Capo, which had direct access to the beach. At a certain point, in the middle of one of the two weeks, Enzo received a summons to Milan for a diaconia called by Father Giussani. He did not hesitate one moment to say yes, and he left for Milan in the morning and returned that evening. (Ciccio Castiglione)

---

25. On this much discussed topic, others remember Claudia Cardinale from "*Once Upon a Time in the West*."

That Naive Boldness that Characterizes Us

It would also happen that some of us would show up in the middle of his well-deserved rest, as happened in 1993 when, starting from Bologna with one car, we went to visit him in San Vito Lo Capo in the middle of August. We had learned to be brief, intense, and university-style, and therefore the whole visit consisted of a one night stay, a game of soccer on the beach, and (exceptionally) even beach volleyball (there were his three young daughters to consider), then a dip in the sea, and the return to Bologna.

And we were not alone:

> Those soccer games with the friends from Modena were epic. Those friends, just "to be with" Enzo, were capable of leaving from the other side of Sicily and returning in a day (and a night), a drive of 700 kilometers total, after going for a swim in the sulfurous waters of Segesta or Montevago. (Ciccio Castiglione)

Later on, Enzo decided to go even further south, where cars could not arrive. But the scenario didn't change much:

> His summer vacations took place at Pantelleria Island from 1996 to 1998. The soccer games were still memorable, which he kept playing even on vacation. He gathered together kids of every age that he met on his walks, and made them play with him and his family. I remember the small caravan of kids, of the most varied ages and social levels, who, after the game, came to look for him in the pubs facing the sea. I remember also that bit of envy I felt with respect to his capacity to catalyze a community. Those local young people, many of whom I did not know, he conquered with a soccer game on a summer evening. I remember that he was willing to travel long and uncomfortable distances, even just for a few days, dragging his family with him in the car, to push his knowledge further, to have new encounters and make new discoveries. (Giuseppe Policardo)

I remember that one year he called me while he was driving back from Sicily, and asked, "What are you guys doing this evening?" I was with family at Sirmione, a guest of my friend Francesco, and I felt a little embarrassed telling him, "Look, Enzo, I can't really go anywhere." I hadn't even finished the sentence when he told me, "Perfect. I will come to you in Sirmione with my son Pietro, and we will play a game of soccer and have a beer." And so it happened. I was a bit cross about organizing a team, and he drove 1,500 kilometers to arrive on time, after dropping off half the family in Modena! I cobbled together a team, and we took to the field against the team of Matteo, who was Francesco's brother and very, very good at soccer. In short, our team of those "escaped from the sword" (as Enzo loved to define our ramshackle companionship) was down four or five goals. But, as usual, we continued for hours until, through the sheer exhaustion of the other team, we were one goal ahead of them. Right at that point, the referee (always Enzo) blew the whistle to end the game.[26] Next came the beers (complete with discussion about Moretti being the best beer), then the Piccinini family started out again for Modena (and the next day he went back to work again after a well-deserved "rest").

We have to make at least one last mention of the most eccentric vacation that Enzo was invited to, shrouded in a secretiveness worthy of the spy novels of the Cold War. Enzo took part in this vacation under a false identity (he was *Dottor Fagiolo*, Doctor Bean) in order to meet up in Sardinia with Father Giussani, the cardinal of Bologna, Giacomo Biffi, and the head of the Memores Domini, Carlo Wolfsgruber. When he returned from that vacation, Enzo related the most hilarious aspects and facts, from the cardinal's habit of going swimming at six in the morning and then of staying in the house the whole day, to his passion for the TV series *Kojak*, to the discussions they had at table, to the visits to neighboring places. He told us that often in the evening Father Giussani would suggest to him in private some topics to propose at table, to find out what the cardinal thought of them: "Tomorrow, Enzo, try to say, 'On this, I think that...'" and he gave him precise instructions. So that was punctually done, as Enzo usually did. Sometimes the cardinal, hearing Enzo's positions, burst out saying, "But Enzo... what are

---

26. Matteo, the day after, was summoned by his father Franco, a renowned hotel owner from Sirmione, who had found out about what had happened: "They told me about yesterday... You see... we have to learn to be humble."

you saying?! How is it possible for a Christian to think that kind of thing?" Enzo then turned toward Father Giussani, asking with a look to be rescued. Gius looked at him and exclaimed, "But Enzo... what are you saying?!" "What?"—Enzo told us—"It was he who had told me to say it!"

On the insistence of the cardinal, one day they went to visit the tomb of Garibaldi, at Caprera. Biffi and Giussani had a way of feeling things that was very similar in many aspects (both were formed at the famous seminary of Venegono). On other things, though, their feelings were very different (certainly about the *Risorgimento*).[27] And so, at the proposal of the cardinal, "Let's say a prayer for Garibaldi," Giussani responded, "Yes, let's say a prayer for all the deceased." And so it was.

THROWING YOUR HEART OVER THE OBSTACLES

A naïve boldness: in Enzo, this fruit of the action of the Spirit was translated immediately into a passion and a constant stimulus not to reduce his aims, even those that were the hardest. For him this consisted in "throwing your heart over the obstacles." And he invited us to do the same:

> He asked me to carry with him questions and burdens that were clearly disproportionate for my age. (Gianpiero di Febbo)

> Enzo invited each of us to take seriously the idea of going to the United States, looking for a job or a thesis to work on there. He was always very clear: whoever had an opportunity to study in America had to make himself available. We did not go to "make" the Movement, but to study in the university, living there the experience of the Movement as we would have lived it in Florence. And so, I left all my responsibilities in the Movement, my boyfriend of

---

27. The *Risorgimento* (Resurgence) was the movement that brought about the independence of Italy and its unification in 1861. Giuseppe Garibaldi played a major role in the military victories and is considered by many Italy's national hero. He was also a harsh enemy of the Pope and the Catholic Church.

seven years (who later became my husband), my family, and I went there alone, for two years. I had only studied English until the second year of high school, and the professor, after having flunked me several times, had said goodbye, telling me, "Astorri, I am sorry, but you will never learn English!" I made a step that was "much longer than my leg" out of a total following of that invitation from Enzo. (Francesca Astorri)

That spring afternoon in 1986, in the hallway of the old CL headquarters in Strada Maggiore in Bologna, Enzo was standing and, with a piercing gaze (which always put me in awe), he called me and another friend, and asked us if we were available to go on vacation with a group of Spanish university students who each year went to Egypt to learn and study the Arabic language and culture. The request had come from Father Giussani who, having met a Spanish priest that had given life to a very lively movement present in the parishes of, called Nueva Tierra, desired that the university students belonging to this movement could meet our experience. Enzo always treated us as adults, putting us in front of a responsibility, respecting and calling forth our freedom. The two of us went, like the disciples Jesus sent into the world to proclaim the Gospel. (Simona Massaia)

My friends from the CLU and I found ourselves without a house, because of a law that made it disadvantageous for homeowners to rent to students. There was a risk we would have to return to our home city. I thought of a juridical and economical way to resolve the problem. When I spoke about it with Enzo, he was excited and brought me to Milan to meet a series of professionals, who could help me to verify the feasibility of the idea and to get the work underway. At the beginning, there was not a week that he did not check in on how the work was going. I was struck by the way he supported me and all those who worked voluntarily for the rental cooperative, a true charity, even looking into the details, sharing the anxiety of the risks we were taking. "You are an adult." I was 22 years old. (Maurizio Carvelli)

He asked me to become the leader of CL in my faculty—I, who practically did not even belong to CL yet! A year later, he asked me to follow the communities in Urbino and

> Ancona, together with a friend from Paraguay. "Me? But I still lack the fundamentals!" (Maila Quaglia)

> I wanted to become a neurologist, but didn't pass the specialty exam. I had entered, though, into other schools of specialization, in one of which I even had a great chance at a career. Everyone encouraged me to accept, even if it was not exactly what I wanted. Enzo helped me a lot to understand what I truly desired, and whether the data of reality could allow me to follow this desire. In the end, I decided to risk waiting a year to take the exam again, knowing that it was probable I would fail again. Enzo helped me even in the smallest details. "You have to become number one, the best neurologist in the world studying Parkinson's!" I was pregnant with my first child, with a huge belly, and he insisted (while I thought, "Does he realize?!"). He pushed us to act seriously, to raise the bar, to love our work, giving the best of ourselves. (Francesca Bisulli)

Throwing your heart over every obstacle: this is not something banal, above all when it is not about a game, when there is a real risk on the table, and the outcome is different from what you imagined after having invested time, energy, passion, money, trust. There are situations from which it doesn't take much to recover:

> It happened often that things didn't go how we thought they would, like hosting the freshmen day in Bologna, the Crazy Bus,[28] without having reserved the buses, and so we had to walk...; the bid war for the study room on Via Mascarella, that we won because we had grossly underestimated the cost of personnel, and so we ended up losing money. (Andrea Pagliarani)

Other times, things were less easy to fix; to pin everything on freedom is a risk. And a happy ending is not always guaranteed.

I happened to write a memory for the 20th anniversary of Enzo's death that summed up his earthly life as "a spectacle of continual exaggeration." That's how Enzo was, always exaggerated, that

---

28. This was an initiative proposed to the freshmen in November: the CLU students rented some buses, duly decorated them, and showed the newly arrived freshmen around the city of Bologna.

is, *ex* (outside of) every *agger* (border). In our barren world, exaggeration is the action of those who want things to appear greater than what they are—and, in truth, things are truly greater than they are. This Christian exaggeration is the antechamber of holiness."

One gets up in the morning and doesn't even notice anymore that he is tired

Enzo's existence was an existence in love; he often spoke to us about falling in love. This was certainly a topic that we young people felt very strongly, but we had begun to intuit that the thing was different from what we thought and that, for this reason, the problem would not be resolved nor limited to our young age.

"Think of when an affection happens. Someone gets up, gets up in the morning, and doesn't even notice anymore that he is tired. I have seen certain amazing changes in this sense, you guys. I have seen the overcoming of every ability and every attempt at self-analysis, in the sense that something else happened, something other, unforeseen. And one feels himself involved with everything around him, the whole world."[29]

It was not just a "naturalistic" experience. Through that natural call, there was hidden (as we had begun to understand) something that pushes us to break through the confines of nature. Through instinct, we were taken on a path that brought us to break through the chains of instinct. "I have never found a sentence like this, so concise and fantastic: 'a longing to embrace that source of love intuited behind the fascination of the human creature.'[30] It is something from another world. We have to put it in the hands of all those young lovers who are 14 or 15 years old and tell them, 'Listen, don't do it. Listen to this sentence, do something, but don't do anything stupid. It's too important.' This is really beautiful; a longing to

---

29. Bologna, November 21, 1985.
30. This was a comment Giussani made on a few verses of Leopardi.

embrace that source of love intuited behind the fascination of the human creature."[31]

Without realizing it, we were walking the demanding road that joins the exalted experience of falling in love with the fulfillment of that love. "The true problem is if you love or not, if you have your face turned toward your stomach or if you look at reality as a continual discovery of something that is not yours. To love in this case is stripped of every sentimental characteristic; it is, naked and raw, the affirmation of the other. In your work, who and what are you responding to? Certainly, you respond to your boss, but in the end the response is to something for which everything exists, for which everything is worthy of respect and time. Without the Presence, there is nothing at all. Not even your wife is present without the Mystery. Usually, instead, for us she is present because you feel her, and when you don't feel her, she doesn't exist anymore. On the contrary, if the Presence is there, your wife is there even if you don't feel her, even if you don't like her anymore. This is life. This is the problem. If you take this away, there is only instinct in relationships. Therefore, we either reason like everyone else, or we change our skin."[32]

On this topic, today as yesterday, today more than yesterday, the Christian perspective on love places us in front of an enormous challenge: we either reason like everyone else, or we change our skin. If we do not perceive this challenge (which comes directly from Christ), Enzo's words seem like just a "way of speaking," a metaphor to interpret, a principle to apply on a case-by-case basis. And we even do this with the words of Christ. "Love is first of all (how strange—this word we are ashamed to say, except in certain caveman-like relationships, in which it is reduced to a certain feeling)... love is not our own construction, because our life is a service to love."[33]

---

31. Bologna, June 23, 1991.
32. Rimini, March 27, 1999.
33. Bologna, November 21, 1985.

"And to love is not a feeling. If this isn't there, you're done for, dammit! You lessen your life in things already known, in little feelings already known. Here we are opening up a new perspective, understand? We are opening up a drama. And a drama is always a dialogue between you and a proposal. So you are alive. The drama is a dialogue, and a dialogue makes you live; that is, it focuses you. Never forget this."[34] "This shortened reason is within the usual things. You see it within the relationship between a guy and a girl—when there is no aura of mystery, there is no possibility of anything other than what we feel or see or do."[35] "How much of the road have they ruined for us, with sentimentalism that they foist on us every day, from kids' cartoons to all the rest that you see on TV or in movies?! Instead, this is life—do you get it? The one you love, before anything that you feel, is a question of truth for your life. And then they say that Christianity is backward on these things!"[36]

All this brought out in us a certain serenity in front of what had become for everyone the "drama of the choice." In those times (we were at the beginning), the anxiety-inducing problem of finding the "right girl" was becoming widespread, a modern problem that one met for the first time in the culture of the Disney dream, walking arm in arm with it. It was a problem of correspondence with our soulmate who has to exist somewhere, and who will be capable of making our earthly existence happy (at the same time making faith completely superfluous). This legitimate preoccupation was translated then, with ever-greater nonchalance, in the widespread method of "disposable" relationships (like single-use razor blades): "Let's see how it goes... if not this one, it will be the next one." And never being "this one," the next ones kept multiplying. Today, we do not even recognize it anymore, because this formula is dominant at every level, having gone way beyond the confines of adolescence (or better, having extended the adolescent phase all the way to old age).

---

34. Florence, September 5, 1998.
35. Bologna, November 21, 1985.
36. Bologna, October 5, 1988.

On this, Enzo was farsighted and provoking, to the point of creating axioms that unfortunately were easily (and maliciously) misunderstood. The most famous was "one [girl] is worth as much as another." Many deduced from this a debasement of women; others, more pettily, an instrumentalization of affective relationships. In reality, it was the opposite. The point was understanding that even the best correspondence (which we hoped for and pursued) would leave us inevitably in front of the limit of that relationship with respect to the infinite desire of our heart. The point was understanding that the experience of love would always bring us to bite the hard rock of sacrifice, of the total gift of self to the other, regardless of the desired correspondence that we may or may not feel. The point was understanding that the dimension of "vocation," of responding to Another even in the affective relationship, is the only dimension that keeps giving new energy to the short legs of sentiment. A bit at a time, we were placed within a perspective of love as a "task," which does not take anything away from the dynamic of falling in love because, on the contrary, it completes it and, within a sacrifice, makes it live again, and differently (the only truly human path to make a passion continue to live).

We were in some way fortunate because the "task" was (albeit in a somewhat rustic and old-fashioned way) clear and operative: "When I see those girls who come to me, either young girls or university students, who complain because their boyfriend is a leader in the Movement and neglects her—how many there are, I could make a list— I look at them and, sometimes, with those that are the most like this, I even say a few bad words to them, but with the others, I look them straight in the face, 'In your opinion, does this guy have any greater way of loving you (than building the Movement), any greater way of loving you than experiencing, loving the presence of Christ? What are you asking for?'"[37] The awareness of a task (whether the Movement or something else, it doesn't matter) is the breathing point for a romantic relationship. "Think about when

---

37. Folgarida, August 6, 1991.

a man and a woman love each other: if there is not this judgment, it is like dogs, it is the same thing. What is different about it?"[38]

All this raised on the horizon the inevitable idea of a sacrifice to be carried out, possible only on the condition of putting oneself in the right position to sustain it. "Can you love a person without putting yourself in the position of asking? Can you have enthusiasm for things or for life without asking? Everything would depend on what you think, what you feel... But in order to have this position, we need to go against the stream. The whole world works together to push another position, which is the opposite one."[39]

Accepting this condition on a daily basis built in us a reserve of the energy necessary for the great decision, the decision of "forever," a "countercultural" decision even back then. It is what the heart desires, but it is also what the heart fears most. "We began to understand that what we had always dreamed of was possible, that is, the 'forever,' and we began to understand why we had fought those battles against divorce,[40] when the whole world was saying, 'If one no longer feels love, how can the couple stay together?' We understood that in the strength of this Presence we could be together for our whole life, even if love was not there, because the truer love is a judgment. We began to understand among us that, for example, in the most incredible aspect of life, which is affection, we do not get married because we love each other, but in order to make Christians and to build the community. These were like punches that left you dead! If you go to any part of the world and ask what is the truest love, they tell you, 'That which is forever,' and you understand very well that you are not able to do it. Here I want someone to get up and assure me that he will be my friend for our whole life, forever. No one would be able to do it. And yet, this is what we desire. So how is it possible? If we recognize this Presence as the reason for everything, then this Presence goes beyond, sharpens our sentiment

---

38. Rimini, December 12, 1998.

39. Catania, October 13, 1997.

40. In May 1974, there was a referendum in Italy attempting to abrogate the 1970 law that had legalized divorce. The Movement participated in the cultural battle against divorce, although the referendum failed.

and makes it persistent—a first move to discover the true reason. It changed everything, you know?"[41] "We need something greater, so that even the situations that you don't understand make sense. We need something greater, so that you may be able to admit that you can even not understand, that things can even not go the way you want. By the way, I don't know how you do it, if you are married, I don't know how you can live, because things never go the way you want."[42]

The awareness that marriage is something that requires a lot more than mutual love can assure had been a rather precocious intuition of Enzo who, at age 22, in the prayer written for his wedding, asked exactly this: "Lord, I thank you that my path is clear. I ask you to give me the strength and the decision that my marriage may not be a private fact, as the world wants, but may be the place where with ever greater firmness we call each other to a life for Christ and for His Church."[43]

The gift of self without measure, without return, is the only possibility of a true and lasting love. "I saw terrible downfalls: young people who were fantastic, full of life, and who as soon as they got married, two or three months later, disappeared, or became sad. Or families that just grind on, searching for a bit of balance: 'Today, I stay at home; tomorrow, you stay. Yesterday, I washed the dishes; tonight it's your turn. I got up once; now you get up for the baby.' We don't think about it, but this is how love becomes a measure. It is absurd, because love is rather the courage to serve always, at all times. I am not just talking to women; it is true for all of us. When a man arrives home, like me, maybe after having had a terrible night, after having operated the whole night, and he expects his wife to put the carpet under his feet, he is wrong. In the same way, the wife, who stayed at home with the baby who has a fever, when she sees her husband return exhausted, cannot think that he still has some strength. 'He thinks only about his recliner, putting on his slippers

---

41. Summer vacation of the Florence university students, 1987.
42. Cesena, March 12, 1999.
43. Modena, July 1, 1973.

and watching TV!' But it is only a love without measure that allows us to understand this. I have also seen people who were strangers become friends. And I saw families that were not doing so well open themselves to an amazing affection between them. I saw my family change. Therefore, it is an urgent invitation that I am making to you. It is possible for everyone."[44]

"When Jesus Christ began to describe the question of the indissolubility of marriage, the disciples responded in a very human way, 'So it is better not to marry,' do you remember? And Christ responds, 'No, for man this is impossible, but for God it is possible.' What saves our life is the awareness of the great Presence within the fragile but irreplaceable life of our companionship. So faithfulness is possible, indissolubility is possible, carrying out the task of caring for children to the end is possible, even when this does not bear the fruit we might have desired."[45]

We were in the years when the strength of family ties was already clearly at risk, and from then on things would get increasingly difficult. Enzo was aware of it, and sought in every way to help us become aware of what this definitive step means, this "forever" of the affective relationship. It was a common practice that his closest friends who were approaching their wedding day would have dinner with him a few months before getting married, to help them perceive his closeness and support for the great and demanding step they were about to take.

> Before my wedding, he invited me and my future wife to dinner in order to help us have a greater awareness of the gesture that we were about to make. "You hardly understand anything of the yes you will say to Christ, and you will have to return to that yes and remember it your whole life; a moment of prayer together every morning and, in the evening, a shared moment about how the day went."[46] (Gianpiero Di Febbo)

---

44. Marche, October 22, 1995.

45. Bologna, June 21, 1992.

46. Of the many trips I took with Enzo by car, I remember very well that every single time he unfailingly made a short call to Fiorisa, even late at night.

His concern for the stability of the sacrament of marriage was not directed only to the younger ones. The judgment and his support continued even for those who had been living for some time the challenge and the effort of the "duration" of the marriage promise. The dimension of sacrifice could not be canceled, under penalty of the deterioration of that same affection: "Excuse me, but is it true or not that faithfulness between husband and wife after 25 years of marriage is at the price of a real transformation of the initial affection? We have all experienced this; otherwise, we would have split up. It is a real transformation of affection and therefore a real transformation of the relationship, because when we said yes, in front of that priest in that church, we didn't understand anything of what we were doing. That yes had an otherworldly importance, and decided our whole life. But who understood? Was there anyone who understood what it meant afterwards? It is clear: now is not like before. In order for that faithfulness to persist in the good and the bad times, that which we felt then has to be transformed and has to become transparent to that initial yes—that is, our belonging to the foundation that allowed us to risk a life together forever."[47]

Enzo always repeated this to the young couples with whom he ate dinner, to help them understand that they have to give priority right away to something capable of transforming the initial sentiment and helping the yes become transparent:

> Before getting married in 1995 (today I have a wife and five children), Enzo asked me and my fiancée to dinner. I remember very well two things, as if he foresaw the difficulties that would come and that have been in my marriage. He told me, "Always forgive her." But the most important thing was this: "Remember that it is Christ who unites you, and if you give your life for Christ, and so for the Church where you have met Him, your union will hold up only in this way." (Gabriele Donati)

The weakness of judgment was singled out as the most fragile point of the affective relationship. The gravest consequence of this

---

47. Pesaro, April 6, 1998.

weakness was not just the end of a beautiful story, but rather the damage toward that which is born from that relationship. "Yesterday evening a couple invited me to dinner (a beautiful couple with two kids). They have just met the Movement, and they want to separate; they have already started the paperwork. I did not know them... they invited me. I saw that they were always bickering, but I did not understand well, and then the problem came out. I didn't know what to say, 'I am sorry, but what about faith?' And they looked at me, saying, 'No, no faith'—'What do you mean no faith?'—'No, no, nothing, no faith.' I say, 'Do you have kids?'—'Yes'—'How many?'—'Two.' 'But then you have to respond to something new. You have to respond to something new between you two. There is not just what you want, what you feel, what you do, between the two of you. If only for a minute, between you two, you could insert in the way you look at each other and think about each other the responsibility that you have in front of the fact that you have brought two kids into the world, and if the memory of those faces could insert itself each time you have the strange attitude of wanting to affirm what you feel at all costs... Only for this you should go back every time. You got married in church, you called on Christ as a witness to your love. It is the memory of that Face, along with the memory of your children, that makes you take in hand a relationship that you feel lost, only because you don't feel it anymore.' Only by responding to someone or something present in what we do, can we take into consideration everything in front of us."[48] "The repetition of self infinitely, says Freud, who was a genius (an atheist, but a genius) is psychological death. The repetition of ourselves (that is, where the law is 'I feel,' there is only what I feel, if I do not feel it, it does not exist; what I like, what I see...) is psychological death, because you just repeat yourself, you have no relationship with reality."[49]

The overcoming of "I feel or don't feel" is what breaks the vicious circle that suffocates a relationship, is what opens up with

---

48. Bologna, October 17, 1993.

49. February 23, 1995.

effort an unforeseen dimension (however painful) to the initial love and makes it become "friendship." "If that stuff doesn't become friendship, what do you do with it, how long does it last?" There resounds in this expression a call full of hope that Father Giussani had made us: "Friendship is always moving, even if it can make you pass through days and weeks and months of dryness! But think about how many men and women, in the responsibility of helping their kids grow up, spend months—months!—in dryness, in which one seems to have become a stranger to the other. They have to accept each other, they have to bear with each other, they have to collaborate, they have to do things together, stay together until, at a certain breaking of the morning, there rises up again in them, they feel rising up in them, much more mature, the emotion they had the first time they saw each other."[50]

Enzo reported to us with wonder a question that Giussani had asked him, creating in him an immediate embarrassment, transformed later into a reflection full of wonder. "Enzo, do you express yourself with your wife?" He was amazed at the thoughtfulness with which Gius shared his passion for a total expressivity, for a fullness of relationship. This same passion Enzo communicated to us:

> We knew that Enzo had the habit of eating dinner with couples who were close to getting married, so, the day after graduation, we "got in line." Enzo listened to us and counseled us ("Give yourselves a point of the day, however short, together"). He was with us until midnight (he was supposed to leave at 10:30!). He never looked at his watch, he was there for us as if our "questions" were the most important thing in the world. He took everything seriously, especially Angela. That evening, an extraordinary gaze happened, unreasonable in terms of time dedicated and questions addressed, so similar, all in all, to the questions of many young spouses, and yet to him so worthy of attention. (Giorgio Guidi)

---

50. Luigi Giussani. *Avvenimento di libertà: Conversazioni con giovani universitari* [*Event of Freedom: Conversations with Young University Students*], Marietti, Genoa, 2002, p. 125 (translation: ours).

When I got married he was my best man and said, "Give in on everything, except on the essential."

But listen: do you love your family?

This "forever" is generative and, once accepted, it leads you, beyond your ability, to discover yourself as "father." The responsibility shared in the years of the CLU was a great training in paternity, the discovery of the source that generates personality. For some of us, it became also a biological paternity, posing the serious challenge of learning what it means to love the one you have generated.

"He [Giussani] asked, 'But listen, do you love your family?' I replied, 'Yes.' 'You love your children?' 'Yes.' 'Give an example!' I don't know who among you has ever been able to give an example of this. I didn't know what to say. 'Look, it often happens that I come home late at night, either because of work or the Movement, and my wife leaves the bedroom doors open a little to hear if the children need help, if they wake up. I arrive and I have to turn on only the entrance lights, because if I turn on the other lights the children wake up and I am in serious trouble, because my wife would get really upset... I turn on the entrance light, I come inside very quietly, I get undressed in the hallway without making a sound. Through the partially-closed doors the light illuminates the small beds where the children are. It is hard to describe, but I am taken by an infinite tenderness in seeing these little bundles in their beds. So I sneak inside, I pick up one of them, and sometimes they wake up: "Papa!"—"Shhh! Or else mom..." I squeeze them a little, give them a kiss...' So I said to Giussani, 'In short, I think I love them.' And Giussani said, 'That is not the way to love them. Look, the true way of loving is that right when this tenderness is at its most intense, true, and thrilling, humanly overwhelming, you have to take a step back, look at them, and say, 'What will become of them?' Because to love is to understand that they have a destiny, that they are not yours, they are yours and they are not yours, that they have a destiny and that it is by looking at the drama that destiny imposes on the relationship with them and with things, in the future and in the present, that you will respect them, you will love them, you will be willing to do anything for them, you will not feel blackmailed whether they obey you or not.'"[51] "The admission of the question, 'What will become of them?'—this dramatic way of being in front of them—means that they are not mine, they have a destiny that I have to love like I love my own. You see, it is poverty that builds hope; that is, it makes a relationship certain. It is a detachment; we have to take a step back."[52]

To recognize that your children have a destiny, that they are not yours, does not imply a position of neutrality, a kind of withdrawal to leave space to their freedom. Freedom is fostered not by keeping equal distance from what has value, but only through a proposal that provokes one to take a position, an increasingly more aware and responsible position. Freedom coincides therefore with taking a position in front of someone who proposes a hypothesis to discuss. "When I am in the operating room, above all during long surgeries, one of the topics I always discuss with the nurses is children."[53] "It often happens that someone asks me, 'Doctor, do you really have four children? Why? Do you know that it is a huge responsibility?' I respond, 'Yeah... I mean, if I had made them...!'"[54] "The other day, in order to explain what it means that there is a challenge in life, we were speaking about normal life. 'Of course normal life cannot be lived without certainty,' I said, just like that, provokingly. And a nurse began to say, 'Yeah, yeah, this is your belief. But how do you think you can deal with your children; how can you teach them something like that? It is a violence! You can't teach them something so certain, like the Christianity you have lived. You have to leave them free, you have to give them more options! They have to discover more options in general, then in the end something will mature.' I looked at her, stopped a minute, and said, 'Listen, you

---

51. Rimini, December 12, 1998.
52. February 23, 1995.
53. February 23, 1995.
54. Pesaro, April 30, 1999.

are a criminal! How do you educate someone, in your opinion? Giving them more options and leaving them free, or provoking their freedom? When has education ever been something that leaves everything just as it was before? Education means "*e-duco*," to bring out. And how do you bring someone out? Telling them that everything is neutral, you think? To lead out the freedom of someone, the proposal has to be clear and challenge one's life, and this means that the cowardice is all yours, because you don't have reasons to propose what you nevertheless believe and for which you live. If a proposal is clear, the other will be forced to bring out the claws of his freedom, and one day you will risk hearing him say "no," but you will have brought out that freedom!'"[55]

"And there I often ask the question, 'Have you ever been in love? Have you ever loved another person?'—'Yes'—'And when you loved this person, when you spoke with this person, what did you do? Did you report to him what the newspaper said, or what you thought? So, you see, the problem is not a question of violence toward the other; it is a question of love. If one loves another, she does not say what everyone else thinks. She says what is true for her. This coincides with the proposal, because the idea of the proposal is the most simple and effective idea of love for freedom.' 'But this absoluteness is not right!' 'What can I do to be useful? As they say in Bologna, just soften the edges, so as to live together more easily? Or maybe freedom is provoked by a proposal?'"[56]

To be fathers means to love the freedom of our children and to do everything for this freedom to come into play. All our paternity comes into play in the hope of the "secret hour," as Peguy would say: "Ask this father if the best moment / is not when his children begin to love him as men, / he himself as a man, / freely / gratuitously, / ask this father whose children are growing. / Ask this father if there is not a secret hour, / a secret moment, / and if it is not / when his children begin to become men, / free, / and they treat him as a man, / free, / they love him as a man, / free, / ask this father whose

---

55. February 23, 1995.
56. Pesaro, April 30, 1999.

kids are growing. / Ask this father if there is not a choice among all choices / and if it is not / precisely when submission ends and when his children become men / they love him, (they treat him), like experts, so to say / man to man, / freely, / gratuitously. They respect him like this. / Ask this father if he does not know that nothing is worth more / than a man's gaze that meets a man's gaze."[57]

And that moment coincides with the maturity of our child, with the handing over of our child (not without pain) to a companionship that takes him by the hand so that he can become an adult, capable in turn of generating. "In order to be fathers and mothers it is not enough to push out children, because even the animals are capable of this. To be fathers and mothers means to give the children which you push out the possibility to live in the world and to know that they can be happy. Because if a woman gives birth to a baby and abandons it, and does not help it to face life according to its destiny, she would be a stepmother, she would be a degenerate mother. Our companionship is your father and mother that takes the torch from your carnal and natural mother and father, because they cannot follow you where this companionship can follow you. There can be many people within the companionship who are not aware of this, but our companionship could not stand up without those who are aware of this. Even if they are the same age as you, it is as if they are fathers and mothers of your destiny, because this companionship is not born from our heart, it is like a gift that invests you, that comes from something else. Because, who can even dream of being father and mother of the other?"[58]

Therefore, paternity and maternity always carry a risk, above all in that they do not always coincide simply with what one says, with what is explicit. Rather, they express themselves through what is not said, the implicit, what can be glimpsed only by paying attention to what is moving a person, to the motive, to what moves the one who makes the proposal. 'And so, one day, I met with my

---

57. Charles Péguy, *"Il mistero dei santi innocenti"* ["The Mystery of the Holy Innocents," in *Lui è qui* [*He is here*], Milan, Rizzoli, 1998, pp. 373-375 (translation: ours).

58. Florence, October 20, 1989.

children at lunch, and I had this thing I had been thinking about for a long time. I said, 'So, why are you in the Movement? It is strange that I have never spoken to you about it.' It is true, I had never posed the problem of the Movement to my family. We have lived like this, I have lived according to what had begun to take hold of me, with my wife and with everything. So, after a bit, my oldest daughter answers, 'You know why we are in the Movement? First, because we have always been struck by the totality of your dedication to the Movement.' How odd—it was exactly the reason that I was less present at home, and it was the thing that had struck them the most. And there I understood that it is useless, you guys, to try to make everybody happy. The enthusiasm of life, the beauty of life, is proportional to your engagement with the ideal! What do you want to calculate? At 20 years of age, come on... 'And the other thing that has always struck us is that when you bring your friends and we see you with them, it was a type of friendship we have always desired for ourselves.'"[59]

This totality of dedication, this commitment without measure to the companionship that God puts mysteriously on our path, explains the reason for Enzo's special devotion to Saint Joseph, the moving and paradoxical figure of a fulfilled, realized paternity. "Even the case of Saint Joseph is not a small thing. That man carried a sense of the Mystery with a nobility and a dignity that I think makes him the most powerful saint in the world."[60]

VIRGINITY IS THE TRUE MODE OF LOVE

Father Giussani often cited this phrase from Heraclitus: "The hidden harmony is better than the obvious one."[61] The implicit, he told us, educates more than the explicit, because it forces us to go to the root of what appears; it forces us to take a position. And so, the most powerful signs of Enzo's paternity are those that derive from

---

59. Rimini, December 12, 1998.
60. Folgarida, August 6, 1991.
61. Heraclitus, *Fragments*, D22, B54.

a dimension that he hardly ever talked about, of which I found few traces in his talks. What he did not speak about is what left the most decisive mark on the vocational path of so many young people. It is a rather unique phenomenon that a married layman, a father, becomes a source for vocations to virginity—many vocations, which were both unlikely and long-lasting.

> In the car with Enzo, I told him everything and I said, "I am afraid, but I have had this nagging feeling for some time..." And he responded, "No, it is not a nagging feeling, it is a suggestion. A discreet suggestion, as the Annunciation to Mary was. Do you remember the painting of the *Annunciation* by Fra Angelico, where we see the angel signaling with a finger to the Virgin to listen? If you don't have a girlfriend, it is right for you to start the *verifica*.[62] You see, whoever lives a full experience of CL has the desire and the longing for virginity, because virginity is the true mode of love. And I too, in a different way, because I have a wife and four kids, am called to live virginity." (Paolo Consalvi)

> Enzo was married with children, but the intensity of his life and his yes to Christ brought me and others to virginity as a form of life. (Luigi Tabanelli)

It is certainly not by chance that Enzo was one of the few (probably the only one) invited by Father Giussani to the solemn annual moment of the "Promise," that is, the definitive entrance into the houses of the Memores Domini,[63] without being a member himself.

---

62. "*Verifica*" is a period in which young people from CL who perceive in themselves the sign of a vocation to virginity have the possibility to be helped to clarify the nature and form of this call (for example, toward the Memores Domini, toward the priesthood, or even toward monastic and cloistered life).

63. Memores Domini is a lay association of pontifical right. It is made up of people from the Fraternity of Communion and Liberation who follow a vocation of total dedication to God, living in the world and practicing the evangelical counsels, assumed with personal commitment. They share a common life and establish themselves in men's and women's houses, where they live a rule of silence, personal and communal prayer, poverty, obedience, and fraternal charity.

"How is it going?" he asked me. I answered sincerely, "I feel a restlessness, a void. I would like to find something definitive for my life." "If you want," he said, "we have started a little *verifica* group in Modena to discover the One who truly responds to our heart." I answered, "Yes," and I felt that evening that I had finally found "the path." Strange words for one who was then 23 years old and already felt too old to be still "suspended." (Nadia Bertelli)

To have seen incarnated in him that "life is a gift of self, a self that is moved," as Giussani had taught him and witnessed to him, is the reason I shared with him the desire of a total dedication to the Lord, so that everything in me could be at the service of reaching a person in any remote corner of the world, as I had been reached. He spoke to me about the Memores Domini, about which I did not know, and of which today I am a part. (Maila Quaglia)

In 1985–1986, I remember that Enzo told us about his discovering the value of the Gruppo Adulto, which then became the Memores Domini Lay Association. The way Enzo described the Memores Domini transmitted a fascination and an intrinsic extraordinariness to that form of life that did not leave me indifferent. But the decisive factor that made me consider the idea of beginning this path was the description of the radical change that Enzo had seen in one of his dearest friends from the CLU in Bologna, who had begun the novitiate. He described this change of humanity with so many details. He was especially struck by the fact that this friend of his, who was particularly disorganized with others and with himself, had become an example of care and order. In September I stopped Enzo while he was going down the stairs at Strada Maggiore 49 (former headquarters of CL) and I asked him about my embarking upon the experience of Memores Domini. He looked at me with an attention and a participation that were so paternal that I still remember clearly today those few minutes we spoke. He told me not to be afraid, and to pray to the Virgin Mary. Then he left me, adding that he would let me know in a few days what were the first steps of this path. (Paolo Gatta)

That the "true mode of loving" brings with it a detachment, a sacrifice, is a condition valid for everyone, in whatever form of life, and it is something evident for whoever has a sincere, a simple heart. I recognized this, with great wonder, at the end of my first year in the university, when, with a group of friends, we went to visit Enzo on vacation, at the summer house of his in-laws, in Serra San Quirico, in Marche. After the classic soccer game in a small field of wild grass, the goals without nets under a blazing sun, followed by an improvised dinner of salami and cured meats from Marche and Emilia, beer, wine, and whatever was in the fridge, we stayed a little longer for a chat. His youngest daughter, Anna Rita, who at the time was four or five years old, was listening to us, wide eyed. I don't remember the content of that conversation. I remember distinctly, though, that the little girl came out with this observation: "So, dad, you are saying that if you love a person, you have to be ready even to separate yourself from her?" It stuck with me.

8.

If Changing Ourselves Means Making an Effort, We Give Up

WHEN SOMETHING GREAT HAPPENS IN LIFE, INCOMPARABLY great, precisely because of its exceptionality there is an inevitable risk of thinking that, from that moment on, everything will be easier, that it will no longer be necessary to work hard, that we will be different from the others because things will finally go "well." So we almost irresistibly fall back into reasoning like everyone else, "with more rules," Enzo said, but once again with "our feet nailed to the earth." Mounier, so many times remembered by Father Giussani and so beloved of Enzo, said that "we have to suffer so that the truth may not crystallize into doctrine, but may be born of the flesh."[1]

The one who encounters the meaning of life is not spared sacrifice and suffering. Not to understand this, not to accept this, makes a Christian dramatically fragile the day after the encounter. The parable of the sower is unfortunately a very real gallery of many friends who were excited to the point of tears because of the spectacle of naïve boldness that happened in themselves. Later, however, they got lost (even badly). "No one can approach something like this and not feel a fascination for it, the intuition of beauty for himself.

---

1. Emmanuel Mounier. *Lettere sul dolore. Uno sguardo sul mistero della sofferenza* [*Letters on Pain. A Gaze on the Mystery of Suffering*], Rizzoli, Milan, 1994, p. 44 (translation:ours).

If Changing Ourselves Means Making an Effort, We Give Up

But this implies the fact that you can't evaluate this companionship with the usual metrics. It means passing through reality and feeling that within the usual reality, beyond appearances, within appearances, there is the seed of truth. It means we have to change. Does it take a bit of effort? Very good, let's give up!"[2]

KEEP IN MIND THAT SOMETHING MUST BREAK

"We have to put our heart into what we do"—nothing better describes Enzo's temperament than this phrase. There is nothing more precious in man than his heart. And yet, there is something that is worth more than man, in front of which it is reasonable to "offer" (that is, sacrifice) what he holds most dear. "Since in our life, at least intuitively, some 'flash' has happened in which that Man, what He says and what He does, corresponds to what we have always desired, loved, and wanted, from that moment on —this is the final twist— to say heart and to say Christ is the same thing. This is the novelty. It now becomes more concrete to say 'I.' If that ultimate criterion for which we exist has as its only corresponding answer One who says, 'I am that horizon' and, having verified this, one understands that not only is He not a strange man, not a crazy man, but in imitating Him, one also discovers that it is even more beautiful to be oneself. Then, from that moment on, the criterion is Christ; it is not even the heart anymore. The heart is Christ."[3]

"To be in relationship with this 'Other than you' (of which your life has a constant need), to be in relationship with this, you have to keep in mind that something in you must break, because it cannot be that you simply agree. The relationship with this Other—give it whatever name you want—has to break something in us."[4]

I remember a conversation in a café on Via delle Moline, in Bologna. We were putting together a flyer, one afternoon, maybe the flyer against the opening speech of Umberto Eco for the

---

2. Florence, May 6, 1989.
3. Marche, June 10, 1997.
4. Pesaro, April 6, 1998.

inauguration of the academic year.⁵ Each one was saying his or her idea, and I also gave my opinion, none of which found Enzo's approval. The issue was rather thorny (and with him anything thorny was always, in some way, just that—prickly). Cornered, I appealed to that which is a life preserver in emergency situations: conscience, the heart. It was then that Enzo told me these words, heavy like a punch in the stomach: "The criterion, for the one who encounters Christ, is no longer the heart." This made me a bit afraid, and it stuck with me. In effect, conscience is and remains an impassable boundary for people, the intimate space of one's relationship with God. What Enzo wanted us to understand was the fact that, on the one hand, it is very easy to make the voice of conscience coincide with one's personal opinion, and not with the voice of Another. On the other hand, the proposal of Christ is the only thing in front of which a restless heart can understand itself, a correspondence that requires something to break.

"The change needed is to begin to take seriously and accept the battle against our own instinctiveness. That is, the truth of things and the true feeling of things is not what we think or what we feel. It is as if feeling and thinking had to be broken and deepened by a judgment, which is that there is more. There is more. And it is my heart that demands this 'more,' and it is reality that admits it, that testifies to it. The work is a fierce, willed, desired, accepted struggle against instinctiveness, against the idea that the law of life is what I think and what I feel. It is the thing that most makes you Martians in this world. Because in this world, it is exactly the opposite: everything is instinct. The law is what we think and feel. Instead, the sense of Mystery, that is, the meaning that exists, decides a way of relating because of which I can no longer entrust myself to what I think and feel. This is what makes us men, not just members of the community. It is a condition for being men."⁶ "You must be

---

5. In 1994, in the Aula Magna of the University of Bologna, Umberto Eco gave the inaugural speech entitled, "The Strength of Falsehood." The CL student office put out a critical rebuttal entitled, "The Jester of the Apocalypse, or When Falsehood Becomes Science."

6. Bologna, October 28, 1987.

loyal with yourselves, even if this can cost the fact that you have to change, that you have to break your measure. You must be loyal (isn't this beautiful?) to the point of breaking your measure."⁷

But this break or, to use a more technically exact term, this "sacrifice" does not find its reasons within the "natural" dynamism of man; no one desires sacrifice. We have to find something that makes this situation reasonable, we have to find the promise, the certainty of a "gain," maybe deferred in time, but certain. "If there is a difficult word today, it is that word. When we speak about sacrifice it is as if the Grace of God went away. The word sacrifice sounds as if it were only something negative, as if we had to mortify ourselves or cut away something. Instead, sacrifice is accepting to make an effort for something greater than what you are, accepting to make an effort for something more, that you must see or that you have seen, because otherwise, if you did it blindly, it would mean that there is something wrong with you. The term sacrifice indicates the idea of 'offering to.' Therefore, the idea of action without sacrifice is not a human action, because an action without sacrifice means that it is not offered to anything but what you think or what you like. It may require an effort, but you do it because you understand, or you have seen, that those who have done it are better off. And so yes, it is reasonable; otherwise, it is losing your head."⁸

"As long as we are on this earth, we will always struggle, right? But, on the other hand, who wants to struggle? No one! So how do we resolve this? This is the problem; it is a condition, but no one wants it. We have to make a sacrifice to get up in the morning. I would like to stay in bed, but the alarm rings and it is time to go to work... It is a sacrifice! We are not made for sacrifice and for struggle. There is a sickness called sadomasochism for those who desire sacrifice, but it is a sickness, therefore it is not good. There is only one thing that allows this sacrifice which is that, in the effort that we have to make, we can participate in something already redeemed. Otherwise, it is impossible for us to offer it as a contribution to the

---

7. Bologna, June 23, 1991.
8. Bologna, January 23, 1986.

sacrifice that redeemed the world. It might be a contribution that is one millionth of a micron, but it is there!"⁹

This "redeemed" mortal condition had become a *habitus*, a form of life, for Enzo, that accompanied him during his thousands of kilometers on the highway, his hundreds of meetings and surgeries. It remained his preoccupation, his exhortation until the end, until his last public talk, three days before his accident. "Why is there still discomfort? The truth, when it happens in life, demands a change. This must become the theme of life. This is what we don't accept. Do you know what this means? It means having the habit of knowing that what I think must always be corrected. Are you on board with this or not? If you are not on board, the discomfort is inevitable. You are out of sync. You are here, but you are not here, not here fully."¹⁰

LIKE THAT UNBORN BABY THAT WHEN IT SAYS "I" SAYS "MOTHER"

"To belong... What does it mean to belong? We said it already: my "I" is within this reality in such a way that it borrows from it, draws from it the criteria for judging, the motives and energies for loving. It is my "I" that belongs to this companionship, with all the intelligence and affection of which it is capable, and we belong where we follow, that is, where we engage our own criteria of intelligence and affection with something greater than ourselves. Then one walks and learns. Otherwise, he repeats himself. Rilke told his wife that, where something that we still do not understand remains in obscurity, it is the kind of thing that does not require clarification, but submission. Continue to follow, and you will understand. This is the condition that makes a relationship last forever. What we don't understand must not cause a break, but a commitment to go deeper. This is the commitment between me and those friends that I told you about, but also with the younger ones, for example Iano, whom

---

9. Porto San Giorgio, February 28, 1999.

10. Ravenna, May 23, 1999.

If Changing Ourselves Means Making an Effort, We Give Up

I see here in front. If there is someone who is different from me, it is him—if only for the hair! I mean, it is amazing because it is a kind of belonging, a friendship to which we belong, that expands, responds to the heart and expands it. Even if many times we do not understand, it is only by staying in here that this obscurity will become light. You guys, this is how it is. It took me two or three years to become friends with those guys, as we are friends now, but it happened only because we put at the center something deeper than the simple recognition of likes and dislikes. This is the newness and so, being together, it is as if the face of each person becomes clearer and clearer."[11] "Our difference is called 'belonging to.' But this 'belonging to' is like that unborn baby who, if it were aware, would recognize that when it says 'I,' it says 'mother'—it is the same flesh! So it is among us; so it is among us and Christ. For this reason, we are a new people."[12]

Belonging, like an unborn baby to its mother, has as its only adequate dynamic a type of relationship that scares and even scandalizes us: obedience. "I think the most difficult thing for us adults is not only saying or declaring our love for Christ, but accepting that this love for Christ is a living reality, a friendship, an organism, and accepting—for this reason—to be ordered to this organism. This is called obedience. Our friendship has only this one goal: to habituate ourselves... not habituate... to educate ourselves to this."[13] "No one in this companionship can claim to say 'you must obey me,' but in the event of this companionship, obedience to this companionship is what allows for personal liberty, because Christian obedience touches the Mystery. Man, if he is himself, can bow only to the Mystery, and that's it. Therefore, I propose that the ultimate criterion for everyone is that our commitment be an obedience to the Magisterium, because the Magisterium is what makes the Mystery present today, and we can bow only to the Mystery. Christian obedience touches the Mystery, and ecclesiastical authority is the place

---

11. Bologna, November 23, 1989.
12. Bologna, January 23, 1997.
13. Bologna, June 23, 1991.

where the Mystery approaches us. It is for the sake of the Mystery that we obey; not for other reasons. All the other reasons can help, can make things more obvious, can corroborate the decision, but it is the Mystery that makes us give way, not the rest."[14]

> I always saw and felt Enzo as an indomitable spirit, with an almost unnatural energy, a kind of "Titan," always in an eternal "peaceful" struggle against all the injustices of life, above all the social injustices, a man little inclined to make compromises. With the same conviction in his path of conversion and with the same strength, he genuflected in front of Giussani and the Church, obeying unconditionally like a lover to his beloved. (Francesco Cerini)

On the other hand, obedience is really an uncomfortable anthropological condition. "There is a pretty lady (pardon the details), fur coat, glasses with the little thingy (what are those strings called?), she stands up, takes off her fur coat, pulls up her glasses, takes out the piece of paper where she had written things down, her pen, and says, 'Doctor Piccinini, it was a beautiful, great, inspiring speech. Thanks again.' Pause. 'Look, I know those CL people. They are all the same. They even say the same words, they have the same inflection, they speak in the same way, but it's not an experience, it's plagiarism. You emphasize the term obedience to the point of exhaustion. The term obedience can lead only to a personal violence that is called plagiarism.' I say, 'What? I don't think you've understood, ma'am. Not only have you not understood very well, but you are also a bit lacking in human experience. Can you live without obeying? Tell me, please, can you live without obeying? Come on! Don't you know that on a normal morning, when it rains, you obey and take an umbrella? Do you give yourself life? In this moment, is there a cell in your body whose development you are determining? You depend on something, you know? Decide. Besides, excuse me, have you ever seen a puppy that suddenly wants to do things on its own? It gets eaten! Do you know what it means to obey? It means *ob audire*, that is, to listen, and listening is a condition of life that

---

14. Bologna, June 21, 1992.

every psychologist and psychiatrist in the world says is more fully engaging for man than doing, speaking, deciding, etc., because it implies intelligence, affection, and recognition. In order to listen, one has to be great, because he has to bring forth something else than himself; a man is a true and great man when he knows how to listen. But tell me, please, can you love without listening? You—I don't know if you are married or what you do in life—can you love your husband or whomever you want without obeying? Listening to the position of the one you love, which means that the other must exist, not that he must exist because of what you feel! And so, why is it a problem if we say that obedience is necessary for life? The problem is your preconception!'"[15]

As an anthropological condition, obedience has to do with the most essential aspects of personal experience—first of all, love. "We cannot love without obeying, and to love is the freest thing in the world."[16] And it has to do with affection, even the most intimate and visceral. "I have a sister who, as you all know by now—almost all of you know—is in a cloistered convent. This sister, as I always say, is the woman whom... I have loved so much, and whom I still love so much, whom in certain respects I have loved the most. It is almost indescribable; it is a great, beautiful, exciting, adventurous affection. It went from banalities—for example, she was pretty and so I brought her with me, because when I went out to dance with my friends, I always looked good with her at my side—to the fact that she had a beautiful drive in life, she had fantastic contradictions. For example, she played at the Circolo Gramsci of Reggio Emilia, which was communist to its bones, and on principle she had also started a school, with only two students, for the principle of Catholic education... not very realistic... I always talked with her, always told her about my whole life. I loved her with all my soul... And it was reciprocal! Well, in six months—I don't know what the heck happened—she broke up with her boyfriend, began this thing called *verifica*, and went into a cloistered convent! At age 18! I was

---

15. February 23, 1995.
16. February 23, 1995.

deathly opposed to it! Opposed with all my strength, with all I could bring to bear on her. Why? Because I was against the cloistered convent! But I didn't even know what it was—in those days, what did I understand?"[17] "Despite this, she wanted me to accompany her to the convent in Vitorchiano. I remember that I did everything I could to prevent her from going. I got to the point of telling her, 'I will go with you, but spend five days with me first,' and I brought her to the most beautiful places in the world, and in the end, before we arrived at Vitorchiano, I even ran out of gas! When I eventually arrived there... now the rite is a bit different, but at the time the Mother Abbess came out, welcomed the postulant by wrapping her in her cloak, and brought her inside. From that moment on, you would see her only through the grate. And I, who at that time was rather tough, started to cry. So Mother Cristiana—the Abbess—said to me, 'What are you doing, crying? A man like you!' And I—I hope no one gets offended—answered, 'Listen, Mother Cristiana, you can go to...' When later my sister came back to say goodbye, she gave me a note: 'You're a good guy! Mother Cristiana.'"[18] "When I went there, to the cloistered convent, it gave me the chills, because to see these young women (especially one like her, whose drive and enthusiasm and intensity I knew well... the instinctiveness with which we lived together), to go there and begin to hear a bell that every half hour, every three quarters of an hour, rings, and she has to drop everything there and go, and she has to ask permission to get up from the table and to get up from her chair, and there is the rule of the 'essential word,' you can't just talk whenever you want... Come on! I always thought, out of an excess of affection for her, that it would be a psychological disaster. That's why I was opposed. I was convinced that I would lose her. Psychologically and humanly. In the end, Mother had said to me, 'So, Enzo, we'll see each other often here!' And I told her, 'Look, I will return only once: to take her away.' I was absolutely determined! This is real, okay? But look, the greatest shock was when, two or three years later, I went there, and

---

17. Bologna, January 23, 1997.
18. Catania, October 13, 1997.

not only had my sister not diminished, she was more free. Absurd! She was deeper, more intense than I was! And so, one of the most amazing shocks of my life began. I could not believe that this could happen within an obedience that, to me, was inhuman! Psychologically devastating. Come on! A bell rings every half hour, every three quarters of an hour, you leave everything and go, drop everything and go! Why? And someone like my sister, of all people! She didn't have any need for psychological surrogates; she knew exactly what it meant to live. There had to be something there, darn it! Now I understand! Now I begin to intuit that this is the path. But how long it took!"[19]

A bell that rings every half hour, every three quarters of an hour, you leave everything and go, you drop everything and go! Why? In the midst of the turmoil of his temperament, almost at the risk of being overwhelmed by it, that bell had begun to ring for Enzo, without negating the turmoil:

> It was the night before the Spiritual Exercises for the university students of CL when he gave that famous testimony, in 1998, that so many people have seen. We had had a heated discussion—even fought a little (it was funny because we fought even about things that were apparently futile)—on the interpretation of the final scene of *Saving Private Ryan*. There was an extremely heated discussion at dinner that had involved other tables as well. He was standing on his chair yelling, "Get out of here!" because, at a certain point—maybe wrongly—I had said that it seemed a bit sentimental. God forbid I said that! That quote from Alexis Carrel, "a little reasoning and much observation lead to the truth," had been reformulated by Enzo that evening into "little reasoning and much sentiment lead to the truth," followed by, "You don't understand anything!!!" And so a brawl broke out—it almost came to blows—with him calling me a Lombard, even though I'm really from Tuscany. At a certain point, a phone call came for him and he went away, coming back looking like a little angel. What had happened? Giussani had called him and asked him to give that testimony, telling

---

19. Bologna, January 23, 1997.

him what he wanted him to say. What had we been arguing about? About the final scene in the film, where there is this Ryan that they all went to save, and they all end up dead. After he returns home, we see him as an old man who talks with his wife and says, "Did I deserve this? Have I been a good man in my life?" Returning from that telephone call —I remember it well—Enzo said to me, "If the Son of God gave His life on the cross for you, you become worthy of it! If you had this awareness when you woke up in the morning, you would not do the things you do in the same way. You would love all that is given you, you would serve Him in every gesture, everything would take on a different light. Every gesture would acquire a usefulness that you wouldn't know how to give it with all your human strength!" I still remember these things. (Davide Prosperi)

The arc of Enzo's life was enigmatic: he was a revolutionary by character, and he recognized that the only true revolution is obedience, is in obedience. "My daughter is in China. Only, she (I don't understand why) writes to Giussani, and Giussani responds to her. Always! Always punctually! I have written to Giussani thousands of times, deep thoughts—in my opinion, things that would revolutionize the Movement—and he never answered me! Never! I don't have one single letter from Giussani, a personal letter in which he writes to me like he does with her. Never! Mystery of life... Oh well! She writes him another one of her letters about what's going on; it sounds like something you would write to your aunt, your grandma, right? 'Dear Giussani...' Literally, it's like that. I could read it all to you; that's how it is! 'Dear Giussani, here we are, I have been in China for a year, I am studying Chinese, blah blah blah...' Just like that, a little story! And so, nothing... there must be a different intelligence, that famous question that one 'sees inside'... I don't know. Anyway, in short, at a certain point she poses a problem, and the problem is this: 'I am here, and they have proposed the idea of staying here to teach Italian at the University of Taipei, and this would allow me to stay here the five or six or seven years that I need for the language and all the rest, and to support myself. But my heart and my mind have remained in Beijing, and I would like to go to

Beijing. Knowing, however, that it would be a precarious situation, and poor, personally, beyond belief... Can you help me?' Listen to how Giussani responds: 'For your, and so for our, future...'— the attack is already unsettling—'For your, and so for our, future, what God will allow you to do is important, therefore'—this is what strikes me, the first passage, and then the last—'therefore, cultivate the desires that most entice and delight you'—cultivate the desires that most entice and delight you—'but don't worry now about the solution, before having clarified the question in its time with your parents and with me'—and it is the finale that is so exciting—'and in this way, to the joy and the satisfaction will be added the truth of obedience.'"[20]

> The most decisive moment for me, among the myriad of moments that I have had the grace to experience with my father, was, I think, when we spoke about China with Father Giussani, at lunch on December 26, 1993. It was an infatuation for me, at that time, and my father had understood it. He said, "It is a passing interest; that world is inhuman" (he had seen this inhumanity at a conference in Hong Kong, which he had attended some time before). That day at lunch my father told me to share with Giussani the desire I had to study Chinese. When I told Giussani, his comment was: "Beautiful!" with his strong and decisive tone, "I will pay for a trip for you and your mother to China, so you can verify together if it is a practicable path." Everything changed. My father went into action much more than I did, reserving the trip, finding people to accompany us, telling me to learn about the possibilities for scholarships, lodging, etc. In short, he took that mission on himself much more than I did. He quickly and immediately inverted his idea and threw himself completely into the new hypothesis. (Chiara Piccinini)

"The concept is clear, and we totally lack it, so we still struggle, unsatisfied: a gesture is cosmically great because of the obedience that lives within it. Not because it is recognized as such, or because it succeeds as such. This is the real problem that Christianity has posed to the world. Mary, the Virgin, received the announcement

---

20. Bologna, January 23, 1997.

of the greatest thing in the world, the most sensational, the revolution compared to which the biggest earthquakes in the world are nothing (the Savior of the world to her, given to her!) and what was the consequence? She walked 150 kilometers to go help her cousin Elizabeth with the household chores! It means that the smallest gesture finds its greatness in the obedience that lives within it, because obedience means the connection with Christ present! Which means that there is finally a connection with yesterday, with the day before yesterday, with tomorrow, with the future, and forever! Nothing is lost anymore! You are at home, a woman, wiping your baby's butt, and you have great dignity not because they recognize it in you, or because your husband is good, but because you know why you do that thing, and what obedience you live within it. You have the same dignity as the President of the Republic, who probably doesn't act like that! I don't know if he does!"[21]

> The last thing my father said to me, before he died, was an invitation to live deeply what had been given to me to live in China (when he died I was in Beijing). In the last conversation we had, around May 20, 1999, I told him that beyond studying for my Chinese classes, I was taking advantage as much as I could of the opportunity to travel around China. He told me, "It is good for you to go and discover all the places you are talking about. Take advantage of the opportunity to see everything you can. You have this possibility only now; later it will be more difficult to have the experiences you are having. Tell me how we can be more useful to you here. We will try to support you in everything." (Chiara Piccinini)
>
> La Thuile, Val d'Aosta. It was the CLU Equipe in 1989. The universities were in turmoil. Pantera[22] occupied the uni-

---

21. Bologna, January 23, 1997.

22. "Pantera" was a student protest movement against the Ruberti reform of Italian universities. It began with the occupation of the University of Palermo in 1989, and then spread to numerous Italian universities until the spring of 1990.

If Changing Ourselves Means Making an Effort, We Give Up

versity buildings, while in Tiananmen Square[23] the protest of the students was being bloodily suppressed. Though I belonged to the Movement, I had the impression that it did not respond to that desire for "revolution" that the world seemed then, in that moment, to call me to... I was very troubled and conflicted. One evening, I stopped Enzo because I wanted him to explain to me why I shouldn't join the student protest, which I felt was a just cause. I wanted him to explain to me what made us different. He answered with few but clear words, that only today do I understand fully and keep with me (soon after this, I left the Movement, but I never forgot that man and those words). He asked me what revolution I was talking about, and then, laughing at my perplexed look, added that my revolution, the true one, I was already living, because I was there, because I had accepted and recognized the Christian event in my life. At the time, I did not understand, but something had struck me, and a worm had made its way into my head. (Goffredo Frontini)

Obedience to the circumstances, repeated and recalled, and above all obedience to the companionship became, step by step, an educational method, that is, a criterion of correction (not always graceful):

During one of these smaller dinners, I intervened to talk about an event we had organized in my university school that had been a great success. He interrupted me, asking me, "With whom did you talk about this?" I insisted on the fact that it had been particularly beautiful, but he asked me again the same question, "With whom did you talk about this?" I continued to support my version, but Enzo asked the same question a third time and then, without even waiting for my response, he changed the topic. Only then did I understand the real reason I was so upset. It was not so much because he had treated me badly, but because I had failed in my relationship with him and with the others in that group. I understood that the value of what I had done was not in the

---

23. In Tiananmen Square (Beijing), from April 15 to June 4, 1989, protests broke out that saw the participation of students, intellectuals, and workers who demanded freedom of thought and of speech from the government. The demonstrations were put down by tanks. There were hundreds of victims.

success of the initiative, but in the point of departure, that is, the communional factor: a unity that embraced everything and everyone. (Gianluca Conti)

It was 1992. I had decided to go on the annual CL pilgrimage to Our Lady of Czestochowa in Poland. I had not told Enzo. It was a decision that I thought reflected what he had taught us on the absolute value of prayer and on a deep, mature, and aware obedience to the leaders of the community. I had to leave on August 4. The day before, Enzo summoned me and the other leaders in Bologna to the CL headquarters, to prepare the annual welcome booths for the freshmen. As always, that day the meeting had taken place with great attention to the smallest organizational details. At the end of the meeting, Enzo looked at me and said, "You take care of it, starting tomorrow." But I couldn't, because I was going to Poland. I told him that I would be busy starting at 10:00 a.m., and explained why. At this point, Enzo got really angry that I had made the decision on my own: "If you want to save your soul by yourself, save it, but we don't care." At the end of half an hour of shouting, he left without saying goodbye—because he was angry and hurt. We understood there that what serves the individual is always in function of the Christian people, and to decide together, sharing our reasons, sincerely facing the comparison and the sacrifice of decisions different from those we would have made alone, is the way we become certain that our own action is useful to the Church and the world. (Giovanni Maddalena)

Sometimes, his corrections and insistence on the principle of obedience ventured into situations that were almost surreal. However, they were always exemplary.

His face immediately darkened, the face we all knew so well, and silence fell. "Oh really, you got yourself a girlfriend? And with whom did you talk about it?" And soon after came the question that brought the discussion to an unexpected and deep level, "You know that, because you are a foreigner, you are here to study and, by getting a girlfriend, you may be asking her for a sacrifice that is maybe not what you are here for? Have you thought of her destiny? And of your task? If

> you don't think of this, it will end badly." This question to our friend from Paraguay shows another characteristic that always struck me about Enzo, which was his focus on destiny and task. Not as a moral doctrine, but rather as the adventure of a relationship with a friendship that goes to the point even of judging the most personal thing there is, love. (Luigi Tabanelli)

The reference to a concrete and daily companionship, to the method of comparison wherever it was possible, was a kind of litmus test of the morality of one's own position—not that we necessarily had to do what was suggested to us. If one had a responsibility in the Movement, he could not use it however he wanted (and on this there was no space for subjective interpretations). When it came to personal choices, though, freedom was constantly evoked, never delegated or taken away. Correction and forgiveness both presuppose freedom.

> It was proposed that we organize a New Year's party for all the university schools, and we were all very excited about the idea. Let's just say the initiative... went overboard... It became a very personal move for some, who used the money and instruments of the community (they even rented a cell phone, with the costs it had in 1994) to bring about their idea of a party. The height was that, at the end of the CLU party, some did not stay to help clean up, because they had already agreed to move to the venue next door to organize another party and get paid for it. Enzo found out about it. He summoned all of us a little later to Pizzeria Nelson in Modena. His face was dark. I remember it well; it was a tense atmosphere that I could feel. He had a paper with a precise report about the misdeeds we had perpetrated in preparing the party, with first names and last names. No one was spared. But what stayed with me and what I will always remember is the judgment that Enzo gave and the proposal he made to us. He said, "The most serious thing is not the money you stole to do your own thing, or the fact that you went to work at another party afterward. It's the fact that you did it alone, you conceived of yourselves alone, you did not answer to anybody... and this is not good. We are people

for whom it is important to respond, and we respond to a unity!" And, after a pause of a second in which not even a fly buzzed, "Are you with me in this responsibility? Do you understand?" And all of us said, "Yes." "Very well." Enzo immediately ripped up the sheet of "sins and sinners," and we stayed up until two in the morning eating pizza by the meter. (Luigi Tabanelli)

Each person has to make an effort: here we come to the word ascesis

"In Buddhism, in Hinduism, ascesis detaches from the particular in order to reach the whole, detaches from the concrete in order to arrive to God. Love for Christ makes us love all the particulars and all the moments of life, the beautiful and the ugly. It's not for nothing that over there they continue to smoke pipes and we invented science! And it is weird to see people chasing these things now, here in Europe, because it is really something totally different. The presence of Christ is the presence within the particulars, that makes us love the circumstances."[24] "Each person, if he loves his own humanity and lives the horizon of a Christian awareness, must continually make an effort. From this comes the word ascesis, to live the approach to human problems from an authentically religious point of view."[25]

We had learned through our CLU experiences that every truly Christian educational gesture contains a request and an "ascetical" proposal; that is, the proposal of the connection between the particular and the whole. Every situation, therefore, was an occasion for this. Every event demanded a greater "purity" in regard to the criteria with which we approached it. In the same way, ascesis is a search for poverty. We were very struck by the fact that we could talk about poverty in a way different from the mainstream, which focuses only on the most visible and crude element, the possession

---

24. Bologna, October 6, 1990.
25. Bologna, October 17, 1993.

of goods, of money. It became clear in time that, more than the "quantity" of things, it was all about the "criterion" for using them. Therefore, it was difficult for a rich man to enter the kingdom of heaven not because he was rich, but because of how he used those riches, for what and for whom. We were really impressed when François Michelin, then president of one of the biggest industries in the world, accepted our invitation to give a talk at the School of Economics. We were thinking about how to pay for the trip (his flight, hotel, etc.). He arrived with his private jet and asked only one thing: "Will you come with me to Mass early tomorrow morning at Santo Stefano?"

Enzo had made a great discovery in the Holy Land, with Giussani and the other friends: "To go back there and see that everything happened in a room that was two by three meters; that everything happened in a house with two rooms, Joseph's house, in a small town that had about four houses and a single well. Everyone knew each other. And there, that thing happened that gave meaning to the world, because of which there is salvation, mine and yours first of all. What must penetrate the heart of each person is that our poverty is not having nothing, or renouncing something, but recognizing that someone Other than us saves us, and that we need salvation. The capacity for tenacity in affection, the capacity for permanence in friendship, the capacity for sacrifice, the capacity for mercy... all are born from here, from a poverty that we call faith. Ultimately, isn't it the same thing, that salvation comes from a companionship like this? To recognize that salvation comes from a companionship like this... For certain temperaments that are more delicate and fine, much more than mine, to see the crudeness, at times, of the companionship... it must be dramatic to believe in it. But it is exactly the same now as it was then: our poverty is faith."[26]

"Poverty is not having nothing. Leave that pauperism to others. True poverty is using what we have in service of the ideal. And so you lack one thing: 'Go, sell everything you have and follow Me.' You can never again say, 'I already gave.' Never again. You can be

---

26. Folgarida, August 6, 1991.

incoherent. You can make a thousand errors, but never again can you say, 'I already gave.' It is without measure."[27]

Among the "ascetical" aspects of our education, there was then the dimension of "unity," understood both as a unity of conception ("If there is something beautiful in the Movement, it is that everything is organic, everything is connected."[28]), and as participation in a human reality, in its works, in its judgments. "What is it that makes Christ present in the world? It is our unity, like a miracle that makes one believe. Because no one can conceive a 'forever' or a bond outside of his particular interest. We conceive of it within an event and it is as if it overrides all our particular interests, penetrates them, and puts them within a greater logic, so to speak. One understands that to build this unity and make this unity grow is the real meaning of life. And so, one studies for this, works for this, gets married for this, raises children for this, gets together for this, plays for this... whatever you can think of."[29]

This unity, Father Giussani taught us, is possible only in following a guide. The principle of authority may be the most "demanding" ascetical aspect in Christian education. "The sense of authority gives man the capacity to be himself, because one grows only if he follows. Therefore, authority, the meaning of authority... it doesn't matter who is in charge, it has nothing to do with it and it doesn't matter at all, because whoever is in charge is the sign that it is Christ who acts. Therefore, he could even be the greatest scoundrel in the world, but it is what he represents that makes him the decisive point of reference. Incredible."[30]

"It doesn't matter who is in charge." Father Giussani told us that holiness is "to give your life for the work of another" but "the work of another, precisely because it belongs to the flow of history, is the work of God. Therefore, it is to God that we give our whole life, but we give it by giving it to a person. Those who fought for

---

27. Colfosco, September 2, 1987.
28. Summer vacation, August 13, 1997.
29. Colfosco, September 2, 1987.
30. Folgarida, August 6, 1991.

Sobieski[31] in the battle under the walls of Vienna gave their lives for Sobieski, even if they gave it for Western civilization or for the Church of God."[32] "To feel that authority is necessary for religiosity is existentially impossible to avoid—this is what authority is! 'Authority' means 'what makes one grow.' It is a more intense face of desire, and a more serious desire. You have met a reality of people who care about themselves, who care about what they have in them, and have a more intense face of desire and of life: it is called authority. Looking at this new face, one perceives that he is pushed further and, first of all, discovers a new happiness! Look, this is true. We are happy not when we affirm ourselves, but when we learn, when we make the discovery of something 'other.' I think this is a normal experience for everyone. When we encounter an authority, an authentic happiness begins to filter into our own life, to cross the threshold of our own personality. Without authority, there is no happiness. There may be satisfaction, there may be pleasure, anything you want, but the human contentment of freedom, of the thought of the heart, of the face, of the word that understands that following that face is how we grow... this will not exist! All this came to exalt what normally happens in nature, which is that we grow by following someone. This is the meaning of authority!"[33] "Either there is a teacher, a guide we follow, or everything falls apart, everything is divided, and the companionship only fosters sediments of useless groups."[34]

Authority has the function of a bank within which the river can flow, and avoid becoming stagnant water. But this function of a riverbank, above all when performed by Enzo, can narrow to the verge of provoking a point of no return:

---

31. John III of Poland (Jan Sobieski, 1629-1696) defeated the Ottoman forces in the Battle of Vienna on September 12, 1683.

32. Luigi Giussani, "Nessuno genera, se non è generato" ["No One Generates Unless He Is Generated"], *Tracce*, June 1997.

33. Florence, November 12, 1992.

34. Bologna, January 9, 1994.

> "You might be wondering what the hell Pirozzi is doing here. I brought Tommaso here as a negative example of all this. He hasn't done anything of all the things that I just proposed to you. He hasn't done it with the head of his school, he hasn't done it in the community, he hasn't thrown his whole self into this adventure, he hasn't understood anything at all. So, if you want to do well, do the opposite of Pirozzi." He didn't add anything else. He didn't allow any possibility for a rebuttal, and after some 10, 20 minutes he concluded the dinner and dismissed everyone. As I walked away, quite dejected, Enzo came up to me, embraced me, and said, "Did you understand what I was telling you?" I remained silent. "I want the most for you, and you need to want it, too. Give your whole self, and remember that you are like a full river, you are a force of nature, but the river needs banks, because if it doesn't have banks, it gets lost and doesn't arrive where it should." I don't know if the words I quoted are exactly those he said, but I remember perfectly the warmth of his embrace, and I remember perfectly that during that evening I kept asking myself why he had organized that dinner against me, but, while I was going home on my Vespa, I was thinking, "How much must he love me, that he organized this dinner just for me!" (Tommaso Pirozzi)

It is interesting that certain episodes affect not only the protagonists, but also those who observe them. Another friend described the exact same scene, viewed from a different perspective, but with the same final outcome:

> "Anyway, you should do exactly the opposite of what he has done this year." He was speechless. We were too. After the dinner, we got up. Enzo went up to the guy that he had just flattened and who was leaving alone and took him by arm. I happened to hear what he said: "Listen, leave the discomfort aside. Did you understand what I was trying to say?" He looked back at Enzo and said, "Yes." Enzo hugged him and they went out arm in arm. How thankful I had been before, that I wasn't in his place! And I envied him now. It was not imaginable that a correction (to use a euphemism that does not quite capture the idea of what I had witnessed) that was so bitter and harsh had, in truth, within it, a gaze for

the good and a proposal of friendship that was so desirable. (Paolo Zambelli)

We breathed in these "embraces" of correction daily and they became ours, in time. This is maybe the "easiest" aspect of following, of ascesis. Father Giussani called it "osmosis."[35] Just by being close to someone who looks at reality in a certain way, because of this closeness, of this time shared together, his way becomes yours, so to speak, by "osmosis."

> The day after I met Enzo, my girlfriend at the time said to me, "The next time you go, you have to bring me, because when you see him your eyes shine." (Achille Fonzone)

> There was the famous gathering of all the movements in Saint Peter's Square with Pope John Paul II on May 30, 1998. After the event, I had the fortune of going to dinner with Enzo, together with a small group of people. At dinner, he told us that he was a bit annoyed to see all that waving of colored scarves while people waited to see the Pope. Then he had looked to where Father Giussani was seated, and had seen him waving his scarf with the enthusiasm and energy of a child, so he began to do likewise. (Paolo Consalvi)

An episode that Enzo loved to relate, to help us understand what this osmosis was (which is not at all a mechanical procedure, like what happens in chemistry), is tied to the visit Father Giussani made to the then-cardinal of Bologna, Giacomo Biffi. Entering the bishop's house, Father Giussani knelt to kiss the bishop's ring. Enzo, behind him, does the same. So Biffi looks at Giussani and comments, in a cross between seriousness and joking, 'You see? He does it, but he doesn't believe in it.' Enzo, as on other occasions, looked to Giussani's face to find some support. And as on other occasions, Giussani confirmed, "It's true!" Silence, chill, and discouragement (it was true)... But then Giussani added, 'But if he continues to do it, sooner or later he will believe in it.' Imitation has in itself a great educational potential, if in repeating the gesture we repeat our

---

35. Luigi Giussani, *L'avvenimento Christiano: Uomo Chiesa Mondo* [*The Christian Event: Man Church World*]. BUR, Milan, 2003, p. 74 (translation: ours).

question of understanding its significance, its meaning, its value. "Do in order to understand," Giussani always repeated to us.

Enzo, gifted with a large personality and capacity for action, always pointed us to Another. He was who he was thanks to the relationship with Father Giussani, one who points to Another. "I am not here for my project, I am here because I was asked. I follow someone. I follow him because he changed my life. You too are called to judge if your life changes, if it is worth it for your humanity to follow someone, who follows someone, who follows someone. Remember that this is true for all of life. The rest doesn't matter." (Giuseppe Capaccioni)

"I want to become your friend even more! How can I be your friend more? I want to be just like you!" Enzo answered me suddenly, "Hierro, first of all, you absolutely have to be better than me! God has given you many qualities, many talents that push you to be better. I am a person with many limits and defects." And then he started to laugh. "Another thing: if you truly want to be my friend, you have to look where I look; you have to follow and love what I love. This is what makes us immediate friends." (Hierro Fanego)

9.

Lord, Make Happen to Him What Happened to Me

> Becoming an adult, what remained in my eyes are not the things he told us (all of which were very beautiful), but what he lived, how he was attentive to the life of each of us, to the reality that was around us. (Giovanni Proietti)

THE ENCOUNTER HAD BROUGHT EVERY ASPECT OF ENZO'S life together in a "task." He looked at each detail in function of a great "work" to be built, the work of the "human glory" of Christ. It was a task that made itself clearer along the way and no one was immediately capable of carrying the load. "So, we are an object of attention and we don't understand why. The level of awareness we have is not yet ready to understand the why and the weight of what we are."[1]

AND SO I ASK MYSELF, "LORD, WHAT DO YOU WANT FROM ME?"

In the continual dialogue with Father Giussani, Enzo helped us become aware, together with him, of this *dulce pondus* ["sweet weight"] of having been chosen. Father Giussani had once asked,

---

1. Bologna, January 23, 1986.

"'What does the age we live in do, to have you in its grasp? Our age does not allow your good intentions to become a work.' My God, how true this is. 'What have you made of the companionship? A good intention that never became a work. The companionship is the instrument with which you have to answer, with which you have to live a permanent responsibility, for which to give a permanent answer. Being here, at this moment, you have to take a position in front of Christ, because there is no other reason to stay here. And if you take a position in front of Christ, you will discover that life has a task, and the task is to testify to Him.' That's it! This is true for all of you, as it is true for me now."[2]

Even three days before his death, Enzo was asking the question that always accompanied him: "And so I ask myself, 'Lord, what do you want from me?' It is right that this question exists. The true change, the true challenge, is that He has made you encounter a history. What does He want from you?"[3] "What is man's usefulness for the world? The value of a human life and of its action coincides with the good that this action represents for the other. It is incredible! My usefulness is certainly not in performing great surgeries. If there is something that we Catholic doctors have to have clear, it is that we don't heal anyone. Our aim is not to heal people; our aim is to help people live with dignity."[4] "My dignity is only in my relationship with God and the more I live this relationship, the more it is useful for the world, even if it doesn't seem like it, even if it does not seem of any particular value to anyone (even less to my own eyes). What you do is not important. What is important is the awareness you have of the relationship of what you do with the Being that made you."[5]

This awareness never had purely interior or pietistic characteristics. It had to do with daily life, with the routine, with "duty,"

---

2. Colfosco, September 2, 1987.

3. Ravenna, May 23, 1999.

4. Pesaro, April 30, 1999.

5. Pesaro, April 30, 1999.

something that you might even try to avoid in the name of the Movement:

> "'What point are you at? You have already been at the university for several years… You still don't understand! We are in front of God! What you study is in relationship with Him, is born from Him, and therefore has within it everything, everything that you are looking for.'" (Flavio Gerardi)

"'It is no longer I, it is another who lives in me'[6] means that I, in order to say 'I,' say 'You.' It is the miracle of a presence that makes 'viable' even the difficulty you have in your heart, a presence with which we can walk and never be alone again. What amazing newness! And still it is a newness that is so livable, that it is enough to open our eyes to see that it has already begun among us—a new way of living that precedes heaven. It is the glory of Christ in time, because the glory of Christ is in this world. Therefore, if I withdraw from this work, I take away some of the glory of Christ in history. This is a crime that we can commit in every moment. If I withdraw from this work, I take away from the world some of the glory of Christ, which is the only thing that makes it worth it to commit myself. Everything else holds us hostage to the outcome."[7]

"Modena was an underdeveloped city, a city between two rivers. There were wolves on the plain; the floods were coming down. Every two or three years, the people had to evacuate because the river flooded and it swept away everything. They were underdeveloped, troglodytes; they had houses on stilts! Well, they made the cathedral! To make something like that, the cobbler, the washer woman, the leader of the people, the head of the police, everyone had to have only one understanding: that the meaning of their life was to build the glory of Christ on earth. This is why one gets up in the morning and sees that sign there and says, 'I am part of that thing, and my life has value because of this.' Life has value in order that Christ may be glorified on earth, and what glorifies Christ on earth is the history of people who make Him present; it is our

---

6. Cf. *Galatians* 2:20.
7. Marche, October 22, 1995.

history. My life has value because of this history. The problem of life is much more than getting your apartment in order! It is the cathedral! 'Now we will get the apartment in order, then, if we have time, we will do something else, if anything is left over.' No, my life has value for this, and that's it; it has value only for this. It will begin to be a definitive way of thinking about yourself. We have to break down this wall. If this does not happen, newness does not exist. We will be able to create the greatest political party in the world, but there will not be newness; the most impressive gatherings in the world, but there will not be newness."[8]

"What does He want from you? That your life be His glory, that is, be within this history [...]. It is not possible without this 'totalization' of life. You can't do it if you don't understand that the Christian fact is totalizing, a totalizing proposal... So the 'what do you want from me?' is right; every evening we have to ask that question, certain that, if we ask God, He responds. All the chaos that was there before is still there—we are messed up, but joyful, ultimately joyful... God wants you to be a presence in what you do, in what you have to do."[9]

This "totalization" toward which he directed us, toward which he invited us by encouraging and giving himself, was not a generic invitation to be generous or to "give time." It wasn't about "how much" time, because the only adequate quantity is totality, the totality that concerns the root of thought, the root of action itself. In this way, life becomes an invitation to be available to what happens, to its deep and mysterious origin. I remember an episode that clarified this adventurous dimension for me: we were at La Thuile, at the summer vacation of international leaders. During a break, we had gathered in a little room with all the friends from Bologna, drinking something together with Enzo. Father Giussani really loved us, he liked us because we were pretty much all "improbable" Christians, a mix of naïve faith and practical godlessness that already in itself made you laugh. And so, for a laugh, Giussani came to meet us and

---

8. Porto San Giorgio, February 28, 1999.
9. Ravenna, May 23, 1999.

spent a bit of time with us. Clearly, we also took advantage of the opportunity to ask him to explain what he had said during the lessons, some of which was not very clear to us (a little like what happened for the fishermen of Galilee). I remember that, at a certain point, I said to him, "Gius, this idea that the *Sign coincides with the Mystery*... it's a bit much!" Already the way of asking the question was very uncouth, considering the theological depth that Father Giussani was clarifying for himself and his clumsy companions. He answered, "You see, we are here having fun and making jokes. And it is something beautiful; that gives gusto to life. It is something that makes me feel good too. Imagine if I, going out that door, met a woman whose husband had just died. I would start crying with her. And there is no break from the previous moment. It is recognizing that both circumstances have a connection with the Mystery that makes them. It is responding to the Mystery by obeying the signs through which He wants to manifest Himself."

Life is a design, Enzo said, "a design that began back then, 2,000 years ago, and I am a flower and a fruit of it, I am an expression of it, an actor in it; even a collaborator. 'I, now, oh God, collaborate with You in Your design.' Time is the development of a design. It becomes positive. If not, it is a monotonous and heavy flow of hour after hour, minute after minute. Time is not time if it is not filled with meaning. Whether I have a pen in my hand, or am leafing through a book, or eating breakfast with friends, or playing soccer, or hiking Mount Senario, or here talking to you, all of this, everything, is part of a design."[10]

> Enzo saw me enter, came running down off the stage, came within two centimeters of my, and, fixing his gaze on me, asked, "Have you prepared yourself for the assembly today?" I mumbled something, I don't remember what I said. He looked at me and said, "We are in front of God, remember that! You can even not contribute, but remember that we are in front of God. Prepare yourself at least for this." Let us say that I don't remember anything of that assembly

---

10. Florence, 1987.

except for that sentence and those eyes fixed on me, which kept rolling around in my brain... (Flavio Gerardi)

IN FRONT OF THIS HARDNESS OF HEART, WE HAVE ONLY ONE CHANCE: WITNESS.

"So, just thinking about life as witness—getting married, working, doing what you do, tending toward this thing... It gave birth to another reality, because it was as if the whole world became in some way the provocation to try... In short, an *apologia* for the existence of Christ."[11]

That everything could become "an *apologia* for the existence of Christ" was for Enzo a slow conquest in time, through many occasions and corrections, like the one received from Father Giussani during their pilgrimage to the Holy Land. "In all the sacred places we went, almost through a strange desire to give offense, wherever there was a church or a sacred place, next to it there was a minaret. Three times, we started to celebrate the Mass or pray in a church, and right away from the minaret '*gne, gne, gne*'... the voice of the Muezzin began. They were playing the tape (now the voice is recorded, they are up to date). The last Mass we celebrated, we were at the place of the resurrection of Lazarus and there is a church there, and a minaret next to it. We start the Mass at seven in the evening—pay attention, seven in the evening, outside the schedule of every Muezzin in the world—and, as we were beginning Mass... *gne, gne*. As soon as he began (by then I had had enough), I got up, determined, saying, 'I am going to do something to this guy.' Giussani stopped me, while I was leaving, while I was exiting the church: 'Where are you going?' I said, 'Listen, what am I supposed to do? You hear that stuff!'—'Now stop here, and we'll talk about it on the bus,' and he said Mass under all the rage of the Muezzin that made me so furious... It gave me a perforated ulcer... After we got on the bus, Giussani said, 'So, Piccinini, what were you going

---

11. Colfosco, September 2, 1987.

to do?'—'Why do you ask me? You know very well. This thing is absurd, an injustice like that is absurd. How is it possible not to react? It's absurd!' And he responded, 'Piccinini, the method of Christianity has never been your method; you are a revolutionary. In front of this hardness of heart, we have only one chance: witness. We have never imposed on people what we think. This is something that Christ never did. But we witness, that is, what is true for you, you say it, and for this truth you are willing to give your life, because it is worth more than your life.'"[12]

The victory of Christ is not a fact of power. The truth within a little people is what in time will conquer, as a capacity to encounter the heart of man and convert it. "Our whole movement began with a school teacher that for four years had only the fruit of five kids who went with him on a vacation in the mountains in Canazei. The number doesn't matter! Once, we went to Alba di Canazei and passed in front of the hotel where they used to go in those early days, and Giussani said to me, 'Look: stop here. I came here in the early days for four years, with four or five kids, then 15, then we went back to 10, and only after the fifth year we began to be 50, 60, when God wanted. The only thing is that I never stopped saying what I always thought and lived.' More than ever, the faith must be proposed to the free acceptance of everyone, in every people, in every nation, because all have the right to know the answer to that cry that is in the heart of everyone. But the communication begins there where you live."[13]

"The communication begins there, where you live." We had learned to name and to bring about this dynamism with the term "gestures." "And what are the gestures of a real humanity? Gestures of charity, that is, gestures that make Christ present, for which people look at us and say, 'How can you be like that?' This is what happened to me that time we asked to use the equipment of the PCI[14] for the Happening. We didn't have anything and they always had

---

12. Summer vacation of the Marche university students, August 15, 1997.
13. Bologna, June 21, 1992.
14. Italian Communist Party (1921–1991).

everything: a stage, tables, chairs, lighting. We asked the PCI for the equipment and they gave it to us, and sent some young people to show us how to use it. I remember that I met one of their leaders in our old headquarters. It was the beginning of July, the exam period, and the place was full of students. Some made the signs, some were putting things up, some were going out to sell tickets, and these PCI guys were really impressed. One of them came to me and asked, 'How do you do it? Because we haven't done these things in a long time; now we have to pay kids to come and set up our Festival of Unity.' We had kids from the university ready to skip exams to support the Happening! These were gestures of charity where the one who sees is forced to say, 'There is something else here!'"[15]

There is something else here:

> He was a missionary, that is, he couldn't do anything but announce in a total way, in a crashing, burning way, the presence of Christ. (Elisabetta Buscarini)

> The synthesis of all the time I spent with Enzo can be summed up like this: Christ is alive; otherwise, a man like this would not exist." (Licio Argelli)

These gestures of real humanity almost always had to do with daily life, with eating and drinking, with the normal and serene aspects as well as the problematic ones, with those capable of depressing us or our loved ones, seamlessly.

> I was little more than 20 years old. My family was going through a dark moment, as my parents had recently separated in a traumatic way. I was living this situation with great difficulty, but I was really helped by the community and by the experience I was living with Enzo and with all the friends at the university. Yet I saw the difficulty of my mom, who, after so many sacrifices, had been abandoned. I saw her pain and my incapacity to be a help to her, to accompany her, to give her hope. So I spoke about it with Enzo and he, without delay, said that he was available to meet my mom if she agreed to it, and that I should organize a lunch as soon

---

15. Bologna, January 23, 1994.

as possible. I was stunned. So I spoke about it immediately with her. She accepted. On Sunday, May 21, 1989, at lunchtime, Enzo showed up at my house. He was elegant, and had brought with him a box of little chocolates. We ate together and then, after being assured that the embarrassment between them had fallen, I left them alone to speak about the questions that my mom would not have been able to discuss with me present. I don't know exactly what they said. Today, my mom lives the experience of the Movement, she has been doing the School of Community for many years, and has rediscovered a full life of faith. Those chocolates that Enzo brought almost with shyness were for me the sign of what it means to make oneself available to Christ, who comes to meet us in the face of people, in the circumstances that call you. (Massimiliano Fracassi)

My friends and I were freshmen and we got totally involved in the life of the CLU, 24 hours a day, with a crazy enthusiasm and dedication. Enzo was very impressed by us, and we were excited to impress him, because we wanted to supplant the generation that had preceded us, and we wanted to become the next leaders of the CLU. Enzo saw something else, and wanted to organize a dinner with all our parents. He wanted to meet them, to hear their thoughts on our involvement, their worries and observations about the life we were leading. The fruit of that meeting was incredible. My mother began to follow the Movement with a passion and a total commitment, because she was able to pass from a traditional faith to a faith full of reasons, and she animated so many charitable initiatives in her city, up until her death, while my father even volunteered at the Meeting. (Licio Argelli)

An "affective" energy, an energy full of affection, had become in Enzo an indomitable power of communication. "It is the Spirit who creates an eminently extroverted personality. This is so true that the first gesture of the first Christians was absolutely missionary—Pentecost is the most missionary feast there is in the Christian life. These men went out, in the middle of the square, troglodytes as they were, fishermen of the lowest order... Peter opened the door wide and started shouting. The first reverberation of the Christian personality is a strange (that is, strange to the world) communicativeness that is stretched, therefore, to embrace the world, everyone and everything. And this is what happened to me."[16] "The only aim of our life is to make this event known, that as many people as possible know this, because what is given to us is to be given in turn with the same gratuitousness. There is nothing more extraordinary than an adult who feels that his life is in service of something greater, so that everything about the adult comes back into a state of tension, like when he was a young kid and hoped for the success of an exam, or of graduation, or of his first love. He comes back into a state of tension, and that tension becomes the full experience of a capacity for construction and edification."[17]

"I was saying, during the closing of the year at Ravenna, that if, with the permission of the Eternal Father, Father Ricci[18] could come here at this moment, what would he say to each person? He would say only one thing: now I see clearly the value of life. The value of life is only one thing, to love Christ. I think he would also add another thing: that the meaning of life is to witness to Christ and spread Him in the world. So, I think that beginning together is always the thrill—real, not sentimental—of telling each other this again: the value of life is to love Christ, all the rest is worthless, and the meaning of life is to witness to Christ."[19]

"So, how do we tell others about Him, communicate Him to others, in a way that others can recognize? There is only one path, which is to ask, 'Lord, make happen to the others what happened to me.' And that's it. This is our missionary position. Imagine going down the street, from the stranger to the one you know, praying, 'Lord, make happen to him what happened to me.' What is immediately overcome? The strangeness. Immediately. That person is no

---

16. Florence, March 18, 1987.

17. Bologna, October 6, 1990.

18. Father Francesco Ricci (1930–1991) from Forlì, who had just died in those days, was a close friend of Father Giussani since the beginning of the Movement, and was an imposing example of the missionary figure in the whole world.

19. Bologna, June 23, 1991.

longer a stranger. You give him your all, not because you like him or don't like him, you know him or not, but because of the destiny you have in common... Just think about your wife! You go home to your wife and pray, 'Lord, make happen to her what happened to me.' If only this were the climate of the relationship! And with your children, first of all—what respect! Second thing: what attention to the smallest details! Third thing: you no longer expect anything from anyone, and you always try. This is our mission."[20]

This passion for the other was an aspect that struck all those who met Enzo. Thus, Lella, his secretary for years at Sant'Orsola Hospital, saw him in action and wondered, even though at the time she did not know anything about CL:

> Enzo made me curious. One day, he sat down in the secretary's office, and when we were alone I asked him the reason for what he did. Considering my ignorance, he expressed himself in the simplest way, and I interpreted his words as if he had made a vow, as if he had to fulfill a "mission." I saw him always as a person blessed by Christ, who spent himself to alleviate human suffering. My duties greatly increased with his arrival, and keeping up with Enzo was not easy. Considering the amount of work, I thought I'd get organized, so I took some clothespins and wrote the names of all the doctors on each one, so that every phone call or note got hung up and seen. But after a little while, I had to change Enzo's clothespin for a bigger one, and even his postal box. Sometimes, I met people who were desperate (morally and economically) and, letting Enzo know about the situation, I said, "There is good work to be done." (Lella Golinelli)
>
> One evening, Enzo had to go to a CL meeting in some remote small town near Rovigo. I don't remember which one, only that it was in the midst of fog. We were in a parish, in the usual little theater, with a stage and dark red curtains and wings and chairs fixed to the floor, the shaped wooden chairs with the backrest that folds, and if you didn't have the same shape as the chair, it is better to stand up. There were 10, maybe 15 people, not that interested in the topic, but

---

20. Marche, February 23, 1997.

sincerely dedicated to the parish. Enzo went up on the stage and began his testimony. It seemed like he was speaking to 1,000 people, as if there was no tomorrow. Enzo was like this, and we were used to it, but that evening was incredible for me, knowing how tired he was. After the meeting, after a few pleasantries, we left. "You drive," he said. I took the keys and I went to the driver's side. He drove with the seat far forward, with the steering wheel practically on his sternum, as if he wanted to arrive before the car itself. Obviously, I didn't change the setup. I took off. I struggled to shift the gears because of the position of the seat, and before I got to the fourth gear he said, very annoyed, "Forget it. Get out." I was afraid he would leave me there. He was really tired, and therefore after a few kilometers I said to him, "Enzo, was it really necessary to come here to this place, with so few people, with all that you have to do?" He turned suddenly toward me, his vein bulging (trouble ahead!) and told me, "Is there anyone who is not worthy to know Christ?" Then silence. (Massimo Savini)

AND HE SENT THEM...

"Those beautiful words, Saint Luke Chapter 9: 'And He sent them to announce the kingdom of God and to heal the sick.' This defines the change of your life. Your life has purpose because of this, if you announce the kingdom of God and heal the sick. He sent them to shout everywhere that there is a reason to live, that there is a reason to suffer, to work, to rejoice, to look to the future; that there is a reason why a mother is a mother, a father is a father. He sent them to announce this positivity throughout the whole world. If, more and more, my life accepts this supreme aim of witnessing to Him, to shout to all people the ultimate positivity of life... this is what it means to heal the sick."[21]

The mission for us, for Enzo, consisted literally in a gesture of "being taken." Father Giussani had said, "God could have been off

---

21. Bologna, October 6, 1990.

by half a millimeter!"[22] Election, preference, is the path by which the Mystery makes Himself known. For this reason, there was an attention to giving value to what the Spirit raised up in us, to identify the young people who were the most struck, attracted, open to responsibility. The "responsible" ones have always been the cornerstones of the method of osmosis, of "cascading" attraction. In this dynamic, during those years, a kind of revolution was developing, compared to how things were before, a revolution willed and supported by Giussani himself. "The other thing that changed was the figure of the leaders. With this idea of having to hold on in battle, the leader was a kind of 'field marshal'—but literally, you know? Now it makes us laugh, like when we talk about certain issues from the Middle Ages. The best leader was the one most like a 'field marshal.'"[23] On the other hand, certain symbolic dynamics, often beyond the limits of common sense, were in service of a fundamental dimension of our education (not only our Christian education): the dimension of authority. During a CLU vacation, I remember, he forced us "leaders" to always eat together at the same table. It was essential that we become friends, and that people could see this authoritative friendship. "In fact," he said, "let's have the engineers build a stage upon which we can put your table, so that you are visible from any point in the room."

But responsibility and friendship were starting to become two sides of the same coin. The attention to the freshmen who arrived coincided with the proposal of these two gifts (responsibility and friendship) that the companionship made accessible and desirable for anyone:

> I was a freshman, reluctantly staying in the CLU apartments. I watched some friends I had bonded with literally disappear on Monday nights. Halfway through the year, I asked, "Where do they go?"—"To Enzo"—"Who is he? I want to go too!" I was invited. At dinner, we talked about everything, including current events. I came from a

---

22. Luigi Giussani, "A Mystery of Election," *Traces* 2001 (March), http://archivio.traces-cl.com/Mar2001/ptn.htm.

23. Colfosco, September 2, 1987.

moralistic, overly pious experience of GS, where I went just to cause trouble. I invited my friends, and making trouble was our way of saying, "Hey! Here we are! Look at us!" They would promptly send us home. In the middle of the dinner, Enzo said, "Morality has become a way of accusing others of immorality." It was the gloomy time of *Mani Pulite*. "To think like this, to live like this, is a betrayal. Morality is not coherence. We all make mistakes. But right after, you go back to looking at the greater good that keeps you on your feet. And that makes you start again without everything being the same as before." My heart leapt—this was my "four in the afternoon!"[24] Who are You who describe my heart so deeply? (Paolino Casadei)

During one of the trips on which he asked me to accompany him, we start a discussion at the end of which I said, "I don't want to be a leader of anything anymore!" After a couple of months, I left for military service, and at Merano I faced a reality that was very far from what I had been used to until just a few days earlier, and was very hard in some ways. One day, the captain called me and said, "There is a doctor who came to see you from Bologna. He is waiting for you in the guardhouse. If you want, I'll give you a couple hours of leave so you can go out." It was Enzo, in his Audi, who had come to visit me… After a few moments I understood that he came just for me, and not only to convince me. "I don't care whether you become the leader or not, if by this you mean a role or something you have to do. I care that you understand, because responsibility means responding to something and to someone for what you are, what you do, what you desire. So anyway, if you live, you have to respond, for what you feel, for what you do, and, ultimately, for what you are. You can respond just to yourself, and then sooner or later you will become sad or angry, because you are needy, and you do not make yourself [in effect, he was showing me a picture of what I had lived there in the barracks those 20 days]. You can respond only to your boss, your girlfriend, your dad, and then sooner or later you will be alienated. Or you can decide to respond to the destiny that now and always calls you, and then you will be free. You choose!" (Alberto Tazioli)

---

24. Cf. *John* 1:35-42.

Enzo met us at the CL headquarters and told us how demanding it will be to be part of the staff of the secretariat. He treated us like adults. I blurted out, in front of everyone, "But... Enzo... I don't know how to do anything... How can I take care of a secretariat with 20 people under me and more than 1,000 university students?"—"Don't worry Chiocchio, ask... ask Daniela, ask Widmer. You are not alone!" And so the great adventure began, made up of availability, dinners to organize, soccer games, cultural events, study vacations for 500 students over two different weeks, in two different regions, all within the whirlwind of the million things Enzo did... (Cristina Chiocchio)

I had just come back to Italy after five years of mission in Brazil, an experience that in many ways was extremely difficult. In the few lines of that short dialogue, Enzo perceived my unease perfectly and took it seriously, not trying to analyze it, but involving me with himself, in a way that over time I recognized was brilliant. Instead of fixating on my difficulty, in fact almost putting it in second place, he proposed that I "give a hand" to that reality of university students that he guided with total dedication. In his request to "give a hand," my need was taken so seriously and given such value that it became a path, a participation in a work that was not mine, a work that opened me to a new horizon, a new perspective. (Father Pierpaolo Pasini)

Enzo was not clerical, you will have understood. He always guided himself directly to the person, to his freedom, and to his capacity to decide. Still (just as, on the other hand, Father Giussani did with him), he never considered the person separate from the relationships that constituted him. He directed himself always to freedom, but he always considered with care the bonds in which freedom could really find its expression.

He asked me to share the responsibility of continuing the work[25] that Novella had begun. I will also say that Enzo

---

25. "Casa Novella," a charitable work that welcomes children, the disabled, and the disadvantaged, founded by Novella Scardovi (1949-1996) at Castel Bolognese, inaugurated in 1996.

wanted to make my wife a participant in this request, "inviting himself" to dinner at my house. (Fabio Catani)

In his final year (1998–99), when Enzo's communities and his commitments had grown, it happened that he would ask me to go with him, thereby taking advantage of the trip to organize his agenda and commitments, or to take stock of the situation. But before I gave him an answer (for me it was natural and instinctive to answer yes), he made me call my husband to ask if he agreed. I called, and my husband always said yes, so it seemed that between Enzo, my husband, and me things were all clear. At the thousandth request I told him, "If you want, I can ask him, but I know he'll say yes." But even that time Enzo did not dispense me from the request, and so I made it, and the scene was repeated just like the other times. (Daniela Zanella)

At the same time, he called for full personal responsibility and challenged us to be adults. He often concluded his speech at the end of the assembly with, "Tag, you're it!" (Elisabetta Buscarini)

After the initial back and forth, Enzo turned to us three new guys and said, "I wanted to meet you because we would like to invite you guys to the diaconia of the CLU, a very important place that asks not just for your participation, but for your whole selves. I invited the heads of your area of study here because it is in the relationship and in the friendship with them that I ask you to give all of yourselves and to begin to spend your life for Christ." (Tommaso Pirozzi)

Enzo answered, "I am not sending you because you are great, but because it is Another who acts, and we are only His instruments. And besides, remember, I am always with you." And so it was. (Daniele Biondi)

In my relationship with Enzo, I never found myself becoming better, or less fragile, or up to the educational responsibility. I became aware of being a man looked at and loved by Another. (Father Gino Romanazzi)

But he said, "I am proposing that you, Cozzella, be the head of the CLU in Pescara." So I asked him ,"Enzo, what

Lord, Make Happen to Him What Happened to Me

does the head of the CLU have to do?" And he responded, "Cozzella, you have to love those people; the head of the CLU has to love the people." (Paolo Consalvi)

"The Movement is the person to whom something unthinkable has happened, something unthinkable, unforeseeable, and who for this reason has changed the connotations of thought and action, which has as a consequence that life has worth for this and not for anything else. It is the same reason why I am here and why certain friends, even very dear ones, with whom we began the first adventure as university students, are now in places like Peru, Brazil, or Chile. I see them once every two years, because maybe they come to the Assembly of Leaders. And, when I see them, it is as if we had always been together. It is a very strange feeling! Two years have gone by, and maybe there are also signs that time has passed, yet I see them and hug them like I did that time at the University of Siena, like that time in Milan when we were all together the last time... and we have not seen each other for years, and I don't even know what they have done! I know only one thing, which takes away all strangeness and all distance, which is that my life is dedicated, just like theirs. There is a totalizing hypothesis in their life, like there is in mine. Whatever we do, whatever situation we are in, that hypothesis binds us, forever. Our 'forever' is a totalizing hypothesis in our life, because of which you, here, he in Chile, you at your house, you who are a manager, I who am a surgeon, the other guy who is a teacher, we are all together. We may not see each other for months, and when we see each other it is as if we had been together the whole time, because we understand that we have done the same thing. Mimmino and I have done the same thing, doing what we have done. We have done the same thing; we have the same love, the same dedication."[26]

> That evening, a table was set for a dozen people in the garden behind the CL headquarters in Bologna, where there is a gazebo. There were already a few people at the table: Enzo, some of the older university students, and a group of younger kids like me (I was in my second year). He asked

---

26. Porto San Giorgio, February 28, 1999.

if we were open to taking even more seriously what we had encountered, and to do it first of all through friendship with those who were there with us that evening. I looked around and saw that each of us had been called together with one of his older friends, with whom he spent every day of life in the university. None of us were there alone. And we were not alone because this was a substantial and essential part of what Enzo was telling us. Never had I perceived a proposal with such scope and clarity. It was evident that he was not asking us to organize the community, nor asking us to spend some time with someone. With that invitation to participate, he was in reality calling into question all of me, and was asking everything. He was proposing to us what was interesting to him, because for him it was the most important thing, something that didn't leave out anything and that was within a friendship. While he spoke, my immediate reaction was a rejection: "No, he is asking too much. He exaggerates." I had never perceived in such a clear, sharp, and all-encompassing way a proposal for life like on this occasion, and never like that time was I on the point of saying, "I'm not in; I'm leaving." (Paolo Zambelli)

I didn't have any doubt about the fact that my happiness was linked to spending my whole life for the glory of Christ. In reality, there was something outside, but I had the impression that it was so marginal compared to what I was experiencing, that I didn't want to face it. I was neglecting the university a lot, and hadn't taken exams in six months. This fact had caused alarm for my parents, who are also in the Movement, and their impatience annoyed me. I didn't know how they couldn't understand that what determined my life in that moment was something greater than my performance in school. During a trip to Marche, Enzo asked me the question he asked everyone: "What's new?" I started in a firm tone, putting the thing on an ideal level, thinking I'd "fool" him. "My parents don't understand. I am giving my life for an ideal and they keep getting under my skin with the fact that I keep absurd hours and am late with my exams..." He interrupted me brusquely, "What does it mean to give your life for an ideal?" "Building the Movement with you," I answered quickly, as if I had been waiting for just that question. "You haven't understood anything! How can you think that your parents will understand that the experience you are having is true? Only if you respond to reality, and if they see you happier. Unless what we live makes you take your studies more seriously and live the relationship with your parents with joy, what we say to each other is incomplete." Then he added, "You shouldn't be content with the natural correspondence you feel now. In time, fascination continues only through sacrifice, that is, accepting this relationship, this different measure, that forces you to look even at what you would not like to look at. If you skip over what we are saying to each other now, ultimately, you will never be free in what you do. To risk in the circumstances is right when what you do can be offered to God." Before I got out of the car I asked, "How can I give an original contribution?" He said, "Creativity is the art of expressing a yes said before. Therefore, the horizon of your talents is the Movement." (Marco Bernardi)

You who love heroic things

A few years before Enzo left us, something absolutely new was happening in the Movement, that would have to do with him personally, leading him to a completeness of "physical" dedication to the service of the Church. Father Giussani was approaching 80 years of age, and his health no longer allowed him to travel far and wide to personally visit the communities of CL now spread throughout the world. It was that circumstance that suggested to him the idea of, in some way, "revolutionizing" the missionary and educational structure of the Movement. He decided to choose three people as reference points for all the regions of Italy—three "visitors"[27] who would "represent" him where he could no longer be physically present. These were not simply delegates. In clarifying this step, Giussani had compared it to the step taken by Christ when he was still alive. Even when He could still have personally reached the places of mission, the Lord decided to send apostles, assuring them, "Whoever

---

27. Enzo Piccinini, Giuseppe Zola, Father Francesco (Ciccio) Ventorino.

encounters you encounters Me." For Enzo, it was a decisive push to that "identification" toward which he had already for some time been dedicating all his affective and mental energies, the "identification" with the charism of Father Giussani. It was not something immediately understood, nor did it lack incomprehension and misunderstanding. Enzo, by temperament, was someone who first jumped in, then reflected or, better, reflected while jumping in. For this reason, he had immediately considered this great new responsibility as an invitation to "do" or to "give" more. Instead, the point was something else: "Like when, many months ago... about the visitors: 'Enzo, but you...'—when Giussani starts like this... I am afraid! 'But you, you of all people, you who love heroic things and have a temperament that gets excited by heroic things, you don't understand the heroism of the Church, that the Church proposes, the greatest paradox. Do you know that Saint Therese of the Child Jesus is the patroness of the missions? That is, the beauty, the fascination of action that the Church proposes, that we call mission! Do you know that the patroness of the missions is Saint Therese of the Child Jesus, who didn't do... anything!' She didn't do anything! It's absurd! So one asks, 'What should I do? Should I also go into a cloistered convent? I don't know. What am I supposed to do?' But this is not the problem. The problem is that mission is precisely this: that incommunicable thing for which you live, within your actions, an ultimate obedience that makes the gesture great. Saint Therese lived until age 24 in a convent, doing the things of the convent, with the rule of the convent, and that's it. Patroness of the missions!"[28] "'You, Enzo, you always have a great defect: you are a child of '68. You think that the Movement grows, develops, because of the sacrifice you make for the Movement, because of the energies you give it. Instead, the Movement is like the housewife who goes to the greengrocer, she goes there 10 times, and on the tenth time the greengrocer asks, "How come you are like this?"' And so, the

---

28. Bologna, January 23, 1997.

Movement is born like this, from a change that is lived dramatically. Because this shines through, and will always strike people."²⁹

"Over the last three years, Giussani has changed the structure of the Movement. He instituted a figure that in the Memores Domini had already existed for some time, the figure of the visitor. I am one of these visitors. Italy is divided into three parts, and so there are three visitors for all of Italy. I am trying to follow (and I hope God gives me the strength) more than 20,000 people. It is a huge task. Because of the intensity of the Movement, it is a huge task. I asked Father Giussani what being a visitor meant, because I didn't know, and I also told him:, 'If I am a visitor, I will have to talk with you all the time.' I saw that everyone was able to talk with him, but I was never able to. So I asked him, 'What kind of visitor am I?' One day, he asked me, 'Will you be my driver again?' On a Monday, when I didn't have to be in the operating room, I jumped in the car and went to pick up Father Giussani, discovering that he also was a visitor. He visited three houses of the Memores Domini. When we arrived at the first house, a women's house of the Memores Domini, he rang the doorbell, and when they answered through the intercom, he said, 'Excuse me, I am Father Giussani. I don't mean to disturb you. Our meeting was supposed to be on Wednesday, but I wanted to ask you if it was possible to do it today. Please excuse me; I am sorry to upset the rhythm of the house.' I thought that if he had come to my house, I would have opened all the doors… If he had come to my house, I would have said, 'Come whenever you want!' But this is what he did. He knew all those women, one by one, and he asked, 'How is your father? Is he taking his medication?' There was among them a bond, an affection unknown to me. So we visited the three houses, all in the same way. That night, while we were returning to his house, Giussani asked me, 'Did you understand?' I answered, 'I am beginning to understand.' We can 'play the role of the visitor', but ultimately being a visitor is to 'be in the Movement,' to love everything and do everything with that belonging in one's heart and mind, with that capacity for connection that is called paternity. The

---

29. Bologna, January 23, 1997.

challenge of the visitor is to let every relationship be maintained with an open wound—it is called conversion. It is also necessary to be a visitor in one's family, in one's workplace; the young man and his girlfriend must also be visitors. It is necessary to keep this wound that is called conversion alive. This is how the Movement is born for us, that is, new relationships. This is the challenge."[30]

> Coming into contact with Enzo was the same as coming into contact with the person of Father Giussani, and for us kids it was literally a re-encountering of the Movement. Enzo was there with us for the entire vacation (and that year there was heavy snowfall). We were amazed that a doctor with a career and four kids would stay with us for four days; it was the evidence that what he said was what he lived. Enzo didn't just make a "nice speech" and then everyone went their own way. For ten years, he came to Reggio every week and with a group of young people we met with him. We spoke about the life of the community that, little by little, was flourishing again. (Ciccio Caprari)

> Enzo lived the paternity of Father Giussani. We understood this by the way he spoke about him, by the way his eyes shone, and by the way he said that he was grateful to him because Giussani had saved him. He was a son who didn't just repeat what he had heard, but embraced and educated with patience as he had been embraced, waiting on the time of each person. How many times did he stay to talk until late, skipping part of the dinner because he had so little time! (Giovanni Proietti)

> He ate up the kilometers on the highway in order to reach each and every one, and I remember that, one Saturday, he had left from Bologna to meet one of the communities he followed in the south of Italy and, when he had almost arrived at his destination, they told him that the meeting had been canceled. There was no anger or resentment, but only the enthusiasm to have a coffee with me, who was waiting for him at the end of the highway. That doctor, who in the early hours of a Saturday had visited his patients at the hospital in Bologna, had then gotten into the car to hurry down and

---

30. Argentina, March 22, 1998.

arrive at a meeting, and then at the end of the trip to return home. All this for whom? (Father Gino Romanazzi)

We carry his signature, all of us who have had the grace to be close to him, the signature of a life lived as a gift, as a true sonship of one who, at all costs, desired to identify himself with his father. (Maila Quaglia)

If I had not encountered him, and through him, the charism of Father Giussani had not become close, fascinating, concrete, and tangible, that is, the verification of Christ present here and now, I would not be who I am today. (Francesca Astorri)

It was a confusing moment for the CLU in Genoa. We were at the end of the Seventies and, at the suggestion of the Center,[31] I called Enzo to see if he could come and give us a hand. He accepted, and I met with him halfway between Bologna and Genoa, in the Ligurian Apennines, at Cisa Pass. We spoke, and what struck me was not so much what he said, which I don't remember well (now my memory is failing), but the fact that he had come and had accepted me with affection and friendship. This is everything. (Father Mimmo Borzini)

At the beginning, we weren't even friends, then we became friends suddenly, always because we looked at the same point. We all looked at Enzo and, looking at him, we were looking at what made it possible to live like him. (Luigi Tabanelli)

When he was sent to support and guide the CLU in Turin, he began this service with a humility that disconcerted me, because at the beginning he was not welcomed with enthusiasm by those who were then guiding the university community. (Father Primo Soldi)

The most fascinating thing was his sonship with Father Giussani, described in the facts that he documented with

---

31. The expression "Center" (regional, national, or international, having to do with adults, university students, or high school students) indicates in CL a small group whose participants are a reference point for the different educational realities in the different territories.

such passion and liveliness that it made me desire continually to conceive of myself in unity with Enzo and therefore with the charism. (Father Gino Romanazzi)

10.

The Poetic Must Become Epic

THE GIFT, THE GRACE RECEIVED, BECOMES, FOR THE ONE WHO welcomes it, a responsibility in front of the world; it becomes a struggle. "Do not conform yourselves to the mentality of this world, but be transformed by the renewal of your mind."[1] Intimacy and affection are fundamental dimensions of Christianity, but they always have an exterior aspect, a "public" task that the Christian takes up in the world. Enzo's combative attitude, his characteristic temperament, was a trait that united him viscerally with Father Giussani: "Every now and then, he says, 'Enzo, I'm not leaving behind the machine gun.' If someone hears this, he'll call Giussani a terrorist, but the meaning is beautiful. 'I'm not leaving behind the machine gun.' This is the challenge. It is like this for everyone. In the family, with your wife, with your children. It is not about imposing a point of view. It means that your personal battle does not stop because you reach a certain age—in fact, it becomes more profound, more true, more restless, more adventurous."[2] "The price to pay is to be countercultural. Companionship with Him is countercultural. We are called to this today."[3]

---

1. *Romans* 12:1-2.
2. Marche, June 10, 1997.
3. Bologna, June 21, 1992.

From here comes that incessant movement, that need to change forms so as not to crystallize in ideology, so as not to allow the world to reserve for the Movement its own little corner, the plot of land where it can legitimately exercise its own interests. "Like the cardinal of Milan said to Giussani, 'You are strange people, like water that is blocked from one hole then springs out from another.' It's true. It's exactly like this."[4]

THIS HOME EITHER OPENS YOU UP TO EVERYTHING OR IT'S A HIDEOUT

"All this has to become mature. It began like this, through an invitation, through whatever occasion. It began as an accent of truth that hit us when we met the community. An accent of truth, small and embryonic. It has to mature so that we can joyfully carry out the responsibilities and the work it implies. But the fact that it matures (here is the greatness) is a miracle that doesn't depend on us. It is our job to welcome it just as it was given to us. That it matures is a miracle that we have to ask for."[5] "What we have said implies an ethical urgency. Ethical means having to do with behavior. It is urgent that every circumstance be tested with fire because of what happened to us, that it not remain abstract or sentimental, but penetrate your way of facing the circumstances, whether personal or historical and collective."[6] "This home either opens you up to everything or it is a kind of animal hideout, sentimental and interior. It is a den. All embellished with religious considerations and inspirations, certainly! But still a den."[7]

> We asked him about everything; literally, everything. From the life of the CLU to national and international politics, advice on books to read or films to watch, and then personal questions, questions about everyday life. He had an

---

4. Florence, March 18, 1997.
5. Bologna, October 17, 1993.
6. Bologna, November 23, 1989.
7. Marche, February 23, 1997.

idea about everything, a judgment about everything, starting from that "we" that was CL, a liberating "we" because this friendship in Jesus that had changed his life, and therefore also ours, did not mortify our personalities but made them grow. It was an extraordinarily fruitful "we." It was not a comfort zone to hide out in... With him, it was not possible to live our friendship as a protective shell, to defend ourselves from the world. We wanted to live everything in the world, to conquer it. Nothing was foreign to us. (Assuntina Morresi)

For me, whose faith was decidedly modest and whose spirituality practically absent, the attraction of those activities was more connected to the form than the content. I liked to challenge myself with things to do, things that were often anything but simple, and I liked to exercise my capacity for judgment on what happened, accompanied by people who were more intelligent than I was. Even though we repeated it to each other constantly, it was not truly clear for me why we did it; it was a mystery that revealed itself a little at a time and, also for this reason, was definitely fascinating. The experience of Christianity managed to pass through that miniscule opening that I had unwittingly left to it in doing interesting things and judging reality." (Andrea Prosperi)

"In short, it is as if we had to stand between two poles: the pole of the discovery of our "I" and the pole of this cultural production, to put the "I" in action in normal things, to understand it at work, in what we feel and what we have always thought in a certain way. When there are two poles, it is like there is an electric arc and, if the potential difference between these is great, lightning strikes. The spark is the potential difference... This discovery of love for myself, this discovery of the "I," and this discovery of a cultural production, to intervene in the world and do something different, as a given within the normal things, changes them."[8]

"When I was in Boston, the community was made up of five or six crazy people, one of whom was called Gandhi. Do you remember, Fabio? I was as ashamed as a dog to go around with someone

---

8. Bologna, November 21, 1985.

like him, because he always brought his own food in weird containers, like he was afraid of being contaminated. When we went to eat pizza after School of Community, he sat down in a corner, pulled out his thingy, and began to eat his own stuff. This guy might have been one of the more sane. It was a very weird group of people, because there were those who came to the School of Community and said they had seen Jesus Christ the night before. Okay, so I was there in this environment, and I remember one day, I was riding my bike through downtown Boston, and there were these huge skyscrapers. Looking up, I thought about myself, about the community, about America, about greatness, about smallness, about faith. There were all these thoughts. I said to myself, 'Wow, this is how it is; it can't be different! Those four or five people there are my salvation, the salvation of Boston, of America, and of the world, because this is how Christianity is, because God makes great things out of small things, if it is He who acts, and if He is recognized.'"[9]

> What always struck me about Enzo was not only his ability to perform extraordinary actions, but the exceptionality with which he lived the normal things, and this was also within my reach. From eating and drinking to a conversation among friends; from decisions on which hung the destiny of the world (the time of the *Pantera* protests was incredible) to a love for wasting time together. (Manlio Gessaroli)

"That the normal things become greater is the miracle of life."[10] "We need everything that we have told each other to go from poetic, from descriptive and profoundly exciting, to 'epic.' That is, it must enter *in medias res* [in the middle of things], it must become the root of our heart, the passion with which we do everything. We do not initiate anything, but the Christian fact does not even begin at all if it does not bring with it, immediately, as a beginning, the passion for changing the world, and one cannot feel that he changes

---

9. Folgarida, August 6, 1991.
10. Bologna, January 23, 1986.

without implicating the world around him, without being a question for those around him."[11]

> I often think about Enzo, about the fatherhood with which he accompanied us, indicating the road to us, the care with which he made us taste the beauty within things, in a work of art or a beautiful song, in front of the mountains or in facing a shared pain. (Simona Massaia)

Every particular became thus an "occasion"—every instant an opportunity to contribute to the great design. As Father Giussani said, "The most amazing thing for me is that his belonging to Christ was so totalizing that there was never a day that he did not seek, in every way, the human glory of Christ."[12] He did so seamlessly, from beauty, to play, to pain, to work.

> That evening, when we went into the operating room, he didn't "wash" himself at all. Those who washed themselves to perform the surgery were his two students, Doctor Ugolini and Doctor Milano. Dad stayed "on the sidelines" for the whole surgery. Like an attentive and scrupulous teacher, he guided, step-by-step, the able hands of Giampaolo, observing and correcting from a distance until the end of the surgery. Thinking about it today, with a clear mind, I recognize that it really took great courage to risk like that, without having the temptation to intervene and correct and to "finish" the job himself with his own hands, without revealing that he clearly would have done the job better and faster. And I am struck even more by the fact that even though I, his daughter, was there present, he did not seem worried about demonstrating his surgical abilities and capacities, but first of all had the desire to show what he held most dear. They joked, they even laughed; they were friends. A rare thing to see in a work environment, above all in an operating room. (Anna Rita Piccinini)

---

11. Bologna, November 21, 1985.

12. Father Luigi Giussani, "Message to all the communities of CL in Italy and in the world on the death of Enzo Piccinini," May 26, 1999 (translation: ours).

THE GESTURE IS MADE UP OF TIME AND SPACE

"If you and I came up here on bicycles (these bikes are really tough; we'd be dead much sooner) ... Let's say we had made it all the way up, and we came here and talked to each other about the places we had all seen. Our words would have some weight, some influence, because we had experienced the passage, and not in an abstract way. What we would do together is a gesture. Do you understand? You and I... There wouldn't be any depersonalization overall. Instead, you and I would feel united in the effort that we make together, in telling each other the things we do... It's you and I. So, it should be like this now. I am not here to make a speech, nor are we here to update each other on the Movement. We are not making a speech, but we are here for a 'gesture.' The difference between a speech and a gesture is that a gesture is made up of time and space, of physicality; it is a physicality, it takes place on earth. A speech is like something that passes by, an idea."[13]

Sometimes I ask myself how Enzo would be today, in the era of social media. In those days, the cellphone was on the frontier of cutting edge technology. Today, time and space have changed a lot, and the virtual has turned the coordinates of our world radically upside down. I imagine Enzo using the new technologies, pushed by an inexhaustible curiosity about human inventiveness, but he would not reduce by one iota, by one second, by one kilometer of the highway, his urgency to share physical time and space with his friends. The dimension of the "gesture" was and is the cornerstone of Christian communication, a physicality that takes place on earth. Our meeting together at table until ridiculously late at night was exactly part of our responsibility to propose concrete and curated "gestures" to our friends.

"This is the beginning of the year, the fact that we are brothers and provocateurs, among ourselves and in the world. Because all this has been given to us, we cannot keep it for ourselves."[14] "Remember

---

13. Florence, 1987.
14. Bologna, November 21, 1985.

that God loves the one who lives—he does not love the one who is in CL; he loves the one who lives."[15] "We began to make our ironic attempts (not cynical, ironic) and it was a great liberation. Irony is the opposite of cynicism. The cynic is the one who stands apart and says, 'Nothing can change anyway. Let's see how it ends.' Irony puts itself in the middle; it feels that the reason for everything is not in the attempt that you make. You make an attempt because you feel that the ideal that you believe is within you, the provocation is within, it doesn't come from what others do. It is within you like an inner force that no longer allows you to stay quiet and to endure the lie."[16]

"We are passing through a period when enmity to the Christian fact is subtle but permanently present. The attack has one aim: to eliminate the social and political presence of Catholics. From 1968 on, people theorized about the disappearance of the Catholic experience, as such, in the social and political world. Now, it is the same thing. The leaven, do you remember[17]? To go around and leaven, not to stand out as Catholics. Go into the world and leaven! The leaven was without labels, without flags, without identity… and we leavened so well that we ended up getting leavened ourselves by the world!"[18]

From here came a ceaseless activity of public, social, and political proposals, all with a dual goal: the witness and the growth (human and also professional) of the person. We lived this activity as an occasion for daily correction, for shared judgment, for the assumption of a responsibility that became, in time, adult.

---

15. September 5, 1998.

16. Colfosco, September 2, 1987.

17. After the second Vatican Council, some large Catholic youth associations in Italy had been promoting the idea that Catholics should be "leaven" in the world, as suggested in the Gospel (*Matthew* 13:33): that is, Catholics should mix in with the rest of society without standing out, without a strong Catholic identity, but rather "leaven" society from within. Many Catholics, however, ended up assimilating to the predominant mentality.

18. Bologna, January 23, 1994.

He challenged us for the thousandth time: "What are you doing for the city? How can people see and encounter the Movement in Reggio Emilia?" And so we started "Atlantide," an outdoor location where people could hang out and eat some watermelon and where we held public meetings, film clubs, water games, etc. (Ciccio Caprari)

Enzo encouraged the creation of a national coordination of "Cattolici Popolari" [Catholics of the People], of which I was a part, together with Massimiliano(Max) Salini, who was then a student at the State University of Milan. After having asked me to confirm the fact that Max and I stopped in Rome only long enough for the meeting, he told me that I had not understood anything of the reason why I went to Rome, and that I was wasting my time. I was astonished. "If your meeting is at 3 p.m. on Wednesday, you should go a day early, to meet, get to know, and then visit again all the people who work in that place (the Ministry of University and Research), telling them who you are, where you come from, what fills your life." A few hours later, in the very early morning, he called me again and, after asking if there was anything new (!), he wanted me to repeat to him what I had understood from our previous phone call. Not satisfied, he repeated everything from the beginning. (Emmanuele Forlani)

The responsibility of the student representatives was connected indissolubly to the life of the community. I participated every week in the "small group" of the CLU (a group of those responsible for the community). On the agenda, there was always a point on how to judge the activities we were doing, with the aim that everyone in the community could know what the student representatives were doing, and remember that the source of the judgment on 'political' issues was the same as the judgment on the existential things we held most dear (our own passions, our girlfriend, our studies, etc.). (Tommaso Agasisti)

"There is a latent danger that a heavy dualism may happen again, as if the faith had to stop where the practical begins. From then on, there are the experts, those who know how to do certain things, etc. The Companionship of Works,[19] with the dimensions which Giussani taught us, is inevitable for everyone, because even a housewife performs a work, whose value does not depend on the judgment of the world; it is her work and the meaning she gives it. Consequently, every action we do with the sense of the ideal present is a work and therefore an ultimate responsibility that we exercise (responsibility has do do with to whom and to what we respond). We also exercise a sane realism, which means taking into account all the factors at play. From here, a particular instrument of connection and help may grow; this goes without saying. It is like the university students who created CUSL, rather than something else. But that student who works for CUSL is entirely part of CL. It is not that, by going to CUSL, he becomes something else because he has a social commitment. We care about this. We may go wrong in our attempts, but the form (which means that which informs our action) has to be complete, otherwise you have already left free space for something else. And then Christ only has to do with it part time."[20]

> I remember that on the first day of my freshman year, in Piazza Scaravilli, I was barraged by eggs with red paint inside of them, organized by a group of far-left students to "welcome" the freshmen to the orientation booths hosted by the CLU. Student representation in the university was given great weight; our campaigning for votes happened with a considerable expenditure of energy and creativity. It went from a simple dinner in an apartment to get to know the candidates, to the organization of festivals where several hundred people participated. (Andrea Prosperi)

"The gesture is made up of time and space" means that these dimensions in which life is played out are the only theater where life can be lived concretely, the place where Christianity demonstrates how unique it is. For this reason, to remove the public dimension

---

19. Born as a mature fruit of the education to the faith received in CL, the Companionship of Works is an association whose objective is to support entrepreneurs, non-profits, managers, and professionals in the development of businesses and professional activities with an orientation toward the common good.

20. Marche, June 10, 1997.

from the Christian experience is not just a reduction but, rather, a radical emptying. "A thing is not truly ours until we are ready to defend it publicly. Remember the famous example of the girl who invites a guy to her house, and he says, 'No, we are just friends... Why should I meet your family? We are only friends... let's wait a bit!' That girl objectively cannot be peaceful about the affection of that guy, because he is not ready to defend it in public. So we need to clarify what it means to say 'in public.' Does it mean that now, suddenly, we all march to Loreto, stand in the town square, and say, 'The time is short, convert to the Gospel,' etc.? They would call the ambulances. Defense in public means that this thing is the true reason for all our civic and public expressions. And what is this expressiveness? What you have, what you do, what you possess, your projects, your successes, your family, your career, your money... Do you want me to specify more? This is public: that all this be for the defense of Christ present in history. So it means that you are ready to defend in public what has happened to you."[21]

You Seem Like a Big Construction Site

"Every person has the same value as myself; he has the same worth as I. The awareness of this, this attention to our neighbor, makes us very sensitive to his need. Sensitive to his need means that we are not people who, at school, at the university, at work, in the city, take a look at something and call the experts in: 'Get us out of this.' We have never been like this. Because of the temperament we have, because of how we have been educated, it is a responsibility that we take upon ourselves in front of a need. We begin to look at what is happening. The second thing is that we start talking to each other to see what we can do, to read the need better, and to be more efficient in our response. The third thing is that we use everything, really everything, so that our response can be adequate. We are people like this. It is not that we see two people hitting each other in the street,

---

21. Marche, February 23, 1997.

hitting a child, and we go and call the police. The first thing we do is go there ourselves."[22]

> Enzo pushed you to make a step, to take a position. With him, it was never a purely intellectual discussion... You had to get to the point of taking action, of taking a position. (Licio Argelli)

"I was struck by what Cardinal Biffi said at the meeting of the community in Bologna, at the end: 'You guys impress me, because you seem like a big construction site.'[23] That's right; it is as if you could feel in the contributions today this great personal work together, this thing that we are building together. It's as if it was a great construction site, with all this work going on, and this is why others meet us and many come with us, because what we are building is interesting for life.'"[24]

It was a work similar to that of those who built the cathedrals. "The cathedral was the sign of the meaning for which they continued to dig out the earth and to go fishing, and therefore it was like bringing out and making evident with a sign what is necessary to live, and to accept and offer the effort of every day. My God, that was a people! See, the concept is this: a common construction in which one understands that what he is building is what he needs to live, is the sign—small or great, fragile or splendid—of the meaning he needs, for studying every day, for being together in friendship and spending free time together, for the sacrifice of traveling back and forth every day, for being far from home, etc."[25]

---

22. Sicily, November 21, 1997.

23. The relationship of Cardinal Giacomo Biffi of Bologna with us was always one of a deep friendship and a fatherhood, which was the outcome of his personal friendship and respect for Father Giussani and for the Movement of Communion and Liberation. He responded to every invitation with generosity, paternity, and Ambrosian irony. This did not stop him from underlining even aspects of fraternal distance: "Cardinal Biffi has never been tender in our regard, because he has always had an attitude... how can I say... like: 'Let's not encourage them too much, because they are puffed up enough already.'" (Enzo Piccinini, Bologna, October 17, 1993).

24. Bologna, January 23, 1986.

25. Bologna, January 23, 1986.

There was an ultimate end to this work, an objective that surely, today as yesterday, is difficult to understand and even to consider as admissible. In the end, all that we built, the work (even economically significant) was in service of growth. But not just the growth of the work; also the growth of the companionship. Many did not understand, and many forgot. "The companionship is not only the instrument that makes possible what we have said, but it is also the work that is born from this labor. Is the concept clear? The work born from this labor is the companionship."[26]

> In the following years, thanks to the work of everyone, we achieved extraordinary results, and not simply in economic terms. the greatest value, the true richness of that experience, was a friendship and an exceptional bond that connected us volunteers, the 160 people hired from among the university students for supervision and technical assistance in the study halls and classrooms, which allowed these young people to support themselves in their studies, and a whole series of adults—not directly involved in the activity—who helped us grow. Once a year, Enzo really wanted to see us volunteer for a dinner. He talked to each person, asking incisive and always frank questions about how, what, and why that experience and that sacrifice of our time had to do with each of us and with the Christian experience. In the end, he was moved and he thanked us because he felt that the sacrifice he had asked, beyond being of value in our personal experience, was a witness of faith for everyone. One evening, while giving me a ride back to my home on via Masi, stopping a few minutes to chat, he said, "Thank you for what you are doing and for how you manage your CUSL." I answered right away that I felt like it was mine, but it was not mine. So he said, "You're right, because this thing has been given to us, but it is not ours. We treat it like it's ours. We are asked to be an instrument for the service of the Church today."
> (Francesco Cerini)
>
> Enzo and Widmer followed our activities with a 'loose' control that allowed us to express ourselves very freely, at the same time also keeping us from running into irremediable

---

26. Bologna, October 28, 1987.

errors. We often discussed practical issues, and from time-to-time met together to remind ourselves of the ultimate scope of all that rushing around. This often happened at twenty-course dinners prepared in the apartment with great care. There was a paternal supervision, present but not invasive, that allowed an original expression of our own personalities, and that didn't allow us to get hurt too much... It was the teaching of a morality understood as a correct relationship with reality, with things. For me, this kind of apprenticeship has been of fundamental importance, and the moment I faced the world of "true" work, I was already professionally mature and ready to engage within the adult context. (Andrea Prosperi)

That experience impressed upon us a method of work, the method for each of us of living our own job. We learned not to waste even a minute of the day, to deprive ourselves of some sleep and leisure to get a few more hours of study, with an attention for each other. Those years marked our way of thinking, made unacceptable any kind of lukewarmness, taught us a passion for not wasting our time, and made us rediscover the desire to love unconditionally. (Daniele Biondi)

Reflecting with a few friends, we noted how the thing that was "naturally" taking shape among us was the sharing of reorganized lesson notes, of the synthesis of texts, of the instruments of study that made test preparation easier. This form of our companionship had happened in a totally natural way among us, generating a "traffic" of useful material that extended even to other friends, and that gave form to our presence without being at all programmatic. It was an offering of the same charity that we experienced among ourselves to all the friends in our school. From here, we used the space that was reserved for us in the building for the distribution of this material, which was then accompanied by study groups, thus allowing us to get to know the friends of the school, with an authentic missionary thrust. After relating the beginnings of this attempt to Enzo in the small group of leaders, he asked us to explain to the whole central diaconia the work we were doing. He noted that the thing was already "latent" almost everywhere... It took only a small spark for a similar "room" and a service of the same type to be built in all the faculties. And so, the Student Office was born. (Marco Mescolini)

> The student office was a tangible demonstration of how the commitment to university life and the role of representation were redistributed in terms of service and facilities for the whole student community. It was a true and proper political activity, in the sense of public commitment for the defense of an ideal. Beyond reaching concrete results, there were an infinite series of relationships in this complex work that often led new people to want to know the profound meaning behind that militant commitment. Often, even professors and university officials, struck by our presence, wanted to know the reasons for it, and were ready to speak with us as equals. (Andrea Prosperi)

The defense of this "good for all" was at the origin of that "fighter" feeling that we have remarked on many times. "Saint Anthony, in the desert, wrote a very interesting little phrase: 'There will come a time when men go crazy and, when they encounter someone who is not crazy, they will turn to him and say, "You are crazy," because he isn't like them.' I mean, there is a notable thing about this position, which is, my friends, that it imposes a dialectic with the world. It becomes a conflict and it has to fight because everything denies it. When this friendship becomes visible, the world does everything it can to sweep it away."[27]

A CERTAIN FATHER LUIGI GIUSSANI TAUGHT ME TO BE A SURGEON

Maybe today, the most well-known and discussed aspect of Enzo Piccinini was his tenacity and his professional courage. It is useful to identify the deep reasons for this attitude, which, on the one hand, go well beyond his indisputable temperamental qualities and, on the other hand, for this very reason, have become the occasion for a true and unplanned flourishing of the professional maturation

---

27. Bologna, October 6, 1990.

of those who lived close to him. "That day (it was the 'Day of the Sick[28]'), they called me to a big hospital in Bari to talk about the organization of my surgery unit—what I do with my assistants, with the nurses, the clinic, etc. At the end of my presentation, someone got up and asked me where I learned these things. Certainly, I have been to America, to England... I had to be clear, and so in front of that enormous crowd of doctors, surgeons, etc., I said, 'I understand that I will cause a lot of confusion in saying this, but I will say it all the same: a certain Father Luigi Giussani taught me to be a surgeon.' Imagine that crowd... a great buzz. 'Father Giussani didn't teach me how to make incisions, or any techniques. I learned those myself. He taught me a human position in which the technique, the sick person, the people around me, what I do with myself, how I manage the human resource that I am, how I become an entrepreneur of myself, are all important, essential things.' And it is for this reason that, because of how I am now, I can say that professionally I have an enthusiasm in doing things that I rarely see in others. And I don't say it out of vainglory, because it is not my merit; I found myself involved in this adventure."[29]

> Giussani was to arrive at the headquarters in Bologna at 5 p.m., and I left school at 4:30. I worked at San Marino di Bentivoglio (16 kilometers outside Bologna). Enzo knew my schedule, but I had thought that for the arrival of Father Giussani, I would try to be at the headquarters early, and I decided to prepare myself and to be at the exit five minutes early, ready to let the kids out of my class. So I arrived at the headquarters before Giussani and Enzo. As soon as Enzo arrived and saw me already there, he asked: "How is it possible that you are already here?" And I happily answered, "I was able to leave five minutes early." His face darkened and he said seriously, "Don't ever do that again." In time, I saw that he never put the commitments of the Movement ahead of

---

28. The World Day of the Sick was established by Pope John Paul II in 1992 as "a special time of prayer and sharing, of offering one's suffering for the good of the Church and of reminding everyone to see in his sick brother or sister the face of Christ." It is celebrated every year on February 11, Feast of Our Lady of Lourdes.

29. Cesena, March 12, 1999.

his responsibility toward his work and his family. (Daniela Zanella)

My work cost me a lot of effort in the first 20 years of my career, because I did not have convincing female models of how to balance family life with work (and, meanwhile, the number of my children grew). Also, in my daily struggle, I was surrounded by a lot of mistrust. You know the typical comments: "Oh, you have small children! How are you able to work so much? You will regret these choices! You can't manage to do everything!" etc. etc. So, when at a certain point I found myself having to make the decision of whether to participate in a competition to become a director, I felt all that uncertainty. Enzo responded, "Of course you have to do it!! Certainly, absolutely, you have to do it!! First of all because you owe it to the gifts you have. But then, you see, you have to think about the Jews." I looked at him, very surprised, because I didn't understand: what do the Jews have to do with it? "For sure, we have to think about the Jews, because we have to learn from them. We are not used to considering ourselves a good for the community. We are and remain individualists. Instead, the Jews consider that any success, any good that happens in the life of a person in the community, is good for the whole community. We really have to learn from them, because a good that happens in your work life is a good that will reflect on the life of so many people. You will be a big sister to so many people. You will do more good if you have more potential to do it, you will teach other people, and you will inevitably increase all the good you can do. So you have to do it!" (Elisabetta Buscarini)

On many occasions, my colleagues noted, and not in a courteous way, that a mother of four children was not well accepted in the hospital environment, in particular in anesthesia and recovery, where surely she would not be up to performing such a demanding profession efficiently. My friends warmly counseled me to quit work and dedicate myself totally to my house and my children. It even seemed to me that, all in all, the circumstances spoke clearly. To my surprise, Enzo told me with certainty that the best thing for me, but not only for me, would be to do my work, despite all the difficulties. I had honestly hoped that he would confirm me in quitting, but it was not like that. He left me free to decide. It was hard. When it seemed like I was sinking, I looked for Enzo and he, wherever he was, called me back. Two words, practical advice. He understood immediately. I set out again. (Alfredina Pezzetta)

Around 1997, the demands and responsibilities that work was asking of me were growing progressively, with short but more frequent trips abroad, getting home later and later, and the worries and problems that began to crowd my mind even outside work time. In front of the thousandth increase in responsibility at work, my wife and I decided to go together to talk with Enzo about it. I had prepared mentally a whole list of pros and cons, to enable him to make a good assessment and draw a conclusion. Enzo didn't even look at me, but turned to my wife: "If you think about him, only about him (and he pointed to me), do you think it is the right thing, a good thing for him?" "Yes"—"And so, accept. And remember that if you go forward, the whole Movement goes forward. And then, both of you pray to Our Lady to help you." (Massimo Vincenzi)

In my last years of studying agriculture, I had a crisis regarding the choice of university that I had made, and I seriously thought about throwing everything away and starting again with a new major. I had chosen agriculture without a specific reason. I did not come from a family that was engaged in that kind of profession, nor did I feel any passion for plants. There was even a time I detested them, to the great scandal of my classmates, who had an unbridled passion for them. In that period, I would have paved everything over!! In my heart, maybe also inspired by Enzo, I wanted to be a doctor. During a conversation with him, I remember well that he let me speak at length. He seemed not to be listening; he was leafing through *Traces*.[30] When I had finished speaking, he lifted up his hand and said, "Of all the things you have studied in these years, of all the exams you have taken, is there anything that for one moment made your heart leap?

---

30. *Traces* (formerly *Litterae Communionis*) is the monthly magazine of Communion and Liberation.

Was there a topic, or a professor, a researcher, in short, someone or something that made you suddenly lift up your head?" I told him that there was a professor, who had an office in the basement of the department of vegetable pathology (plant sickness, something that comes close to medicine...) who did not count for much, but it seemed to me that he liked me, and I liked his classes. And then, in vegetable pathology, you could wear a lab coat! He said, "Go and ask to do a thesis with him, attach yourself to him like a mussel, and if he accepts working with you, you will have found a teacher and, praying to Our Lady, you will be thankful for the choice that the Mystery had you make." That professor accepted my proposal. He became my teacher and was even the best man at my wedding. He wanted me with him everywhere. One day, a Dutch multinational company asked the professor if he had a good student they could hire and he, understanding that there were not great possibilities at the university, told me, "I am sorry to lose you, but I insist that you go to that company and stop working with me, for your good and for your future." He was truly great; he loved me more than his project. I did it reluctantly, and from there began my professional path, that led me to start my own company and, thanks to the companionship of the Movement of CL, to experience an enthusiasm in my work that today, at 55 years of age, is not so common. (Simone Pizzagalli)

Work, for Enzo, had become more and more, in time, what Father Giussani had defined as "the most concrete, most arid and concrete, most tiring and concrete aspect of one's love for Christ."[31] And for this reason, after a very risky surgery on a mutual friend, the two men had called each other and Giussani had thanked him. "And in the end, he said to me, 'Thank you for being the instrument of a miracle.' So, you see, this is the true position in life, because I could not even boast about all that I had done. 'Instrument of a

---

31. Luigi Giussani, *"Natale: motivo della vita come lavoro"* ["Christmas: Reason for Life as Work"], *Litterae Communionis-Tracce*, December 1998, insert (translation: ours).

miracle' means that I did not do anything. If this is the position in life, excuse me, what is there to fear anymore? What can stop us?"[32]

THAT STUFF THERE, WHICH I DON'T UNDERSTAND, IS MADE FOR A GOOD DESTINY

His attitude toward the whole of reality was contagious, not so much and not only for what concerned his professional skills, but much more for his underlying relentless "positivity," lived tenaciously in front of any eventuality, even the most dramatic. Enzo was contagious because he carried hope. "It is a question; you go within reality with this question and you love everything. Everything is interesting to you! And you feel bad about everything, you are a man and, in the morning, drinking your cappuccino, you suddenly hear that with one attack they killed 16 people, young people, children, maybe in Pakistan. You can no longer drink your cappuccino like before, if you are a man! We need hope to go forward, the certainty of a promise that even that stuff there, which I don't understand, is made for a good destiny."[33]

> In 1996, just after graduation, I decided to follow Enzo and choose general surgery as my specialization. He suggested that I do my first year abroad, and proposed that I go to Chicago to study genetic therapy of colon cancer. He told me that first we have to talk about it with my parents. We decided to go to dinner in Rimini at my parents' house, and he talked the whole evening about how important it is to have an experience abroad, but also about how Chicago is the most dangerous city in the United States, with the highest crime rate. At the end of the dinner, he asked me why my mom was so worried about the decision I had already made to go to Chicago... So I took courage and told him about my sisters, who died in a roadside accident as children. I still remember his sudden braking, and where we were. He told me that the same thing had happened to him and that

---

32. Rimini, December 12, 1998.
33. February 23, 1995.

when he was a kid, while walking with his brother Sergio, a truck had run over his little brother and killed him. Then he said, "Remember that in the friendship between us there is already the seed of victory over death." (Simone Zanotti)

Not even two years after the death of my mother, in November 1988 (I was in my third year of university), my father died of a heart attack while we were at dinner with some of his work colleagues. After all the commotion (ambulance, hospital, doctors, etc.), late that night some friends from the Movement invited me to sleep at their apartment, so I wouldn't have to return to my house, now empty. When we arrived at this apartment of students from out of town, the phone rang (the land line, obviously; there were no cellphones then). Enzo wanted to speak with me. It was a short conversation, at the end of which he said these exact words: "God gives, God takes. Live this thing as a Christian. Ciao." They were the only sensible words I heard in those days. Words of strength and hope. (Francesco Vignaroli)

Giampaolo (Giampa), a classmate and friend of mine, returned home and threw himself from the roof of his house, taking his own life. The morning of his funeral, Widmer called me and said, "Enzo wants me to tell you this: Courage! Life goes forward with its head up. Tomorrow, at the end of Mass, get up and tell us about your friendship. But I beg you, try not to let yourself get overwhelmed by emotion, because what has to come through is the certainty of the Resurrection. Without the cross, we don't understand the Resurrection!" (Paolino Casadei)

I remember a conversation between Enzo and the CL secretary about the condition of a guy from the community who was nearing the end of his life at a little more than 20 years old. At a certain point, Enzo raised his voice and turned toward the secretary, who had asked if it was not better to cancel the Holy Week *Via Crucis*, and said, "We cannot think of cancelling the gesture of the *Via Crucis* because of this! We cannot act as if Christ had not conquered death!" (Alberto Paltrinieri)

I experienced personally the force of this "violent" hope, almost a punch in the stomach that challenged the small faith with which even we Christians judge the facts of life, above all those facts that are most painful. I was in my third year of university and I had been invited as a leader to the freshmen day, which that year was held at Fognano, above Faenza. On the trip, a car with five of my dear friends was hit by a truck. I start going up and down the emergency rooms in the area. I saw a gurney pass by, quickly loaded onto a helicopter. Others were kept there at the local ER, some with uncertain prognoses. In the afternoon, the outlook was very bleak: two dead, one in a coma, and two badly wounded. Beri, a freshman, lived with me. He was someone I had invested much of my time and my hopes. 'What kind of businessman is God?' I was brooding on the side, crying. Enzo came to me and put me literally with my back to the wall, saying, 'You don't have the right to do this! You look at life and death like everyone else does. What use is it to be a Christian? And remember that your friends are looking at you and see this!"

"Yesterday afternoon, I was randomly at Gudo Gambaredo, where Giussani lives, and I saw there, in the house, that they have a beautiful phrase that says, 'The Lord will bring to completion the good work He has begun in you' (*Philippians* 1:6). This here is hope. The only hope for which it is worth it to be together is this certainty. And, when we were leaving, Giussani told us, 'Please be humble; it is the Lord who does it.' Amazing! It is absolutely true. Without this humble but certain position that it is the Lord who does it... And what does He do? He will bring to completion what He has begun in your life, whether your life is a disaster or good, doubtful or certain, with the temperament of a protagonist or of one constantly undecided. It doesn't matter, understand? He has taken initiative and will bring it to completion. Be humble, that's it, be humble! This means to recognize that it is God who does it. The first thing is this."[34]

---

34. Porto San Giorgio, February 28, 1999.

11.

Gusto for Life Is Proportional to Your Engagement with the Ideal

THIS LAST CHAPTER DEDICATED TO THE EARTHLY JOURNEY of Enzo Piccinini tries to delineate, as far as possible, the most mature achievements of his human path, the ideal peaks that he had reached by the day when, just before his 48th birthday, he was taken from our friendship. His daughter Maria, a few days after the accident, had shared in a letter a perception she had of those last days: "Everything seemed meticulously prepared for his death."[1] There remains, in many of us, the question about what would have happened with him at our side in these past 25 years, in which so many new and unexpected things have happened. But there remains, even more, the gratitude of having seen in him the passion of one who scales the Everest of humanity. There remains the responsibility to tell what we have seen. And to continue the climb.

ON THIS "BREATH OF A YES" GOD HAS BUILT THE MEANING OF HIS HISTORY

The secret of the human spectacle offered by Enzo can be summed up in one word: "availability." This is the attitude that made everything

---

1. Maria Piccinini, June 2, 1999.

possible. After all, for him, it was also a structural condition of human nature, the condition for its realization. "There was there, in Boston, I remember like it was yesterday, an auditorium with a huge screen, and this young lady was speaking: 'Welcome... this and that... how beautiful... blah blah blah.' And then they opened a huge screen with a sensational image (to knock you out—a sensational image). There was a man and the peak of a mountain this high! A man was free climbing, alone, with his fingers all bandaged up, all taped up, hanging like this, over the void. The image zoomed in on his trembling hands and then, bam, he fell! And so you heard everyone shouting, 'Oooooh!' It gave you a shock. And then you saw that he was connected to a rope! It was an image that knocked you down; it psychologically knocked you down. It is an incredible image that makes us understand what the attitude of availability means because, without this attitude, we are like that individual there, who tries to stay attached to life with his fingers, but it is inevitable that he will only last a few moments and then fall. The Bible, the most important book, the most important message in the world, that changed the world, finishes with an invocation: 'Come, Lord.' Not with a social program but with an invocation, 'Come, Lord.' The problem is exactly this total availability, 'to put yourself in the hands of,' and it is an event with no turning back, because if you ask and you put yourself in His hands, He responds, always! The only way not to make Him respond is not to ask."[2]

I still remember a very strong expression that Enzo often used, which was, "There is only one way to put God's back to the wall: to ask. Because if you ask, He responds. The problem, though, is that He responds as He wills. And, at that point, it's up to you." He responds as He wills. He did this by intervening in history. From then on, availability has necessarily changed its face. "He put Himself in, He saved you, without asking for anything from you in return. He died for you without waiting for your response. We normally say, 'We need to abandon ourselves to...' It is not about abandoning yourself to something. Availability is more radical than

---

2. Bologna, April 21, 1991.

abandonment, because abandonment is still a feeling that comes to you, for which you take the initiative. Availability strips you, because availability is availability to something you don't know, something you can't define. Faith is being available to Christ, to the Mystery that revealed Himself to you in the companionship, through the very particular way with which He came to you, through our most personal vocation. You know that friend, you know that invitation, you know that phone call, you know that companion…? Like this… totally personal. No two vocations are the same."[3]

Availability is a position in front of an initiative already taken, in the precise, historic form where the Mystery decided to meet you. "The Angel appears to a 15-year-old girl, something that could have been diverted, cancelled from her mind by closing her eyes, like a bad thought, as if from an exaggerated imagination. She believes it and it changes her life, it changes the life of the world. Here is the beauty of our experience and above all the genius of Giussani: 'On this breath of a yes, on this invisible point, God has built the meaning of His history.'[4] It is beautiful to hear that it was the breath of a yes. It wasn't 'YEEESSS!!!,' like I would have done. No. This is a breath of a yes, something so human, because she had to feel the weight of history, a young girl, she must already have imagined what would happen to her, how people would look at her. A breath of a yes. From this breath of a yes, on this invisible point, God has built the meaning of His history. What has happened to us, comparable in all respects to this? Why are you here, do you remember? A flyer, a phone call, a group of friends? Is it not equal to an angel? Does it not have the same fragility as an angel who says, 'Christ will become incarnate'? It is incredible. It is identical; it is exactly the same dynamic, because it lives in a sign, so all your freedom is exalted."[5]

Therefore, availability is within the daily circumstances, in which the Mystery reverberates. "The way to live the normal things,

---

3. Bologna, April 21, 1991.

4. In Luigi Amicone, *Sulle tracce di Cristo: Viaggio in Terra Santa con Luigi Giussani [In the Footsteps of Christ: Journey to the Holy Land with Luigi Giussani]*, BUR, Milan, 2006, p. 30 (translation: ours).

5. Folgarida, August 6, 1991.

without becoming imprisoned by them, is to feel the normal things connected to something greater than you, than your own thoughts, than your own aims. Try to imagine if this had to do, even minimally, with the relationship you have with yourselves and with others. First of all, there would be a total positivity in your relationship with reality—your studies, the CL welcoming booths for new university students, the pain of the loss of two friends."[6]

It is like a revolution, but in daily life. "There is another thing that this Christ brought into the world: the greatness of every action. I really want you to understand this! It's that there is nothing left to throw away, nothing. 'Even the hairs of your head have been counted.'[7] What kind of newness it imposed! The hairs of your head! They blow away with the wind! There is nothing that is not known, that is not within a will, that is not wanted! There is no longer anything banal. The six hours, or the eight, or the two, or the ten hours that you spent yesterday studying in your room, where it seems like there is nothing else than the effort you have to make to store away all that is written in the book, and the fear of your exam... Try for a minute to imagine that you discover in your life that even the hairs of your head are counted. In the same moment that you are there studying, don't you understand that it is an incredibly great gesture?"[8]

"The seed has a strange mechanism and dynamism in the earth, something inexorable. It mutates the earth; it changes it. Its falling to the earth changes the earth, and changes it by changing itself, growing as a seed, taking root as a plant. The only condition is that we recognize it within our life; not next to or outside of life, but within our life—in the university, in my affections, in my family, in my hope for the future, in the thought that I have about my past. The earth is interesting only when it is involved in a process that builds, that generates, that transforms that inert mass into something useful for me and for you. My morning, my eating, my

---

6. Bologna, October 28, 1987.
7. *Luke* 12:7.
8. Florence, 1987.

working, the hour of pain, the hour of injustice, the hour of rebellion, the hour of temptation, the hour of joy, the hour of study, the hour of affection, is sown in truth."⁹

From this awareness, an aspect already present in Enzo's temperament is confirmed and flourishes in full maturation: attention to the particulars.

> At a certain point, I heard a door open and Enzo said, "This is what it means to love the Movement—to notice even the cigarette butts!" (Cristina Chiocchio)

> At the end of a Beginning Day with the CLU in Turin, where he spoke after a long and exhausting operation in which a patient, the father of a kid from the CLU, had died, I gave the final announcements in a distracted way, so much so that when he greeted me, visibly exhausted, he told me that it didn't make sense to give the announcements like this, without the smallest awareness of the connection between our companionship, the things that we ask each other, and Christ. (Gianpiero Di Febbo)

> Enzo listened to us attentively and told us something that we would never have expected to hear, "Good, but you are living by approximation. If you continue like this, you will never build anything." For him it was as if every instant and every circumstance were always important, and had an infinite value. (Simone Magherini and Francesca Fontanella)

> It didn't matter whether it was a dinner together, or an assembly, or one of the games of soccer on Saturday afternoons in the outskirts of Modena. The most impressive trait of his method was precisely this: an attention to everything he did, down to the smallest detail, and always. (Raffaello Vignali)

So many of us remember with what "maniacal" care he tended the banana tree, the magnolia, and the statue from which the water in the garden fountain flowed at the CL headquarters in Bologna. These were "obsessions" of Enzo, in which the particulars in the end decided the morality of the act.

---

9. Florence, May 6, 1989.

Gusto for Life Is Proportional to Your Engagement with the Ideal

"From this breath of a yes God has built the meaning of His history." Progressively, the things in Enzo's life acquired this sense, a "sacramental" depth. "I have always had difficulty understanding the question of the Holy Spirit. I remember that, when I was a small kid and I went to catechism class, my pastor always said that the issue of the Holy Spirit is fundamental. But I never understood, until one day I heard it explained, and the comparison was suggestive. I still remember it well, because it is clearly the only thing that resolved my question about the Holy Spirit, because He was compared to the wind that blows wherever it will. And I recall that I was really impressed by this comparison. It happens to me sometimes in the morning, when I go to the hospital on the road that skirts around Modena, and I have in front of me the mountain range of Cimone and Cusna—and sometimes there has been a storm or a light snowfall, and the wind sweeps away all the mist, all the fog—that everything takes on a perfect outline. It takes on its own outline in a way that you had never noticed up to the day before. It is extraordinary, because the blue sky provides a background in the early morning, and everything is clearly inscribed as it should be, with its correct outline and dimensions. This makes one understand the action of the Spirit. It is like that wind, and it is a sense of presence, of present meaning that gives back to things their correct outline, their correct dimensions. It is as if this mysterious presence, in looking at the friend you have next to you, gave him back his right place, no longer determined by what you feel, or by the heaviness of your morning or of your feelings. You see, we need to feel reality according to its right proportion, its right significance. I need to look at you feeling that the strangeness is not everything, that the fact that you are, that I am here, by chance, is not everything."[10]

"It is necessary, now, that the beauty of normal things and of the things we encounter or of the things we love, the beauty of the normal things not imprison us. The beauty of normal things does not imprison us when it is seen, conceived, approached, and lived according to its profound nature, which is that of being a hint or

---

10. Bologna, October 6, 1990.

a passage to meaning, to destiny. We need to begin to feel normal things as connected to something else that is not just our reaction. Like dawn is connected to midday, so we need to begin to feel ourselves and feel normal things as connected to something greater, without interruption."[11]

"For this reason, we are finally free to embrace everything, without cautious estimations. And immediately I feel that I could die for you now, if God helps me."[12] "I love you (you, whom I have never seen) and I would be ready to give my life, in this moment (if God gives me the strength) for you. And it doesn't matter if you are good, not good, if you can give me something, if you have given me something, who you are..."[13] "He created you like no one knows how to create. Therefore, we love Him with an infinite love and therefore there are people who give their lives for this."[14]

Everything has worth if it is offered to Him!

"In a beautiful poem by Victor Hugo, there is an eagle that, flying high in the mountains, speaks with the sun and says, 'You who illuminate the peaks of the mountains and illuminate and make clean and serene the air where I fly (so much so that it's beautiful to fly around when you shine), why do you get mixed up in the mud of remote valleys, where without your intervention only that filth, that rot, would remain? Instead, you go to find that filth. Why? Remain here and illuminate the mountains, without getting involved with that banal normality!' And the sun turns to the eagle, saying, 'Climb on my rays.' The eagle climbs on the rays of the sun and suddenly—it is a visible sensation—seeing the sun that illuminates, it is as if the mountains became one with the valleys, as if everything was illuminated in the same way, with the same intensity of light.

---

11. Pesaro, April 6, 1998.
12. Marche, October 22, 1995.
13. Bologna, January 23, 1997.
14. Sicily, November 21, 1997.

Gusto for Life Is Proportional to Your Engagement with the Ideal

Everything all of a sudden takes on a beauty that could not be conceived before. To go home and have to wash clothes for the tenth time, always those same clothes; to have to pay the phone bill; to balance the weekly budget; to be quiet when your husband gets too angry... All these things would be mud and filth, things that make life distasteful. But, illuminated by the ray of this sun, of this ideal that strikes us and has struck us, they are no longer banal. The ideal illuminates everyday things and makes them feel no longer just like everyday things (that is, less than other things). The ideal illuminates life day by day, minute by minute, and the normal things become great because they are connected to the Mystery, permanently connected to the Mystery."[15]

"We finally glimpse an ideal. Then life begins to work like this: from the mosaic that it was, that is, study, then the weekend, then sports, then fun, then vacation... but the problem is what we want to do with it all, and the meaning of this destiny (Mystery, God) begins to respond to this question that is fundamental, that distinguishes life as a mosaic from a unified life. And this thing—the ideal meaning—makes it possible to risk. When I ride my bike through the university and I see the tables and booths set up by the CLU, I see those kids there, who are more beautiful, humanly more beautiful, compared to all those who pass through the halls of the university. What makes them like that? What is it? Simply the fact of a certainty about themselves and an ideal meaning in life, and that makes them risk, and they set up tables and come there to give you a copy of the lesson notes. But what do they get out of it? It is the ideal meaning that makes them feel that what they feel is right should be built immediately. Otherwise, you stay there calculating whether it is worthwhile and whether you lose hours of study, then you swallow the nonsense and you slowly burn out."[16]

> The only way to act exactly like him was actually not to imitate him at all. Not in his actions, not in his character, not in what, remaining on the surface, could seem a frenzy, but

---

15. Marche, October 22, 1995.
16. Florence, November 12, 1992.

only in his integral dedication to the ideal that he served and that had completely captivated him. (Paola Belletti)

"Everything has value concretely as an offering to Him if ultimately it has one aim: that this history, which makes Christ present, may grow. We don't have anything else to say. The gusto for life is proportional to your engagement with the ideal. Keep this in mind. There is nothing else to say. Whoever sits there calculating will have nothing to enjoy. The gusto for life is proportional to your engagement with the ideal, directly proportional, and that's it. Whatever age we are!"[17]

"I remember still, it had happened, in fact, with the father of some of us, that, operating on him, there were complications, so I re-operated... complication... I re-operated.... We went forward for almost a year, and then he died. I could never get over this. Never. One day, I was coming out of the meeting of leaders. I was there in the hall, and Giussani came up and said, 'How's it going?' I said, 'Not bad.' He said, 'What do you mean, not bad? What's going on?' I said, 'No, stupid things. After what we were just saying in that meeting, these are stupid things. Come on, let's go, it doesn't matter.' He stopped all of a sudden. He was really tired but he stopped all of a sudden (in the hallway—where there were people passing by): 'Excuse me, Enzo, with all the stupid things we say to each other, when there is something that really counts, we don't talk about it?' He had me nailed, so I said, 'Sorry, look, but this thing happened and I blame myself a little. In short, I am not able to sleep. That is, I sleep for an hour, then this thing comes into my mind. And even my wife is worried because, after an hour of sleep, I get up, and it goes on like this.' He looked at me and gave me an answer that was the most unexpected thing ever; I couldn't ever have imagined it. He looked at me and said, 'But Enzo, you of all people,' with a disappointed face, 'You of all people act as if Christ did not exist?! It is as if everything depended on your hands. How do you think you can go on like this? You will no longer do the things you do, you will act like everybody else—trying to do what hurts you

---

17. Porto San Giorgio, February 28, 1999.

least, what makes you feel comfortable. You will no longer take any risks.' Then he said, 'Anyway, I want to talk about this again. Can you come as soon as possible?' Of course! Two days later I was there. So we met for lunch and he said, 'Tell it to me again.' 'Listen, Giussani, I don't want to take up your time, because now I understand. There is a little chapel in my hospital and now, before going into the operating room, I go there and say a prayer, and things are coming back together. I am more calm.' He snaps, 'Enzo, what's this about praying?! The problem is not praying; it is that you don't know how to offer.'"[18]

> Everyone has a vanishing point, that moment of truth that on the one hand you seek, and that chases you, looks at you, judging you with mercy; present at night, at work, with friends, in jail, when you thank God and when you want to say something to leave with the one you love. For me, since June 1999, it is on page 12 of the book *'Tu sol pensando o ideal sei vero'* [*Just Thinking of You, Oh Ideal, You Are True*][19]. It was the testimony of Enzo on December 12, 1998, at the Spiritual Exercises of the CLU in Rimini. Can 12 lines mark the path, the life of a man as a continual call, written and readable whenever needed (and how many times they are needed in life!)? Yes. I think this is the miracle of the Church, that a man named Enzo had lived a relationship that was so significant with another man named Luigi, and he gave witness of it to me, and I continue to read to myself and my children those 12 lines in order to understand Who was at the origin of that dialogue Who was called Christ, Whom I didn't meet 2,000 years ago, but have met now through these friends. If someone may have forgotten those 12 lines, this is what they say: "Enzo, what's this about praying! The problem is not praying, it is that you don't know how to offer. Your problem is that you don't know how to offer, and offering means that reality is not something you hold in your hands, it is not yours, and that everything one does is as if it had within it a desire that the Lord, master of this reality, reveal Himself, because this is how one lives, and you,

---

18. Rimini, December 12, 1998.
19. *Litterae Communionis-Tracce*, 1999 (6).

look (I told you, but I will tell you again), you will stop doing what you do, and you will be afraid to risk." Ultimately, when you have a saint in front of you, you can become a saint in a simple and dramatic manner, by following. And that is what Enzo did. (Antonio Simone)

"And in fact it was true, it was incredibly true. For two months, I had been saying to my two older assistants, 'Guys, enough with these surgeries. We don't need problems. I have a career; the less problems, the better.' Then, continuing the discussion, Giussani said to me ,'Do you know what it means to offer, to recognize that reality is not yours, that you did not make it, that you are not the master of things? It means that you are in front of reality with a poverty that is the truest, most authentic way of being in front of things: you are seriously more realistic, you take things into consideration, you recognize the limits you have. If you do not know, you will ask and you will ask, and you won't have to defend your image, your position.'"[20] "This is the point that allows us to accept it: the circumstance is an occasion. Everything is an occasion and, in a special way, the circumstances that constrain you the most, because they can be lived only by offering them. And 'offering them' means recognizing that they have a meaning even if you don't see it, or if you don't immediately feel it. You can be patient and go forward, embracing them with this tension in your heart. It is right to say that this difficulty makes us grow; it is the only way."[21]

"We can live life (live, not just survive) only if we offer it. How true this is! It happens when we begin to understand that all things are made in this moment, and that a hand is giving them to us right now. That notebook that you have in your hands, that jacket that you are wearing, and, at the same time, widening the field, that friend that you have next to you. It is as if a hand were giving these things to you at this moment. You have to say thank you, because they are not yours, and if you want to possess anything truly, you have to give it back to Him. That is, offer it. No particular is banal,

---

20. Rimini, December 12, 1998.
21. Bologna, May 24, 1992.

Gusto for Life Is Proportional to Your Engagement with the Ideal

if a mysterious but real hand is giving it to you. Imagine what this means between husband and wife, if they begin to think this way when they get up in the morning, or after a fight, but also in the middle of a fight. And imagine what it means with your children. Think what implications it has in the work environment, with your boss who harasses you from morning till evening, but you begin to feel that even he is offered to you. It changes the world, it changes everything. Life has an intensity without compare, an equilibrium without compare. It is the offering, 'You are Lord, not me.' It is foolish to the philosophers and scandalous to the moralists, that God is so close. He is so close that it makes me change the things I have in my hands and the way I carry them. The Mystery emerges perceptibly, becomes an experience, and like a potter begins to shape things and to make life different."[22]

"Let's not think that sitting on both sides of the fence puts our life in order. Let's not start calculating how much time we can give to the Movement, how much to family, how much to work... Come on, stop it! What are you trying to do? Life is not a jigsaw puzzle! Do what God assigns to your life with a single concern: that everything has worth if it is offered to Him!"[23] "How can we live those things that are absurd? How can we live if it is not possible to offer them, that is, to understand that there is something more than what I see? How is it possible to live them?"[24] "For the Christian, the only right attitude in front of the things that happen is offering them to the Lord. Offering them to the Lord means, in concrete terms, handing them over to the companionship we have met. Be faithful, at all costs, to the friendship. Even your solitude will no longer be a problem."[25]

> Twelve days before he died he was in Ferrara, invited by Cardinal Caffarra, for a lesson on the topic, "Living the Church." After the meeting and the dinner with friends from

---

22. March 22, 1995.
23. Porto San Giorgio, February 28, 1999.
24. Bologna, November 21, 1985.
25. Modena, February 22, 1980.

the community that went until late at night, while I accompanied him to his car, he said to me, "Thank you. You are a beautiful community, but always remember that your unity is a gift and must be guarded as such. It is not yours. (Carlo Tellarini)

When he asked me for a judgment on the community and I told him all our "successes" and the things that were going well, he corrected me and said, "It doesn't depend on you! We have to help each other in the things that don't go well; a simple mention of the rest is enough." (Gianpiero Di Febbo)

When a patient or a patient's family members said to Enzo before a surgery, "Doctor, please, we are in your hands!" Enzo always responded, "Don't worry; my team and I will do everything possible. But remember that we are in the hands of Someone else." (Giampaolo Ugolini)

"It is the amazement, the wonder of finding ourselves in front of something great that makes life permeable to grace. The capacity for wonder (as Jean Guitton said in his beautiful little book, *Arte nuova di pensare*)[26] is the first movement of the man who lives. And he compared this experience to someone who leaves the hospital and finds the same air, the same courtyard, the same building as always, but when he leaves the door of the hospital, almost instinctively he says, 'Ah! What freedom!' And yet it is the same thing as before. What happened? He has regained the capacity for awe; it is like he rediscovered something he had desired and didn't have anymore. Our life is like this. If you lose the capacity for wonder—this art of being amazed at what is around you, at what you could never imagine, at the miracle that you are—if you lose this, what taste is left in being alive? The rest is an attentive analysis of your own psychological states, or a hope in some kind of good luck. But it is not life. We care about a new humanity; this new humanity begins with the fact that one starts to understand that there is an immense grace around him, there is a gift, something that has never been his,

---

26. Jean Guitton, *Arte nuova di pensare* [*The New Art of Thinking*], ed. Paoline, Bologna, 1954.

and that he would never have been able to create. To think of ourselves like this... life begins to change, because when you understand that life is a gift, that you do not give it to yourself, you understand right away that to save your life means to give it. Its nature as a gift remains if life is given back again, not calculated or held tight."[27]

"The one who lives like this is certain, secure, because everything that he has as security is something he has received, that happened, that was given to him. I couldn't be secure if I had created it myself, because I know that one day I feel it and the next day I don't; one day I'm okay and the next day I'm not. Instead, what I believe in, what I base my life on, is a gift! You can't get more secure than this... It is a fact of life. You can't get more secure than this! I have received everything. What I am, I have received—everything! I am certain of this."[28]

Offering, gift, gratuitousness... To put these three dimensions together is like making our humanity explode, but above all it is what can convince us not to spare even one comma, not to hold anything for ourselves, not to defend anything. It is what makes us understand the advantage of "totality." This had become the style of Enzo, of his embraced person. It was the aspect that most struck those who encountered him. And it was no longer just a matter of temperament; it was a new face, it was the profile shaped in him by the embrace to whom he had given himself. Totally.

> It is difficult for me to talk about Enzo. It always was ever since, after he went to Heaven, I was called, on various occasions, to talk about him. The source of my discomfort is the sense of "unattainability" that I always felt around him. And there were so many occasions to be close to him. At the end of the '70s, before Father Giussani decided to send me to Rome, he wanted me to go to Modena to be close to Enzo. We had important conversations with the bishop of that time. Everything seemed to have been worked out. Then, other considerations intervened that changed my little personal story. But in the meantime, for close to a year or

---

27. Bologna, October 5, 1988.
28. Riccione, December 16, 1998.

maybe more, I came to Modena on many occasions. Enzo wanted me to meet his friends. These were unique moments, very simple, mostly around a table at dinner, with salami and strong wine. I was impressed by the beauty and the strength of the friendship Enzo had with his young people—a pact for life. Within that simplicity, there was the demanding presence of Enzo, gruff and smiling, with an attention to the particulars that was all his own, and also very like Giussani. He appeared to me like a teacher, a rigorous father, an educator. He was not yet the Enzo of Bologna, the one who would create a very numerous people, whose flourishing we still enjoy in their children and grandchildren. It was a sonship that was beginning, but that already showed its totality. It was precisely this totality that scared me. I thought, "How will I keep up with him?" I was concerned: "Will I always understand him? And when I do not agree?" I knew many saints in heaven, but I struggled to recognize the saints on earth. (Bishop Massimo Camisasca)

Before talking about a particular episode, I have to underline the impression that Enzo made on me from the very first encounter. I was struck by his blazing temperament and by his dedication to Jesus without ifs or buts, as well as his indomitable commitment that led him to take on a pace of life that was almost humanly unthinkable. His death itself happened like a total offering of self to the living God, Whom he loved with all his strength. The memory of his person remains very alive in me, starting from 1991, when I became bishop of Grosseto. Then our relationship intensified, thanks to him. He often came with a group of university friends with questions and observations on the life of the Church and on the way Father Giussani's charism could implement the announcement of Christ starting from a belonging without reserve to the community. When, on the morning of May 26, 1999, the news of his passing reached me, I happened to be at the Vatican, and felt the urgency to go to Saint Peter's for a prayer. It was there that I understood that Enzo's death, beyond the pain of his family and of the whole companionship of Communion and Liberation, would not be a loss. The time that passes, as well as your work and the cause of his beatification, demonstrate this. (Cardinal Angelo Scola)

I participated in so many meetings where Enzo spoke, told stories, gave witnesses, explained, responded to questions and requests, had conversations, got angry, embraced those in front of him with his eyes, with his words, with the movement of his hands... He embraced, understood, contemplated even those who were not present, those who were there once, those who would arrive next... His voice grew, reared up, and with it the whole world and the universe rose up behind that fire that blazed and blazed. When Enzo spoke, moved, played, laughed, shouted... he did not just direct himself, first of all and above all, to those present—or to himself—but to something and Someone greater than him and all of us. (Silvio Cattarina)

In the first days of July, he had the regional leader give me an invitation to the International Assembly of CL, that would take place in August. I had already organized a vacation in Sardinia for myself, and so I let him know that I would not be participating. In September, he came to Abruzzo and so we met. In addition to the epithet of "bourgeois," he confronted me, as was his style, in a lively verbal "clash." I could see clearly, though, in him and later also in myself, the pain for one of "his own" who had decided to live for less than everything, for less than happiness, for less than the human glory of Christ! (Gianpiero Di Febbo)

I did not speak, because I was the youngest person there. As soon as we got up from the table, he stopped me, putting himself in front of me as if to block my path. He asked me with a serious and almost regretful face, "Why do you hold back?" (Alessandro Vato)

Once I told him I was very tired and he told me, "Of course! The slogan for the *Pavesini* cookie advertisements is true: *The one who loves burns!* Don't be afraid to burn up." (Silvia Poisetti)

The radicality of faith with which Enzo faced every situation was the aspect that struck Father Giussani himself: "Therefore, the most melancholic thing, the saddest thing, are the people who are forced, or invited, or give in to the suggestion to give their life for something less. It is the great lie of the world. Once, the telephone rang in the morning, at my house on Via Martinengo. I picked up the phone: 'Ciao, it's Enzo,' with a voice… 'What's going on, Enzo?'—'You know, I'm here and I'm scared to death'—'What happened?'—'I did a surgery and I, when I operate, don't see anything else anymore, I don't notice anything anymore, not my wife, my children, my friends…. I don't think of anything else (and lately, I can barely follow you and say, "I offer it to you, Lord"). So I operated on this person who was sick with AIDS. I did the whole operation well. I was ready to close him up, and I saw that there was a stitch I could have done better. So, in the moment, I did not reflect anymore and I tried to do it better, and I poked myself. So now it could happen to me.' For four years it was like this, without anyone knowing, not even his wife and children—he spent four years scared to death. But this is beautiful! And Enzo is a simple leader of the Movement, the visitor for central Italy, center-north-east!—'And also Puglia'—Also Puglia? Anyway, this is beautiful! In that moment, he gave his life; he would have given his life for something true. Otherwise, he would not have nurtured his total dedication to his work! We need to have total dedication to our work, because our dedication to our work is our dedication to the design of God."[29]

JOY IS THE FEELING OF BEING ON THE RIGHT PATH

"He was at dinner with his friends. These are the most beautiful chapters in John, the testament of Christ. He was at dinner with his friends. He knew that He was going to die, that in a little while He was going to die. What kind of courage and awareness must He have had, saying to his friends that He would give them his testament, what He had most loved and understood and wanted for

---

29. Luigi Giussani, *Affezione e dimora* [*Affection and Home*], Rizzoli, Milan, 2001, pp. 433-434 (translation: ours).

Himself, and therefore for all those who followed Him, and He says it like this: 'I have told you everything I have told you so that my joy may be in you, and your joy may be complete.' (*John* 15:11) It is extraordinary to think about this. This work that awaits us and therefore this commitment is for a joy, the joy of living."[30] "I deeply believe that the ideal we have, the Christian fact, is the only thing able to keep life in play always and totally, never to allow the game to be played less. Your sufferings will grow, and you will walk away with a wounded heart, but it doesn't matter because your head is high."[31] "Joy is the feeling of being on the right path. Christ says so, in this antiphon from the Ambrosian liturgy: 'The world will notice the glory of my power through the joy of their hearts.' Joy is the discovery of being on the right path, on the right path that makes us discover what the world, instead, wants to reduce in us. So it's right, my friends, for sure."[32]

"The dogma of hell... if it did not exist, we would have to create it. We would not be able to understand that we are free, if it is not possible to say a total no to the Creator. He is the only One I know, in every possible and imaginable history, Who has truly loved, that is, created another in His image and likeness, allowing him to say no to the One who created him. Find me something else like this! Try finding even among yourselves a freedom like this!"[33]

> Enzo accompanied my personal and professional vocation, helping me find my path, and he never took sides for one choice or another. (Pietro Lorenzetti)

> I met Enzo the first time in November 1986 in Siena, in the city center, in a hall filled with university students. Some friends had invited me, but I could never have imagined running into, hearing, and seeing (Enzo was one you had to "see") such burning passion. I am certain, though, that it would have remained only a blurry memory of a particular

---

30. Bologna, October 17, 1993.
31. Bari, February 13, 1997.
32. Bologna, November 22, 1986.
33. February 23, 1995.

encounter, if a girl had not come up to him and shouted in his face, "You can't say that Christ is the truth! You can say that he is your truth, but not that he is the truth. Who the hell do you think you are?" Enzo responded decisively but without rejecting her, "I repeat to you that Christ is the truth, and I ask you to go to the depth of your path, of what you believe, of your ideas. To the depth, though! To its extreme consequences, as I have done, with loyalty, and I am sure that we will find each other again." And he added, "I have done it, and am doing it. Are you in? If you want, I am in for you, too." Everyone around was distracted and was trickling out. I was transfixed by him, stuck there in my place. Enzo didn't want to convince her. I would have expected a sea of perfect, logical citations that would have left her speechless, or that would have repaid her with equal rudeness, and instead no, just the opposite. "I have met a true man," I said a few hours later on the phone with my father. I still didn't know why I had said "a true man," but, in time, I understood and relished it. Enzo never left anyone alone. I had never seen such freedom! (Francesco Prioglio)

At the end of university, having just graduated, Enzo proposed a job to me: to go to work in Rome in preparation for the Jubilee in the year 2000. Partly because the stereotype of an economics graduate that was popular around the halls of my university didn't seem to correspond to that proposal, partly because I saw the thing as too open-ended, without a precise direction, and short-term... in short, I didn't like the proposal. I told Enzo no, trying to explain all these things, and he came back asserting that Rome is Rome, that one thing is born from another, one relationship is born from another, etc., etc. After a few days, I thought about it again and, more out of the displeasure at having told him no than because I was convinced, as soon as possible I went to him and told him that I had thought about it again. On that occasion too, his answer amazed me. I don't remember the exact words, but in substance he told me that I had already said no, and now it was too late. I was disappointed there, too;,but I quickly understood something good. I don't know if things were really how I am about to say, but I think that Enzo understood that he had to let me do what I wanted;

not that he agreed, but I had the perception that he thought this was the best path for me, and for this reason was ready to 'sacrifice' even the project he had. (Andrea Pagliarani)

I had started working in the university, but had been abandoned by the professor to whom I was apprenticed, who had turned to politics. Anyone who lives in the academic world in Italy knows that, without a 'boss,' you don't go forward in your career. It was hard, without any prospects, as well as a starvation wage. I had had a very interesting job offer that brought with it also an improved financial picture. So I went to Enzo to tell him everything about the work I was doing and the proposal I had received, to ask him for his judgment. Enzo answered right away, categorically, "No, you have to stay at the university." To my objections about the situation I was living (it was objectively a dead end), he answered, "You still haven't gone to the depths of your experience of work in the university," explaining to me that to go elsewhere would be to avoid the circumstance God was giving me, and therefore to betray my vocation. So I asked him, "Excuse me, Enzo, many people have come to you asking the same question and you told them to go. Why are you saying no only to me?" He responded, "Because the other ones had already decided; they only wanted a stamp of approval. You came truly to ask, and I felt free to tell you what is best, not for me, but for you." (Raffaello Vignali)

I HAVE TAKEN YOU AS MINE AND I PLACE YOU IN THE MIDST OF ALL THE PEOPLES

"This community inherits that great conception that belonged to the Jewish people, a chosen people, willed by God, made holy because God had taken them to Himself, and in this it generates an otherworldly revolution. It makes this tradition its own, not basing it on ethnic belonging as the Jewish people did. The early Christians came together only because of the common interest they had for Christ. They were brought together because of the relationship they had with Christ; therefore, men and women find themselves together. This initial community went outside the confines of one nation, one ethnicity, and embraced all those who accepted the name of Christ as true for their lives. There were no longer differences of politics, culture, or sex."[34]

"Holiness makes clear the first characteristic of the tradition that Christians inherit and fulfill. It is not moral conduct, because they betray a hundred thousand times. Holiness makes clear the initiative that God takes with some people (and in that case with a particular people), preferring them to others and putting them in the world as His instruments, in service to Him, so that the whole world may recognize Him. This community, therefore, inherits the awareness of being holy not through its own capacity, but through a choice it receives, God's choice of the people who compose it. *Sanctus* [holy] means 'separated,' 'sanctioned,' 'detached from.' Holy means this, first of all. 'I have taken you as Mine and I place you in the midst of all the people, so that they may see My glory.'"[35]

"So that Christ may appear as everything in everyone, so that the glory of Christ may appear as the form and content of everything, there is a choice or election, made by God, by the Mystery, by the Father. Outside of this choice or election, there can only be the reality of a crowd of tramps, of beggars, who collect the crumbs that fall from the children's table, exactly as the Canaanite woman said: even the dogs can feed on the crumbs that fall from the children's table (*Matthew* 15:27)."[36]

> We are such people that one just needs a glance at us to know what happened to us together. And Enzo had understood what was happening. Like the others around him, who argued with him, worked with him. It was Christianity that was happening. Like at the beginning, identical to the beginning. Not even Christianity as a cultural phenomenon, but it was Jesus Christ happening among us, thanks to the gaze of Father Giussani on life and the gaze of the other saints.

---

34. Florence, March 18, 1987.

35. Bologna, February 14, 1993.

36. Luigi Giussani, *Il tempo e il tempio* [*Time and the Temple*], Rizzoli, Milan, 1994, p. 14 (translation: ours).

The saints, for the first Christians, were not those who were perfect, but those taken by Him, His companions on the road, the living members of the community. Enzo, a saint; Father Ricci, a saint; Father Ciccio, a saint; Father Giacomo, a saint; Luigino, a saint; Father Fabio, a saint; Emilia, a saint. And the others who are still alive, saints because given to me by Jesus. I saw Christ happening, with all the holiness and the human ambiguity of the beginning, with all the strange and revolutionary weight of the most incredible news in the world. (Davide Rondoni)

"It is in doing what you were called to do (the most incredible Christian word for defining the person is called 'vocation,' that is, someone who calls you, even if you are here for the first time), the grace of God reduces these 'buts,' these doubts, these 'ifs.'"[37]

A few years after that first encounter, around 10 years, unexpectedly he had someone search for me and gave me a private meeting in Udine. I had to wait a long time and, when he entered, without losing time, after fixing his eyes on me, he said, "I am looking for men who love Christ more than their own lives." (Francesco Prioglio)

For me, it was the so-called "moment of transition" before the imminent beginning of my career. Discussion, exchange of ideas, stories, then our days together ended. Enzo started off again, getting in the car, but after 50 meters he stopped, drove backwards, pulled up next to me, rolled down the window and said: "Go, don't worry, we are all with you!" At a certain point he stopped, looked me straight in the eyes, literally seeing with his gaze the unease that I was living, and told me, "You have to live what happened to Jacob, who wrestled the whole night with the Mystery, getting crippled in the end, and thus carrying the mark of this struggle for his whole life. The mark of Christian life as a continual struggle." (Paolo Datore)

Forty years ago, at the end of an assembly at the university in Ferrara, where there were just a dozen university students present in an empty hall, after his heated exposition,

---

37. Bologna, April 21, 1991.

which would have merited a packed hall, he left with just one observation: instead of complaining about the few people that we had brought to the encounter, he corrected me brusquely about the inconsistent and taken-for-granted tone with which I had given the announcements in the last two minutes. Then he dragged me to the best restaurant in Ferrara to drink whisky and, looking me in the eye with his decisive tone after having me tell him who I was and where I came from, he said, "If you want to be with me, you have to leave everything that you have—the nun you meet with regularly and your friends from GS. You have to stay with us and that's it." (Carlo Tellarini)

One day, I was humanly in pieces, I don't even remember why—probably a disordered relationship with some girlfriend was damning me—when the phone rang. "Malfo, this is Enzo. (silence)... How are you?" For the first time in my life, I answered, "Shitty!" I had never been sincere like that in front of a question so common and so true. I had always responded to whomever, "Great, awesome, fantastic..." But to Enzo, to his disruptive phone call, I simply responded with my "I"! (Francesco Malfitano)

"We do everything and we get involved without an ultimate handing over of ourselves. And so every action, even the most perfect, is ultimately disappointing. Handing ourselves over means that what I am is wanted and loved, and I am in front of a reality through which it is possible to understand that God loves me. So a woman who is in the home all day lives those moments with dignity, or a man who commits himself and then the world crumbles in his hands—they live those moments with dignity, not because they are strong, or good, or capable, no! They live so because they are ultimately handing themselves over. And this handing over is not a formula, a certain modality of commitment. It is the thought that comes to you, a flash, while you are there opening the car door when you leave in the morning: 'Lord, I offer you this.' But it's not like it even needs to be said. And everything acquires the place it should acquire, returns to the right place."[38]

---

38. Bologna, May 24, 1992.

"It is very clear to me that everything I am I have received; all has been given to me. Therefore, there is a gratitude that I cannot escape."[39]

"Therefore, in the end, it is a gratitude. As I began, so I want to finish: it is a gratitude that characterizes my life. Therefore, I am not afraid to give it all."[40]

---

39. Rimini, December 12, 1998.
40. Rimini, December 12, 1998.

12.

The Day After

> "Amen, amen, I say to you, unless a grain of wheat falls to the ground and dies, it remains just a grain of wheat; but if it dies, it produces much fruit."
>
> —John 12:24

WEDNESDAY MORNING, MAY 26, 1999, I WAS ON A TRAIN. I was going up to Milan to teach my lesson in music history at the high school of the Sacro Cuore Foundation.[1] Enzo had suggested that I combine this work with the work on the Spirto Gentil collection.[2] My phone rang. It was Macio, president of the CUSL Cooperative. We hadn't spoken in a while, because it had been many years

---

1. The Sacro Cuore (Sacred Heart) Foundation of Milan is a recognized private school, born in 1985 from the educational charism of Father Luigi Giussani. With more than 1,200 students and 100 teachers, the Foundation offers a complete educational track, from preschool, to elementary school, up until middle school and three high schools (classical, scientific, and artistic lyceum).

2. In May 1997, Father Giussani accepted the proposal of directing a musical collection as an "introduction to music" dedicated to the works and the composers dearest to him, and that over the years he had made known to the followers of Communion and Liberation during assemblies, meetings, and spiritual exercises. The collection produced 52 CDs with written commentary by Giussani, and were widely appreciated throughout Italy and around the world.

The Day After

since he graduated. I picked up, wondering about a phone call at that hour, and I heard him, totally out of control, "Widmer, listen. I'm not joking." He repeated to me five or six times, "I'm not joking..." Why would I ever think that? "The highway police called me. An accident happened to the Cooperative car last night. Whoever was at the wheel died, and they are not able to identify the driver because the car went up in flames." I hung up quickly and started to check with people. I called Daniela, the secretary, and asked if she knew anything about Enzo. Nothing. I asked her to try his home, to call Fiorisa, to see if Enzo had returned home. He had not. But even this happened sometimes. When he was really tired, Enzo went to sleep directly at the Sant'Orsola Hospital in Bologna. I called Alberto Savorana, and I told him how things were, and asked what we should do. We waited.

I arrived at Sacro Cuore and went to the office of Father Giorgio Pontiggia.[3] I said, "I'm sorry; I can't do my lesson this morning." I explained to him the reason, in tears. We were there together for a few hours. The hope that things might be different was growing slimmer. Then the confirmation arrived: the driver was Enzo. We went to the chapel and said a prayer, then to Father Giussani's home in Gudo. He wanted to speak to us. I had never thought that one could hope under the cross. I thought that one could do so only after it had passed, or when there was at least a hint of its passing— not "during." I hardly remember anything Giussani told us; only this perception of hope remains indelible.

> After Enzo's funeral, which took place in Bologna, I had to go back to Gudo right away for a meeting with the Memores Domini and, given that I was so sad, I went to say hello to Father Giussani, who lived there. He was in the living room of his house. I cried and he also cried. I told him, "Father Gius, I've lost a father," and Gius answered, "And I've lost a son." Then he stopped crying and said, "Enzo was all that I ever wanted to be. You know the difference between

---

3. Father Giorgio Pontiggia (who died in 2009) was then Rector of the Sacro Cuore Foundation. He was a great educator. A friend of Father Giussani, he founded Portofranco, a free tutoring center that has spread throughout Italy.

me and you? It is that now I am certain that Enzo is more alive than before, and you are not. But if you pray every day to have his faith, you will realize it, and will become like him. But you have to ask for his faith, not his image (the cars, the kilometers, etc.)." (Giovanni Maddalena)

In the afternoon, we moved to the CL headquarters in Milan, on Via Porpora, and Fiorisa and the children Pietro, Maria, and Anna Rita arrived (Chiara, in those days, was in Beijing). I think that none of us was able to comprehend what was happening, to make sense of it, to take it simply into consideration. Those words that he had spoken five months earlier in front of 7,000 university students resonated: "It is a gratitude that characterizes my life. Therefore, I am not afraid to give it all." No one could have imagined the prophetic force of that phrase.

Other words of his resonated in our minds that none of us could have imagined would describe literally his earthly trajectory: "A humble and certain boldness, but not founded on the self. It is founded on the grace that was given us of a Presence that will never fail. And then I would like to conclude reading a prayer of Father de Grandmaison that seems to me the best synthesis of this meeting: 'Holy Mary, Mother of God, preserve in me the heart of a child, pure and clear like spring water; a simple heart—hear how centered it is, psychologically and humanly—that does not remain absorbed in its own sadness; a heart generous in giving itself, quick to feel compassion; a faithful and generous heart, that forgets no favor and holds no grudge. Give me a humble, gentle heart, that loves without asking to be loved in return, happy to lose itself in the heart of others, sacrificing itself in front of you Divine Son; a great and unconquerable heart, which no ingratitude can close and no indifference can tire; a heart tormented by the glory of Christ, pierced by His love, with a wound that will not heal until heaven.'"[4]

Giussani quickly wrote a letter to the whole Movement throughout the world:

---

4. Bologna, April 21, 1991.

The Day After

While returning to Modena after a day working as a highly esteemed surgeon, and after coming to Milan for a meeting of CLU leaders, Enzo, we don't know how, ran off the road and was killed in a terrible accident.

Deeply grieved, I ask every CL community in Italy and in the world to join together to say a Mass to pray to God to allow us to inherit his same faith.

This is certainly the greatest grief that God has sent as a trial for all of our Fraternity at this time, because Enzo was a man who, from the moment of intuition he had in a dialogue with me 30 years ago, said his "Yes" to Christ with an astounding devotion, intelligent and total in outlook, and he dedicated his life completely to Christ and His Church. The most impressive thing to me is that his commitment to Christ was so all-encompassing that no day passed when he did not seek in every way the human glory of Jesus Christ.

What does the mystery of God ask of us in a trial like this of great suffering? It asks us to always remember Christ as the meaning of life, at all levels and in all fields: "Christ is all in everyone."

Thus it becomes clearer to us, as time passes, that salvation, that is, the positive affirmation of being, always involves as a condition the cross: *Ave crux, spes unica* [Hail to the cross, our only hope].

We pray to the Virgin, who long before us went through a similar trial, that his wife Fiorisa and children Chiara, Pietro, Maria, and Anna Rita be as true as he was.

Our friend Alberto, returning from America with the joy of reporting to everyone the depth of our charism, witnessed also by the most recent great assembly at the UN, as he got off the plane received the first phone call from Widmer, announcing to him the very sad news, and his response to the contradiction inherent in the history of all men was: 'Cross and Resurrection.' Grief would not be reasonable, if it were not redeemed in the affirmation of Christ.

This, my friends, remains, in any case the contradiction which nothing in the world can resolve. Only in faith in Christ is there the possibility for the peace and joy which the mystery of His Resurrection gives us in Him.

> Thus we ask also Enzo to help us remember all of this, before the world assails our heart and destroys in it all positiveness and thus all hope.
> I write to you as to friends.
>
> Father Giussani
Milan, May 26, 1999

We returned to Bologna and we met continually with the leaders. It was difficult even to comprehend the weight of the events that happened. It was up to us now to witness to what Enzo had taught us in so many tragic situations that we had faced together. We would have never expected to have to repeat for him the indications that he had taught us in front of the death of so many friends. We began to take care of all the particulars. We set up the funeral chapel in the crypt of San Vitale and Agricola, which he loved so much, the beating heart of Christianity in Bologna, where we met to pray with the Fraternity. People arrived from all across Italy and the world. The funeral procession to the Basilica of Saint Petronius stopped at the heart of the city. Thousands of people participated—friends, patients, colleagues, regular people. The Basilica was packed (it is one of the biggest in the world). Cardinal Biffi, in the homily, spoke as if to a friend:

> We are dismayed here in front of this very dear brother of ours, snatched away suddenly by a pitiless fate that in one blow cut off a precious and intense life, snuffing out in an instant a patrimony of extraordinary humanity, spiritual richness, unreserved giving, plans, and high purpose. My soul too is troubled and suffers for the loss of a friend, the friend of days of rest and serenity and of days of work and commitment, of days animated and comforted by our shared ideal of active witness to Christ and belonging to the same Church, and of days intent on and directed toward the best possible service to the Kingdom of God mysteriously present in history. The souls of all of us are troubled, and we spontaneously want to demand of the Lord—who nonetheless did tell us that He wants to come sometimes like a thief in the night—an account of this death, which we experience as a theft, a robbery that has ripped into lasting and profound

affections, that has plunged many of us into a grief that won't go away. [...] God knows the roads that bring the life of his own to a more ample and decisive fertility, and transforms our pains into redeeming energy for the benefit of all our brothers. Persuaded of this, the apostle Paul can daringly write, 'It makes me happy to be suffering for you now, and in my own body to make up all the hardships that still have to be undergone by Christ for the sake of his body, the Church.' (*Col*. 1:24) Today we lay into this Emilian earth the mortal body of our friend Enzo. We lay him there as a seed, that is, as a promise and a certainty of invigorated and expanding vitality for the groups of Communion and Liberation, for all this people of ours, for the entire human family.

Cardinal Giacomo Biffi
May 29, 1999

I was the last friend to see Enzo alive. After the meeting of the central diaconia of the Movement in Milan, we went out to eat like so many other times, at a restaurant that they called "The Egyptian's," close to Via Porpora, where those meetings with Father Giussani were held. Discussions, discoveries, I was the youngest one, I looked, spoke out, learned. I saw him again putting his bag in the trunk of the car and saying goodbye to us, between 11 p.m. and midnight, I think. I left a few minutes earlier, a few minutes earlier I had passed that point on the highway where he flew away. The dinner together, and "Ciao Enzo, see you later," and we left. You shouldn't have flown away, I should have. But that's how it went, God knows, and ciao Enzo, holy teacher and friend, yes, we'll see each other soon. (Davide Rondoni)

The days went by. A little at a time, we started living again; we had to live, almost out of obedience. A little at a time we start to understand the enormity of what had happened. And a little at a time we saw signs of a particular development of this tragedy; we saw, here and there, unusual signs. The first to notice them was his daughter Maria, who wrote a message to her friends in Milan (where she studied) in which the death of her father had a particular, strange character. It was a death that did not signal an end, but a beginning—an intuition that caught me unawares.

The first person who then spoke to me was Giussani, telling me (with an unexpected positivity—he loved Enzo like a son) that my father would remain forever, and even more than before, and would do greater works than he did in life. Now I have the impression, thinking again about many particulars, that everything seemed meticulously prepared for his death. Everything: the friends he had around him at work, at the university, in the Movement, and in the family. Even the garden, which he particularly loved, had, so to speak, reached perfection. We have to tell everyone what happened, as I said to my classmates, "Come down here, because miracles are happening!" It is clearer now than ever what my father said at his last *Equipe*:[5] Friendship is mission." (Maria Piccinini)[6]

Another fact found me unprepared as well, a few weeks later. In agreement with Father Giussani, I went to visit Cardinal Biffi. Certainly, my state of mind still had not recovered; I had not much more than a remotely hidden hope that miracles could happen. I wrote Giussani a very depressing "report" of my visit: the cardinal had given me the impression of an "abandoned factory" (he, who had defined us as a "great construction site"), maybe because he had told me that the task of his generation was coming to an end. A few days later, I was hurrying to leave for the summer vacation of the CLU (almost a thousand university students to guide) and I took a look at the mailbox and noticed an envelope. I opened it and my eyes fell on the signature: Father Luigi Giussani (I remember Enzo saying that Giussani never wrote to him...). I read:

> Dearest Widmer, thank you very much for telling me about your meeting with Cardinal Biffi. The task of his generation is not finished, and the "abandoned factory" has within itself an infinite number of stone quarries from which Enzo, with the strength of the Spirit, will tear out the pieces of rock necessary to rebuild the Church that the passivity or lack

---

5. The "Equipe" is a moment of work proposed to the national leaders of the CLU that takes place at different times throughout the year, normally in Milan, but also in the mountains, during the time of summer vacations.

6. June 2, 1999.

of intelligence, the small heart of many Christians, has not been able to use. Enzo will make you all capable of renewing the strength that God has given you to recreate in the world the continual glory of Jesus. Dear Widmer, I hope that God gives me time to speak to you about the dramatic beginnings of your service to God and, therefore, to the world.

Luigi Giussani

"Pieces of rock necessary to rebuild... to recreate in the world the continual glory of Jesus." It is difficult to take note of all the facts that happened connected to Enzo from that May 26th. Certainly, other books will be written. Some facts, though, happened right away. Not sensational facts, but decisive ones for those who kept that simplicity of gaze that Enzo witnessed to us for years.

A few moments after the news of his death, I, who at that time was the oldest one in the group, had to go to make the rounds in the department and to communicate to all of his, all of "our" patients (Enzo wanted us to look at all the patients as if they were our "personal" patients) what had happened. One patient, who had been operated on by Enzo, seeing us so weighed down and shocked, told us in a totally unexpected manner, "Guys, I understand that you are sad, but now you have a great responsibility! I have gone to many hospitals, I have undergone many operations and, beyond the positive outcome of the surgery that Doctor Piccinini did on me, I wanted to tell you that I have never seen a group of doctors and nurses work together in this way, with such a peaceful climate among you, and so right for us patients (both professionally and humanly). To be cared for in a place like this is what every patient desires. I ask you not to stop working in this way, and it would be beautiful if each of you could go to a different hospital and begin to build something similar!" A little while ago, then, I received this letter from the son of a patient we had operated on: "What struck me above all was your capacity to look at my mom, my dad, and me. A gaze that was not yours. This is evident from the fact that you, Isacco, and Davide are very different, but this gaze is embedded in your DNA. I remember clearly when you hugged my dad, and he came back so moved by that embrace, so much so that in that day of suffering, the embrace for him was 'the thing' that dominated, more than the second surgery and the pain of my mother." (Giampaolo Ugolini)

We had just finished our third year of high school when, in the summer of 1997, a few friends and I went for the first time to a meeting held by Enzo. We already attended GS with a certain enthusiasm, but what happened there was something totally new and unexpected. He spoke about friendship, romantic relationships, the ideal, and so much else, but the things that struck me the most were the force of life and the unity of his person. All that he was saying to us was a gift that was so concrete… It was impossible to perceive it as abstract, because it was there, in front of us, alive, in his person. We began to go to meet him every time he came to the Adriatic Coast around Rimini. We were so happy; we had found a friend, a guide, a gaze on reality that we all immediately desired. On May 26, 1999, as I was leaving school, the news of his death reached me. I got home, I closed myself in my room, and began to cry desperately. A long and inconsolable cry. The longest and most inconsolable that I had ever experienced as an adult; a cry for a person I had known a little more than a year, and met only a few times, but who had sparked something extraordinary in me, an "impossible possibility": that life could be lived in such a full manner, so intensely, truly, passionately, like I could never have imagined before. That year, I went to Bologna to study economics and there, with different faces, the encounter I had had a few years earlier was renewed. I see happening to others what happened to me and my friends when we went to meet him at the exit of his clinic: people moving, elbowing like children, attracted by a presence that was filling their lives with gusto. The life of the university, the studies, the friendships, the romantic relationships, everything was lived within that relationship. I saw that anything I kept for myself, anything I did not open to that life, was dying in my hands. And so, slowly, joyfully, I started to give everything. I remember as if it was yesterday when a friend asked me to start working for CUSL. "It's not for me," I said, "all my friends are somewhere else; they do other beautiful things and I want to be with them." "The problem of life," the friend answered, "is the ideal horizon for which you do everything. The only thing that makes a difference in life is this ideal." (Giovanni Pirozzi)

Seven years after the death of Enzo, Carras, his close friend, came to Columbia to meet me, because Enzo had left him the task of staying with me when he visited people of the Movement in South America. I had been estranged from the Movement and this outreach of friendship brought me back into the Church. (Aureliano Palmieri)

For reasons connected to a serious illness of my wife, I met so many of his friends from the community in Bologna where, together with my family, I found welcome and support for a long period. Here, there was the great surprise of finding a community of people truly marked by their relationship with him. They had, that is, assimilated, in so many years of life together, his gaze of faith, of openness, and of charity toward one's neighbor. (Giuseppe Policardo)

I asked myself after his death how it was possible that a man with a demanding job and four children could have time and desire for one like me, and the best answer I found was in Alberto Savorana's book, *The Life of Luigi Giussani* (I cite it as I remember it): "God is one who comes to pick you up with a teaspoon." That is, you are down at the bottom, dissolved, and God, in my case through Enzo, picked me up drop by drop, putting me all back together. Today, I have a predilection for the "losers." When I coach, I like to pick the worst ones and help them win; I like the excluded ones, the rejected ones, the delinquents, the ugly ones, those whom nobody loves. I have been volunteering for a little while in a jail, and I am moved every time I enter. Thanks to what happened to me with Enzo, I feel that those people are closer to me than so many successful people who have everything in life but no longer desire anything. (Gabriele Donati)

I have been a teacher for 30 years, and it happens that the parents thank me for the dedication with which I do my work, or for the attention that I pay to their children. I always say, even if they don't understand, that I am like this because I had an encounter in my life that changed it, and gave me the capacity to do those things that they recognize in me, but that are not mine. (Francesca Astorri)

For me, Enzo is not dead. I don't want to sound like a pseudo-theologian giving a speech, but what he followed and what probably made him do, in his availability, what he did, is still alive and well. In short, God has not left me alone. (Gabriele Donati)

Afterword

THIS BOOK HAS TOLD A HUMAN STORY—AN EXTRAORDINARY story, in many respects, but, in so far as it is human, a story that has a precise beginning and ending. Such are all human facts.

Still, after 25 years, after all these things that have been told, the category "human story" is too narrow to define the temporal arc of the life of Doctor Enzo Piccinini. "It is, if it works,"[1] Father Giussani always repeated to us. That is to say, something is real, is living, if it influences reality now, so much so that someone who runs into it is led to ask, "What is the energy that moves these people now, and makes them so special, so united, even while they are so different?"

The category of "recollection" is very human. And being very human, it shares with human nature the same destiny, which is that it has an expiration date. Memory (as we have been taught) is different from recollection, because it is capable of changing the present with methods that are recognizable and can be traced back to their historical origin.

The human trajectory of Enzo Piccinini has the characteristics of certain phenomena that are structured, that are implanted within a continuity that is alive, living, with an exceptional vitality, that precedes them and exceeds their limits. It is a story that presents unmistakable traits, because it infuses life into life, making it an inexhaustible energy. Enzo has gone to take his place in this "unnatural" curvature of time:

---

1. Luigi Giussani, "È se opera" ["It Is If It Work"s], *30 Giorni*, 1993.

Afterword

> Then came, at a predetermined moment, a moment in time and of time,
> A moment not out of time, but in time, in what we call history: transecting, bisecting the world of time, a moment in time but not like a moment of time,
> A moment in time but time was made through that moment: for without the meaning there is no time, and that moment of time gave the meaning.
> Then it seemed as if men must proceed from light to light, in the light of the Word,
> Through the Passion and Sacrifice saved in spite of their negative being;
> Bestial as always before, carnal, self-seeking as always before, selfish and purblind as ever before,
> Yet always struggling, always reaffirming, always resuming their march on the way that was lit by the light;
> Often halting, loitering, straying, delaying, returning, yet following no other way. (T.S. Eliot)[2]

Enzo has gone to take a position in this inexplicable, "unnatural" process, in which "time, which for everyone is synonymous with decay, works positively,"[3] to the point of breaking down its natural constraints:

> *Mors et vita duello conflixere mirando:*
> *dux vitae mortuus, regnat vivus.*
>
> Death and life have contended in that combat stupendous:
> the Prince of life, who died, reigns immortal.[4]

On April 3, 2017, Giorgia Galasso was in the car with my son and would not return from that trip. I had not yet had the occasion of meeting her parents; her death introduced us to each other. It was a strange death. It went against nature. What, by definition, should separate, united, inexplicably, going against the current of the torment.

---

2. T.S. Eliot, *Choruses from "The Rock,"* https://www.poetrynook.com/poem/choruses-ôç£the-rockôçø.

3. Rimini, December 12, 1998.

4. From the Roman Missal, Easter Sequence.

Afterword

I asked Diana, Giorgia's mother, to read these pages while I wrote them. She was the only one to do so, because (as I had told her), "I need someone who does not know these things to tell me what works." I wanted to know the impact these pages would have on someone who didn't know Enzo, Father Giussani, or the Movement of Communion and Liberation, because this book was written for those who don't know, and for those who, while knowing, have maintained the only true virtue, a childlike naivete that makes you welcome as new what you think you already know.

Diana's comments are a confirmation of this unnatural curvature of time for which what is here now explains what has been, and what has been explains what is here now, and they explain each other with the mysterious relationship that we call love, which is at the origin of life and is its final destiny.

We can love only what is present.

Therefore, it becomes permissible to smile within the torment that has been redeemed, knowing that Giorgia smiles with Enzo, looking at us smiling, bewildered but without embarrassment.

> I devoured it like I do with your articles, without breathing... and I don't know if this is good because, given that I am "ignorant" of the context, I'm not entirely getting it... I see Enzo, his methods, his exuberance, and all the rest, but it's because ultimately I got to know him through you. I also took a look at his videos, his speeches, because you had spoken to me about them, and I was curious. I watched them because I thought, "Maybe through Enzo, through Giussani, I can understand Bellini as well." (Diana Falcione, after reading chapters 1-3)[5]

> I don't know if it can have the same effect on others as it has on me. I see him as he says these things, his arms moving, hitting the table, his hand goes like this 👌 Who knows, maybe even he was surprised by the things that were coming out 😊. Are there others like this among you? (Diana Falcione, after reading chapter 4)[6]

---

5. January 12, 2023.
6. February 19, 2023.

Afterword

I am very impressed by the history of the Movement... Maybe I am about to say something silly (tell me if so)... the intuition of Gius is so simple, but so simple that it becomes genius! He re-established a Companionship of Christ, simply stuck to this companionship, and it is extraordinary! No special effects to convince us, no demagoguery, nothing of the sort... It's like when you, an adult, try to solve a math problem for a first grader... You don't know how to do it because you think it is impossible that it could be so simple... Certainly... we need the Holy Spirit, for sure, to come down and do His thing... on Enzo, on you, and on this whole companionship, singing. (Diana Falcione, after reading chapter 12)[7]

---

7. May 15, 2023.

Biography of Enzo Piccinini

1951–1965

ENZO PICCININI WAS BORN ON JUNE 5, 1951, IN VENTOSO DI Scandiano (Reggio Emilia) to Ilde Ferretti and Angiolino Piccinini. His parents were married in 1943. At the time of his birth, Enzo already had an older brother and sister—Romano, born in 1948, and Giuliana, in 1946. The members of the family of the two spouses were Catholics by tradition and practiced the faith rigidly. His father was also president of the local chapter of Catholic Action. In the family, Catholic teachings were put into practice and the commandments were considered rules to be followed as a moral duty. Enzo's parents, especially his father Angiolino, were very strict, and the children were treated with rigor and often punished if they disobeyed.

On June 10 of that year, Enzo was baptized in the parish of Chiozza with the name Eugenio, but his mother and relatives called him "Enzo" right away. In the following years, he would add this name to the registry records, so that his certificates and many documents appear with the double name "Eugenio Enzo."

Before he was one year old, the whole family moved to Bagno (Reggio Emilia), where they lived in a large farmhouse with the paternal grandparents, Desolina and Giuseppe, a married uncle with a son, and Aunt Maria. The family of origin later moved to Rivalta for several years, and eventually established itself in Sabbione in 1991, a few years before Angiolino's death. In 1954, Enzo's brother Sergio was born. On June 24, 1958, the youngest two siblings were born, the twins Giovanna and Giovanni. Enzo received Confirmation in the Parish of the Nativity of John the Baptist in Bagno the same day.

In 1962, he finished elementary school. He wanted to keep studying, but the family could not afford to pay for their son's further education, despite the fact that the child showed much promise and was brilliant in his studies. Father Girolamo from the Order of the Servants of Mary helped him, welcoming him into the private boarding school Saint Philip Benizi in Montefano, in the province of Macerata. In the Marche region, Enzo attended middle school. Every year, he returned home to his family, but only during the summer vacation. In the summer of 1965, on June 29, the feast of Saints Peter and Paul, while he was going to Mass on his bicycle with Sergio, who was pedaling in front of him, a truck skidded and struck Sergio, killing him. According to his mother Ilde, Enzo was troubled for the whole summer, wandering around the fields, and was unable to sleep at night.

1965–1970

After middle school, between 1965 and 1967, Enzo attended his first two years of high school at Saint Joseph Boarding School, run by the Servants of Mary at Ronzano, Bologna. In 1967, he transferred to Ancona, residing at the boarding school of the Servants of Mary and attending the "Carlo Rinaldini" public high school, which was not affiliated with the religious house. Here, his classmates call him "Super Enzo," because he was interested in every subject, he constantly spoke out in class, and because he began to dedicate himself to sports, preferring soccer above all others, with strenuous training. In those final years of high school, he began to participate passionately in the social and political debates that animated the student environment at the time, and that eventually led to protests, occupations, and demonstrations in the 1970s.

In high school, he met Fiorisa, his classmate, a native of Ancona, with whom he began to have a special relationship already in those years. In the following years, their relationship deepened and strengthened into marriage while they were attending university.

Between June and July 1970, Enzo took the high school graduation examinations in Ancona. His past as a "rebel boy," for which he had previously received an eight in conduct and a demerit from Father Bruno of the Servants of Mary, contributed to lowering his final grade to 45/60.

After obtaining his diploma in classics, during his stay with his family in Reggio Emilia, he came to reject the Christian faith and rebel against the Catholic Church. He began to attend meetings with a group of kids who had left the Federation of Young Italian Communists (FGCI), which called itself the "Worker-Student Political Collective" and gathered in the center of Reggio Emilia, at Via Emilia San Pietro 25. At this address, young people of different extractions, belonging to different Communist groups, but also Catholics belonging to groups that were active in the social sphere, entered into debates and political conferences, with invited speakers that included activists coming from *Potere Operaio* [Worker Power], *Lotta Continua* [Constant Struggle], *Avanguardia Operaia* [Worker Vanguard], *Servire il Popolo* [To Serve the People]. In particular, they discussed the Marxist ideology and the political consequences of it. The place was known as the "Apartment" and Enzo participated there actively, motivated by an elementary need for justice and for a change in society. In those meetings, which often lasted hours, there were also young people who belonged to the Catholic group One Way, linked to *Gioventù Studentesca* (GS), which had started a bookstore called "Nuova Terra" [New Earth] in the center of Reggio. Enzo took notice, was struck by the friendship among them, and began to follow them to see what they did together. He realized that they gathered every day in the crypt of the cathedral nearby, to say Vespers. Curious, he asked to participate in their prayers, but initially the members of GS were afraid of him, because they knew he was part of the group of the Apartment. With different excuses, they always kept him outside the crypt. Finally, on the insistence of Enzo himself, they were convinced to welcome him. It is there that Enzo encountered GS, which later became Communion and Liberation, CL (he spoke about this with Fiorisa in a letter dated July 27, 1970). Thanks to this new interest, Enzo reconciled with the Church and rediscovered a faith that was now enriched by experience and by reasons for living it. Others from the Apartment, instead, went into hiding and became a part of the Red Brigades.[1]

In the summer of that year, he spent many days in Como, with his Uncle Bruno. While there, he wrote about the new experience he was living in the Movement of Communion and Liberation, which he was loving more and more and where he decided to remain. In September, he returned to Reggio Emilia and enrolled in the School of Medicine and Surgery at the University of Modena, which he entered in the fall.

1971–1973

He began to be one of the leaders of CL in Modena, and at the end of September in 1971 he participated in a gathering at Gatteo Mare (held by the future Cardinal Angelo Scola), from where he wrote to Fiorisa. His many activities made it difficult to attend the university and forced him to slow down a bit in taking his exams. On July 1, 1973, he got married in Modena.

At the end of that same year, his first child, Chiara, was born.

1975–1977

Starting in 1975, he attended, as a student intern, the Institute of Special Surgical Pathology and Clinical Propaedeutics at the University of Modena with Professor Angelo Conti. At the beginning of Advent, he was given the responsibility of the CL community in

---

1. A far-left terrorist group responsible for several acts of violence, including the abduction and murder of former Prime Minister Aldo Moro in 1978.

Modena. He began to work assiduously also with high school and university students in Modena. The witnesses of people belonging to the community in those months speak of a daily contact with him. He organized gatherings in the flatlands and foothills around Modena, where they spoke about the position of the Church on debated topics like divorce, abortion, and political events. Many people adhered to CL thanks to those public encounters, repeated even in the following years, in Modena and in the communities where Enzo would take charge, in particular in Bologna.

Between 1976 and 1977, Father Giussani asked a few of the CL leaders in Milan to meet Enzo and help him take care of the CL community in Modena and the surrounding province.

On November 5, 1976, Enzo obtained his degree in Medicine and Surgery with a maximum score. In the same month, he successfully passed the state exam for qualification in the medical profession. Continuing into the following year, he carried out scientific research and experimentation on animals (dogs, rabbits, and rats), in collaboration with the Institute of Pharmacology, Human Physiology, Anesthesia, and Resuscitation of the University of Modena. The results were collected in his first publication in the *Rivista di Farmacologia e Terapia* [*Journal of Pharmacology and Therapy*] in 1977.

In 1976, he also passed the admission exam for the School of Specialization in Vascular Surgery. From November, he attended the Institute of Special Surgical Pathology at the University of Modena, with qualification as a "university medical intern with care duties."

That summer, Enzo's favorite sister, Giovanna, made the decision to enter the convent of the Trappist Sisters in Vitorchiano, undertaking the path of cloistered life as a Trappist. Enzo initially disapproved of this choice. While being fascinated by a life lived in total consecration to God, he did not understand that this could be done by totally rejecting immersion in the world, preferring the retirement of the cloister, being closed within a convent and with little contact with the outside world. Mother Cristiana Piccardo, the abbess, a decisive and intelligent woman, began a dialogue with him on the meaning of the choice of the cloister, until she convinced him of the goodness of the life undertaken by Giovanna, who became Sister Chiara in the year she took the habit.

In 1977 Maria, his second child, was born.

1978

In the months of May and June he held the role of "assistant in charge" of the division of Thoracic Surgery of the Local Healthcare Unit 34 in Turin, in the Piedmont region. On that occasion, he got to know the CL community in that area. Between August and October, he was nominated as "substitute university assistant" in the Chair of Special Surgical Pathology at the University of Modena.

That year Pietro, his third child, was born.

1979

As the children of the young adults in the CL community of Modena began approaching school age, the need was felt to give them a solid education inspired by Christian principles. Hence, the idea of founding a cooperative of parents and teachers to open a school grew. The decision was founded on the awareness of the educational capacity of the Christian community. Initially, in the preceding summers (1977–1978), they organized summer camps of a few weeks, led by teachers, young people, and adults of CL who were engaged in the world of education, whether in Modena or in the lowlands around Modena, where a community of young workers and families had been growing. On May 2, 1979, the cooperative "La Carovana" ("The Caravan") was established. It took charge of and managed a nursery and primary school, beginning in September of the school year 1979–1980, which coincided with the start of obligatory schooling for Enzo's oldest daughter.

The same year, with some university students and adults, he gave life to the activities of the cultural center named "La Collina della Poesia" ("The Hill of Poetry"), which organized meetings and public initiatives with a social and political interest.

On October 22, Enzo obtained his specialization in vascular surgery at the University of Modena, receiving the maximum grade and honors.

That year Anna Rita, his fourth child, was born.

1980

His work moved to Bologna, as he followed his professor, Angelo Conti, while retaining his residence in Modena. He covered different responsibilities at the University of Bologna and at Clinic III of the Sant'Orsola Hospital, where he carried out research and teaching activities, as well as patient visits in the department and surgeries.

At the initiative of Giancarlo Cesana, it was proposed to Enzo to also lead the CLU in Bologna, which in those years was one of the biggest communities in Italy. After a difficult beginning, during which Enzo clashed with the students, above all in the medical school, because of his severity in giving grades for his exams, he began to introduce his radical way of sharing the Christian experience. This, in time, conquered the group of university students in Bologna.

Starting on November 24 of that same year, Enzo was in Irpinia, in southern Italy, to help those affected by the earthquake in Castelgrande. He remained there a couple of weeks, helping the families, the elderly, and those who were alone to organize themselves in tents and then in trailers. He also worked as an urgent care doctor for the local public medical service.

1981

Enzo was given the responsibility of the whole CL community in Bologna. Starting that year, he began to invite those belonging to a smalle, more deeply committed group of the CLU to meet regularly every Monday, to discuss life and daily events, as well as to put themselves at stake in the way they lived the Christian fact in the university. From this proposal, a friendship was born that spread like wildfire. This way of meeting at regular intervals with the university students continued for generations of students up until his death.

In the meantime, the experience of CL in Modena also continued to grow thanks to the contribution of Enzo and through the works begun there. From one of his letters dated March 18, it appears that the La Carovana school had begun, and that there was an idea of continuing with a middle school.

1982–1983

Enzo's responsibility with communities of university students grew and expanded to other universities. For example, two university students from Bologna started going to Florence to work with students there.

At the suggestion of Father Giussani, Enzo deepened his relationship with the bishop of Bologna, Enrico Manfredini. After the premature death of this bishop, Enzo visited, together with Giussani, the newly-elected Cardinal Giacomo Biffi, who had already had a long familiarity with the founder of CL during their years of seminary at Venegono, where they had been classmates. With time, there would flourish a deep friendship between Enzo and Cardinal Biffi, founded on their common belonging to the Church, up until Enzo's death.

In the hospital, Enzo created a network of relationships that would help him to grow professionally and take care of patients in a total way. Some university students in the medical school were starting to connect themselves more closely with him, even to discuss career choices.

1984

In the summer, in the center of Carpi, a town in the province of Modena, in the Piazza Martiri della Libertà,[2] a group from CL organized the first edition of "The Craziest Festival in the World" under Enzo's guidance. This was an event that lasted for a few days, with games, soccer tournaments, concerts, and testimonies next to tents with food and drink. The organizers, in addition to Enzo, were a group of young workers and adults. The aim of the "Happening" was to publicly propose the Christian experience through the CL Movement.

Among the freshmen who came to the university of Bologna in September, that year there was a small nucleus of students enrolled in different schools at the university who developed a particular affection for Enzo. They were destined to engage with him in a radical way, to the point of sharing with him the responsibility for the communities that Enzo was now visiting daily throughout Italy.

On October 27, he obtained a second specialization in surgery with honors from Professor Mario Vellani, rector of the University of Modena.

1985

Father Giussani called Enzo to the CL National Council and assigned him the role of "visitor" of the communities of Italy, in one of three zones into which the country had been divided. The area that he had to cover went from Trentino, Veneto, and Friuli in the north-east of Italy, to Puglia in the south, along the whole Adriatic Coast.

Enzo was moved by the meeting of Father Giussani with a group of the extreme left in the Comuna Baires Theater in Milan. Those present included Brandirali, Casali, and Todeschini from

---

2. One of the largest piazzas in Italy, dedicated to the "martyrs of freedom" killed by the Fascists in 1944.

Lotta Continua. That encounter resounded loudly in the leftist press, and Enzo spoke about it in public meetings.

1986

In September, he was invited to be part of a small group of Father Giussani's friends who went with him on pilgrimage to the Holy Land.

In Modena, the project that had been in the works for a few years was finally realized and a middle school was acquired. This school was founded by the Salesians in Modena and legally recognized in 1931. The La Carovana cooperative took over management in the 1986–1987 school year. The first year of activity started with a sixth grade class of 10 students and a seventh grade class of three.

Enzo continued to hold public meetings each week, sometimes having more than one a day, in different cities where he had responsibility for the CL community. In the fall, he began to meet personally and diligently with students from the CLU in Florence, in agreement with Father Giussani.

1987

That year, in September, a terrible car accident occurred near Faenza involving a few freshmen who were known by many in the communities of Modena and Bologna from the experience of GS—Alessandro Beri and Elisa Beatrice were killed. Enzo accompanied and embraced the friends and parents of these young people, helping them stay in front of the pain and suffering of their sudden loss. He underlined with words and gestures of friendship that death is not the last word.

Enzo began to take steps to travel for a few months to the United States, to Boston, where he applied as a Research Fellow in Surgery. In August, he was in London for his first experience of an Anglo-Saxon country, to learn English and prepare for his American experience. During his time in England, he did not miss the opportunity to contact the local CL community, and met members of the Memores Domini house in that city.

On November 15, he left for Boston, where he worked at Massachusetts General Hospital with Professor George L. Nardi, one of the world experts in colorectal surgery. The initial challenges were many. Enzo left his family in Modena and lived in a run-down apartment with other young people who worked in the neighborhood of Harvard. He still did not know English well (he had studied French as a young man), and he struggled to communicate with his colleagues at the hospital. With tenacity and the help of both Italian and American friends from the local CL community, he managed to improve his knowledge of the language, eventually understanding well what he saw and heard in the hospital.

In the six months he spent in Boston, he met the CL community, made up mostly of Italians who lived there for work, but also Americans who had begun to follow the School of Community and were becoming friends. He also found the time to visit other cities in the United States, including New York and Washington. He went as far as Sacramento, California, where an Italian family from CL lived.

1988

He returned from the United States in the middle of May and immediately began to apply, at the hospital in Bologna, the surgical techniques and the methods of patient care that he had learned in the preceding months in Boston from Doctor Nardi and Doctor Glenn LaMuraglia. With the latter in particular, he began an intense collaboration, which brought Enzo many times to Mass General. In the letter that certified the work Piccinini had done in America, Doctor LaMuraglia asked that Enzo be permitted to return to Mass General the following year, to continue his experiments on the use of lasers in general surgeries.

When he was about to return from his experience in the United States, two children, his wife Fiorisa, and his older sister Giuliana met him in Boston and they visited the city together, as well as Walt Disney World in Orlando, Florida. He would comment on that visit in his public interventions when he returned to Italy.

1989

In April, Enzo was in Paris, where he attended an internship at the Broussais Hospital at the VI University, learning experimental surgeries from Professor J. H. Alexandre. He remained there for a month (with his wife and two of his children), with the aim of updating his knowledge of surgical techniques and bringing them to Italy to the Sant'Orsola Hospital.

In August, Enzo went to meet his younger sister, Giovanna, for the first time in Venezuela, where she had moved with a small group of sisters from Vitorchiano, to found a new Trappist monastery in Humocaro Alto, in the province of Barquisimeto, in a remote and poor area of Venezuela. During his trip to the new foundation, whose buildings were still under construction, Enzo exhibited a different attitude from that of his past discussions with Mother Cristiana and the sisters who lived in the cloister. He was amazed by how the sisters were growing and were even more attentive to the facts of the world than the people who lived outside the monastery, despite an existence separated and far from society.

In October and November, he accepted an invitation from Doctor LaMuraglia and returned to Mass General in Boston to work with the American doctors on experiments in the use of lasers in surgical operations. During that time, he went to meet the surgeon who allowed him to undertake the American experience, Professor George L. Nardi, who was now at the end of his life because of a pancreatic tumor.

1990

In the month of May, he was in Bordeaux with his wife Fiorisa and two daughters, for a period of observation and specialization at the local hospital, with the aim of studying the most up-to-date surgical techniques.

In June, he was back in Boston at Mass General. He also brought his oldest daughter and enrolled her in an English course. During the trip, he again met the CL community, for the most part made up of a few Italians and a small group of Americans. In the same period, he visited New York and Washington.

During that whole year, when he was not abroad, he dedicated himself to the CL communities in Emilia, with a special concern for the CLU in Bologna, which now numbered more than a thousand members, and other cities in Emilia, in Tuscany, and in Piedmont, and above all the CLU in the city of Turin. He also went many times a week to Milan to see Father Giussani, to participate in the meetings of national leaders of CL and other gatherings that happened periodically, at least once a month.

1991

At the invitation of Father Giussani, he began to meet regularly with Bishop Angelo Scola, who had been named bishop of Grosseto, in a diocese that was a bit isolated from the principal communities of CL in Italy.

In August, he went to Penafirme, near Lisbon (Portugal), where he was subjected to a few "tests" from the Portuguese CL community: he had to face a (small) bull in a bullfight, and take a swim in the ocean, managing to resist the strong tide.

1992

In the meetings with leaders, judgments were made on the political and international events of the day. That year, in particular, Enzo often commented and discussed the invasion of Bosnia and Herzegovina and the siege of Sarajevo, which lasted a year. In internal politics, the beginning of *"Mani Pulite,"* which would also involve some people belonging to CL and many Italian business people, was discussed in private debates, but also in public meetings with Enzo.

In June, Enzo was in Tampa, Florida, where he met Professor Ludovico Balducci, a doctor from Rimini who had moved to the United States. Enzo began a professional collaboration and a friendship with him that was initially controversial because of the doctor's aversion to the CL experience (which he overcame in the ensuing years). The occasion allowed Enzo to meet the local CL community, which was beginning to take its first steps. A new reality in that group was the presence of adolescents and young people from GS, with whom Enzo got involved suddenly and a bit impetuously. Many people remember those moments and still live the Christian experience thanks to that encounter.

Enzo's professional results were reported in different international conferences in which he participated in Hungary and Greece—in Athens in September and Crete in October—where he observed and shared the results of his research on digestive and colorectal surgeries.

He returned to Paris for a brief period after the summer, for professional commitments.

On October 16 and 17, 1992, on the occasion of the 10th anniversary of the pontifical recognition of the Fraternity of CL, Father Giussani gathered all the adherents of the Fraternity in Lourdes to celebrate the anniversary. As often happened, Enzo took advantage of it for an "out of town" trip around France with a group of four people (they went first to the Camargue region, to Saintes-Maries-de-la-Mer, Carcassonne, Avignon, and finally arrived in Lourdes to participate in the celebration).

1993

In the summer, for two weeks between July and August, for the first time the Piccinini family went on vacation to Sicily, to San Vito Lo Capo, in the province of Trapani. During the vacation, Enzo was invited to meet the local CL communities in Trapani and Palermo, and also held a few public meetings. That summer, some of the CLU students from Bologna reached him, traveling more than 2,000 kilometers in two days to spend a day with Enzo. A friendship was born between the surgeon, his family, and the local CL community, such that also in the following years, up until the year before his death, he and his family would spend their vacation in Sicily, with every now and then a few days on the island of Pantelleria.

On September 18, the stay in Munich with his daughter Chiara, who had begun to study German in the School of Foreign Languages at Bologna, was an occasion for one of the many "out of town" trips with some university students. The principal aim was to bring his daughter back to Bologna after her time there, but it also afforded the opportunity to spend an evening drinking beer at the Oktoberfest.

From the professional point of view, Enzo was now a recognized surgeon. He participated in many international conferences, and at the same time followed many communities throughout Italy. Every day, after having operated on patients at Sant'Orsola, he got on the road and drove hundreds of kilometers to carry out the responsibilities that had been assigned to him, and to be close to all the CL friends who asked for his help.

From December 3 to 5, Enzo participated in an International Symposium on Surgery in Hong Kong, where he brought the results of his research.

1994

Enzo was awarded a scholarship for six months in Paris, where he went to study surgical techniques with Professor Parc, spending part of the week in the French capital and the other days in Bologna, for his activities at the hospital.

After his daughter Chiara's decision to undertake the study of Chinese in the university, Enzo did his best to facilitate her first reconnaissance trip to China, together with her mother Fiorisa, between the end of May and the beginning of June.

In June, Enzo was again in Tampa for professional reasons, and also to cultivate the relationship with members of the CL community there. At the beginning of July, he was in Mexico for a conference on colorectal surgery.

During the first half of September he was in London at Saint Mark's Hospital as an "observer." There, he had access to the departments and to the operating rooms, as well as the outpatient clinics, where he learned the modalities with which Professor John Northover and his team managed patients, from the visits, to the diagnoses, to surgeries, and to post-operative recoveries.

Again, in September, he won a scholarship of specialization for six months in Paris, where he went to study surgical techniques with Professor Parc at the VI University, alternating brief stays in the French capital each week with work at Sant'Orsola in Bologna.

On October 23, Enzo's father, Angiolino Piccinini, died. The funeral was celebrated in Sabbione, where his parents had moved with Enzo's older brother. Many of the friends of Enzo's youth in Reggio Emilia were at the funeral, as were adults and university students from the nearby cities of Parma, Modena, and Bologna.

1995–1997

Enzo was more and more engaged in his responsibility as visitor for the areas of Triveneto (Veneto, Trentino, and Friuli regions) and the eastern side of Italy along the Adriatic Sea (he followed the communities of Marche, Abruzzo, Basilicata, and Puglia). He asked his friends from the CL leadership of Bologna to help him keep a close eye on the situation of the various groups.

In those years, he encouraged the university students to participate in the political life of the university, and every time there were elections, they fought to send as many people as possible to vote.

On November 15, 1995, in the Aula Magna of Santa Lucia, in Bologna, Father Giussani held a lesson for the university students entitled, "The Risk of Education as Creation of Personality and

History." The event was curated by the university students and had a strong resonance both at the public level and in the CL Movement. On that occasion, the deep affection and the common intentions of Father Giussani and Enzo were made evident.

From November 15 to 19, 1995, Enzo was in Barcelona to participate in the international conference of surgery called, "Eurosurgery-95."

In October 1996, he was again in Tampa to meet the community and to work with Doctor Balducci. In December of that same year, he returned to Saint Mark's Hospital to work with Professor Northover and Professor Ralph Nicholls, in London, where he was again welcomed as an observer.

He continued to follow, as the visitor, the communities situated in Triveneto and those along the Adriatic Coast. His visits extended as far as Trieste and Udine in the northeast.

He traveled to South America to establish collaborative relationships with specialized surgery clinics in some universities, with the intention of realizing a project for the formation of doctors in those areas.

1998

On January 5, 1998, a terrible tragedy happened in Padua during the "*Pan e vin*" ("Bread and Wine") bonfire, organized for the Feast of the Epiphany, where two people died and more than 40 were injured. Enzo stayed with the people recovering in the emergency room from the evening of the incident up until the next day. The tragic event became an occasion of prayer and support for the community in Padua also in the following weeks, on the part of all the communities that Enzo visited and at his invitation. Enzo's closeness and competence, which step-by-step accompanied those wounded in the tragedy, as well as the family members who had suffered the loss of their loved ones, impacted the community and bound them deeply to him.

In March 1998, he went to South America, to the Universidad Nacional de la Plata, in Argentina; to the Universidad Mayor Real y Pontificia San Francisco Xavier de Chuquisaca, in Sucre, Bolivia; and in other South American cities to conclude the agreements and start the administrative procedures necessary to implement the so-called "Alfa Project." The aim of this project was to train South American surgeons in European universities where there are faculties of medicine and surgery and where there are specialized departments in colorectal surgery, including the University of Bologna, the leader of the initiative.

This provided a good occasion to "pass by" and greet his sister Chiara in Humocaro, Venezuela, accompanied by Giuliana, his older sister.

On July 1, he celebrated 25 years of marriage with Fiorisa in Modena with friends from the CL community. His children were all studying out of town, in Bologna, in Milan, and in Lugano. His youngest daughter Anna Rita began to study medicine that year in Bologna.

In September, he was again in Paris with Professor Parc.

In October, the inauguration of the "Master in Colorectal Surgery" was announced in the newspapers. It was sponsored by the European Union and the University of Bologna, together with the Universities of Vienna and Paris. Enzo strongly desired this course of study. It involved the participation of specialists selected by the Argentine, Bolivian, and Uruguayan universities, who would be guided by professors and surgeons from France, Austria, and Italy by attending both theoretical and practical courses. The leader of the project was the Department of Surgery and Anesthesiology in Bologna, of which Enzo was the head.

On December 12, he gave a testimony at the CLU Exercises in Rimini, considered his spiritual testament and the public moment that summed up most maturely his encounter with CL.

1999

In agreement with Father Giussani, he began to again follow the CLU in Florence starting in January, meeting with a small group of leaders every two weeks on Monday evening, up until the Monday before his death.

He was again in Paris in February.

That same month, in Milan, the Medicine and Person Association was officially introduced, and Enzo was among the founders. Its aim was to promote interdisciplinary studies in the health environment, to create places of dialogue, and to affirm the medical profession as a personal, free, and responsible answer to the needs of the sick person.

On March 12 he performed a few surgeries at the San Lorenzino private hospital in Cesena. After a particularly difficult surgery, he held a public meeting for doctors and health personnel entitled, "The Patient: A Person Before a Disease." It was one of the last testimonies Enzo gave about his vocation and his work.

In mid-April, a dinner was organized in Bologna with the leaders of the CLU on the occasion of the departure of his oldest daughter for China. This was the last time Chiara saw her father.

On May 23, Enzo climbed Mount Cusna for the last time. He loved to do this often, with a group of close friends and as a proposal to forge bonds with new friends.

On May 25, at 6:30 p.m., he participated in a meeting entitled, "Doctor–Patient Communication: An Open Question," organized as a debate in the Caravella Santa Maria Hall of the University of Life and Health at the San Raffaele Hospital in Milan.

On the evening of May 25, Enzo was in Milan for a dinner with a small group of CLU national leaders.

On May 26, on his return, close to 1 a.m., while he was driving his Audi on the A1 highway between bridge 92 and 93, just past the highway exit for Fidenza, Enzo's car went off the road and burst into flames. He died immediately.

The funeral was celebrated by his friend Cardinal Giacomo Biffi at the San Petronio Cathedral in Bologna. Over 7,000 people attended. The coffin was carried in procession on foot from the CL headquarters in Bologna to San Petronio Church, in silence. The frenetic life of the city of Bologna stopped for an instant as the column of people passed, walking behind the coffin.

PIER PAOLO BELLINI is an associate professor at the University of Molise where he teaches Sociology of communication in the Department of Humanities, Social Sciences, and Education. He is the general editor of the musical collection Spirto Gentil by Father Luigi Giussani.

CHIARA PICCININI, daughter of Enzo, is a researcher in the Department of Linguistic Sciences and Foreign Literatures at the Università Cattolica del Sacro Cuore in Milan.

ENZO PICCININI (1951-1999) was a surgeon from Reggio Emilia. He participated actively in the movement of Communion and Liberation, where he was a point of reference for many. Father of four children, he died in a car accident at the age of just 47. Following his death, in 2002, the Enzo Piccinini Foundation was born to pursue the educational, scientific, and religious ideals that inspired him.

www.ingramcontent.com/pod-product-compliance
Lightning Source LLC
Chambersburg PA
CBHW031135160426
43193CB00008B/147